REFRAM
THE WO
IN THE
WINDOW

Jennifer Sliwka

DULWICH
PICTURE
GALLERY

This exhibition catalogue has been generously supported by The Elizabeth Cayzer Charitable Trust

First published in Great Britain in 2022 by Dulwich Picture Gallery, Gallery Road, London, SE21 7AD on the occasion of the exhibition *Reframed: The Woman in the Window* at Dulwich Picture Gallery, 4 May–4 September 2022.

Design and creative direction by James Hunter and Stephen Coates
Copy edited by Susannah Worth
Printed in the UK by Pureprint
Reprographics by DawkinsColour

ISBN 978-1-898519-46-1

Acknowledgements
We would like to thank the following people for making *Reframed: The Woman in the Window* possible.

The generous lenders for parting with their artworks
The Ashmolean Museum, University of Oxford
The British Library
Bradford District Museums and Galleries, CBMDC
British Museum, London
The Courtauld, London
Daniel Katz Gallery, London
Gagosian
Government Art Collection
Her Majesty the Queen
Hauser & Wirth
Irish Museum of Modern Art
Jack Bell Gallery
Katrin Bellinger Collection
Leeds Museums and Galleries
The Leiden Collection, New York
Louise Bourgeois Trust
Maureen Paley, London
Mr & Mrs William Iselin
The National Gallery, London
National Trust Collections, Polesden Lacey
Piano Nobile
Royal Academy of Arts, London
Russell-Cotes Art Gallery & Museum, Bournemouth
Simon Ray, London
Simran Janjua
Steph James
Tate
Tullie House Museum, Carlisle
Victoria and Albert Museum, London
Victoria Miro
Wilson Centre for Photography

With thanks to all of our private lenders

Exhibition supporters
This exhibition catalogue has been generously supported by The Elizabeth Cayzer Charitable Trust

Exhibition supported by The Tavolozza Foundation

Official Paint Partner

EST. 1884
MYLANDS
HOUSE OF COLOUR

Digital Exhibition Guide

Bloomberg Connects
Digital Experience Supported by Bloomberg Philanthropies

All members of the Desenfans Circle of Patrons, The 1811 Club, and Dulwich Picture Gallery Friends

This exhibition has been made possible as a result of the Government Indemnity Scheme. Dulwich Picture Gallery would like to thank HM Government for providing Government Indemnity and the Department of Digital, Culture, Media and Sport and Arts Council England for arranging the indemnity.

Our thanks also go to William Brown, Carol Warner, Camilla Stephens and Vernon Rapley and the V&A team for their advice and support.

The expert contractors
Exhibition build: MER Services Ltd
Exhibition 2D design: Jana Vodickova
Exhibition graphics: Displayways
Exhibition lighting: DHA Designs
Art handling: Patina
Transport and logistics: Momart
Conservation: Alice Powell, Painting Conservation Studio, Keith Taylor

The Dulwich Picture Gallery team of staff and trustees
Exhibition Curator: Dr Jennifer Sliwka
Content Advisors: Jennifer Scott and Jane Findlay
Creative Producer: Alexander Moore
Exhibition Management: Hannah Edwards and Abigail Kikuchi
Collection & Programme Committee: Helen Macintyre, Dame Janet Vitmayer, Benedict Brogan
Creative Conversations project: Kelly Robinson, Eve Travers and all of our community participants.

Front/back cover:

Ajarb Bernard Ategwa, *Posing with my Parrot* (detail), 2021, acrylic on canvas, 237 x 199 cm
© Ajarb Bernard Ategwa / Jack Bell Gallery

Sandro Botticelli, *Portrait of a Lady known as Smeralda Bandinelli* (detail), c. 1470–80, tempera on panel, 65.7 x 41 cm
© Victoria and Albert Museum, London

Director's foreword 5

Introduction 6
Window gazes: a cultural history
of the woman in the window

Origins: windows in the ancient world 9

From envious gazes to sacred visions 19
in Early Modern Europe

Restricted views in Renaissance 31
poetry, painting and portraiture

Protestantism, the reformed gaze 37
and its inheritance

Changing views: political, psychological 51
and cultural conceptions of the window

Modernism, photography and film 75

Post-war window gazing 83

The artist at the window 97

Epilogue: the pandemic window 107

Biography 110
Bibliography 111
Picture credits 116

Curator's acknowledgements
This study is greatly indebted to the research of many scholars working across a variety of fields ranging from art, archaeology and architecture to psychology, advertising and gender studies. The research of Daniel Jütte, Anne Friedberg and Sabine Rewald on various aspects of the history of the window and of window gazing were especially helpful. The preparation of this catalogue has also benefited from the knowledgeable staff and invaluable resources at the Warburg and the Courtauld Institutes and the Tate and British Libraries in London. I am particularly thankful for the institutions and individuals who have generously lent to this exhibition and to the directors, curators and conservators of those collections who facilitated my visits to study their works of art.

I would also like to express my gratitude to those individuals who assisted me with special access to objects, information and expertise: Charles Asprey, Jack Bell, Katrin Bellinger, Gareth Brereton, Alessandra Cereda, Clare Coombes, John Chu, Harriett Clapham, Martin Clayton, Cristina Colomar, Nicholas Cullinan, Tom Davies, Ana Debenedetti, Oliver Durey, Donato Esposito, Darren Flook, Sam Fogg, Susan Foister, Flavia Frigeri, Kendal Grady, Arnika Groenewald-Schmidt, Hannah Gruy, Oscar Humphries, Kudzanai-Violet Hwami, Lindsay Ingram, Jill Iredade, William Iselin, Andrew Jackson, Sabina Jaskot-Gill, Joost Joustra, Danny Katz, Robin Katz, Thomas Kiely, Hope Kingsley, Teresa Krasny, Karen Limper-Hertz, Erin Manns, Susan May, Steven McNeil, Lucy Peter, Antony Peattie, Clare Pollard, Laura Popoviciu, Leslie Primo, Mia Prvan, Simon Ray, Guy Robertson, William Robinson, Fiona Römer, Helen Record, Matthew Reeves, Cait Schuyler, Joyce Seaman, Karen Serres, Matthew Stephenson, Tim Schmelcher, Matthew Travers, Robert Travers, Alex Truscott, Duncan Walker, Nigel Walsh, Ittai Weinryb, Francesca Whitlum Cooper, Rachel Whiteread, Annette Wickham and Lara Yeager-Crasselt.

Thanks also to the individuals who have facilitated the loans: Ilenia Scerra, Lucy Scanlon, Pamela Keeton, Carlota Iris, Julia Blanks, Chloe Le Tissier, Petra Wright, Jess Topping, Sarah Mcfadden, Paulina Shearing, Hannah Widgington, Jenny Foot, Lauren Porter, Sophie Nurse, Poppy Fairfax, Lauren Murphy, Melissa Viscardi, Christina Kennedy, Livia Schaafsma, Sarah Murray, Sara Smith, Kim Kruse, Alice Joiner, Oliver Evans, Samantha Saward, Claire Hallinan, Richard Dark, Suzannah Brown, Phoebe Meiklejohn-McLaughlin, Martha Graves, Stephen Wright, Hannah Murray, Claire Sleightholm, Elizabeth Loughran, Sara Mittica, Polly Fleury, Clementine Williamson, Annabel Niekirk and Luke Farey.

I would also like to thank Jennifer Scott, Jane Findlay, Alexander Moore, Abigail Kikuchi, Sam Dorman and Hannah Edwards at Dulwich for all of their energy and enthusiasm for this project and Stephen Coates, James Hunter and Susannah Worth who transformed my text into this beautiful catalogue. For their constant encouragement and support, I would like to thank Ryszard, Anne and Daniel Sliwka, Clare Wells and Federico Carafoli.

Dr Jennifer Sliwka

DIRECTOR'S FOREWORD

In the seventeenth century, as legend has it, a painting was displayed by Rembrandt in the window of his house in Amsterdam. Passers-by looked at the girl and wondered why she had been standing still for so long. This was recounted by an early owner of the painting, the artist and diplomat Roger de Piles, and is attractive for many reasons: it makes us consider the ultimate goal of painting, to imitate nature itself, so that oil paint on canvas can convincingly be mistaken for flesh and blood; it makes us consider of the skill of Rembrandt in rendering movement in a face that at any moment might snap to attention to see us looking at her; and most of all, it makes us consider the enduring image of a woman – nameless and unknown – seen at, through, behind, within, a window.

I think of de Piles' anecdote often, particularly when travelling by train at night, speeding past windows lit up from within. Through glimpses into living rooms and kitchens, we can snatch a sense of the private world of strangers. The mystery of the personal space of women, transformed into a public stage through the construct of a window, has inspired artists, and captivated viewers, for centuries.

This exhibition is a window in itself. With reflective selections and inspiring research, Jennifer Sliwka opens up a new way of looking. Mid-way through the chronology of this selection, women as artists take on the motif for themselves, embodying a powerful duality as both subject and creator, adding to the resonance of this topic.

I am deeply indebted to Elizabeth Cayzer for seeing the scholarly potential in this project and supporting this publication from the outset.

My thanks also to Katrin Bellinger and the Tavolozza Foundation for supporting the exhibition.

Thank you to our partners and lenders, and the Patrons, Friends and Volunteers of Dulwich Picture Gallery, who have stood by us through the past two difficult years.

I wonder what Rembrandt's *Girl at a Window* [cat. 12] thought of the artist's painting of her. Perhaps she was flattered by his presumption to immortalise her in paint. Perhaps she was annoyed that he included everyday details such as suntan lines and insect bites on her arms. Or perhaps she never existed at all; a figment of an artist's imagination, flesh and blood with a light in her eyes, a construct of fiction.

As we look through the window at the faces within this ground-breaking exhibition and book, we encounter multiple perspectives into distinct spaces, from Ancient Greece to today. The world marches forward while the women framed in these images remain suspended in time. Life is short, but art, and the stories it tells, is long.

Jennifer Scott
Director, Dulwich Picture Gallery, London

'What one can see out in the sunlight is always less interesting than what goes on behind a windowpane. In that black or luminous square life lives, life dreams, life suffers.'

Charles Baudelaire,
'Les Fenêtres', 1863[1]

INTRODUCTION
WINDOW GAZES: A CULTURAL HISTORY OF THE WOMAN IN THE WINDOW

In his 1863 poem, *'Les Fenêtres' (Windows)*, Charles Baudelaire adopted the persona of a *flaneur*, a man roaming Paris at random, extracting visions of beauty from the chaos of the city and 'framing' them with words.[2] Seeing a middle-aged woman through a window, he observes her physical appearance, dress and gestures, and imagines her life. As he strolls through the streets, Baudelaire collects these window scenes in his mind, transforming them into a kind of living gallery of pictorial *tableaux* upon which he projects his own fears, longings and fantasies. Much the same can be said for visual artists who take up the composition of the 'woman in the window'. This book, and the accompanying exhibition, explore social, anthropological, architectural, cultural and art historical accounts of this enduring theme and consider how works of art might reflect, contradict or even subvert contemporary practices of window gazing.

While this study cannot be exhaustive, it explores the long history of the representation or evocation of a woman in a window and identifies key civilizations, cultures and time periods for which the theme has a particular meaning. From ancient murals all the way to contemporary photography, video and installation art, this survey demonstrates how artists have long used the window as a visual device for presenting the female figure to the viewer and conditioning a particular response, ranging from empathy to the sense of being a voyeur. The window may suggest the protection or confinement of the woman or a combination of these aspects. Artworks on this theme usually concentrate on notions of identity and the gaze (both of the subject and the viewer) but often also explore ideas around sexuality, psychology and social convention. The motif is one that frequently appears deceptively simple but can be deliberately enigmatic or ambivalent or may have become so over time in cases where the original context or meaning of a work has been lost. This book highlights some of the historic 'misreadings' of these artworks to demonstrate how women's bodies have long been used by artists and their interpreters as carriers of meaning, as 'canvases' upon which to project ideals, morals and fears that reveal a great deal about the preoccupations of a particular social group or society at a given moment.

Fenestration: a brief history

While a window is commonly defined as an opening in the wall of a building, often fitted with glass in a frame, that can be adjusted to admit light, allow air to circulate and allow people to see out, it may also be understood as a charged threshold, a site of observation, communication or as a signifier of wealth or spiritual meaning. Early windows in the Middle East and Western Europe were unglazed apertures, sometimes protected by shutters or veils, while in Asian, Indo-Islamic and Arabic contexts, windows more often took the form of translucent, carved or pierced screens.[3] In addition to providing practical and sanitary functions, windows offered important social, aesthetic and pleasurable experiences for their users. Indeed, before the invention and wide accessibility of telephones, televisions and the internet, windows were the primary sites of informal communication and the practice of simply gazing out of a window was one of the most popular leisure activities in Western Europe.[4] Testifying to this custom are the 'accessories' designed and used to facilitate window gazing from the Early Renaissance up until the 1960s, such as special stools and cushioned boards on which to rest one's arms while leaning out of the window.[5] Although popular during the Early Modern period, the practice of looking out the window was especially debated in relation to ideas of decorum, morality and religious beliefs, for both men and women.[6] These concerns were intensified in cases where women appeared at a window and recur in periods and cultures in which the visibility and movements of women were (and still are) highly controlled, such as in Muslim and Hindu communities practicing *purdah*, screening women from men or strangers. Artistic representations of women at a window may be interpreted in several ways: as an extension of this controlled visibility, as surrogates for these 'invisible' women, or perhaps as fantasies for the 'male gaze'. This term, derived from feminist theory, is helpful in considering works from any culture that take up this motif, as it refers to the practice of depicting women and the world from a masculine, heterosexual perspective, one which often presents women as sexual objects for the pleasure of the male viewer.[7] Indeed, most of the historic works that take up this composition were made by men and for men, a tradition that only really began to change, with a few key exceptions, in the 1960s during the women's liberation movement which campaigned for legal and social equality for women and saw female artists taking up the subject to powerful new ends.[8]

Notes

1. Charles Baudelaire, 'Windows', 1869, in *Paris Spleen*, trans. Louise Varèse (New York: New Directions, 1970), p. 77.
2. Sima Godfrey, 'Baudelaire's Windows', *L'Esprit Créateur*, vol. 22, no. 4: The Poet as Art Critic (Winter 1982), pp. 83–100.
3. On the use of glass in windows see Anne Friedberg, *The Virtual Window: From Alberti to Microsoft* (Cambridge, MA: MIT Press, 2006), pp. 103–22.
4. On the popularity of window gazing as a leisure activity see Daniel Jütte in 'Window Gazes and World Views: A Chapter in the Cultural History of Vision', *Critical Inquiry*, vol. 42, no. 3 (Spring 2016), p. 612; Horst W. Opaschowski, *Pädagogik der freien Lebenszeit* (Opladen, 1996), p. 22.
5. On window stools, see Thomas Bernhard, *Old Masters*, trans. Ewald Osers (London: Quartet, 1989), p. 142, and on the window cushions, see Mark Twain, 'On Renting a Flat in Berlin,' in *A Tramp in Berlin*, ed. Eva C. Schweitzer (New York, 2013), p. 41; visual evidence of these stools is also found in works such as the Master of the Pfullendorf Altar, *A Prophet* (c. 1500), Staatsgalerie Stuttgart. This image, showing an unidentified prophet, is one of the earliest depictions of a window cushion.
6. This has been persuasively argued by Daniel Jütte in 'Window Gazes and World Views: A Chapter in the Cultural History of Vision', *Critical Inquiry*, vol. 42, no. 3 (Spring 2016), pp. 611–46.
7. The term 'male gaze' as we understand it today derives from the work of feminist film theorist Laura Mulvey. See Laura Mulvey, 'Visual Pleasure and Narrative Cinema', *Screen*, vol. 16, no. 3 (Autumn 1975), pp. 6–18.
8. A particularly powerful example of this is Betye Saar's *Black Girl's Window* (1969). Saar, a key activist in both the feminist movement and Black Arts Movement, gives her composition an immediacy and urgency by representing a woman pressed up against the front of the windowpane, fixing her gaze on the beholder. Her use of an actual window frame in this assemblage deliberately blurs the real and the represented, the frame and the window, in order to create a very personal, autobiographical work. This work was recently the subject of an exhibition and accompanying catalogue; see Christophe Cherix, Esther Adler, *Saar: Black Girl's Window*, exh. cat., MoMA One on One Series, Museum of Modern Art, 2019.

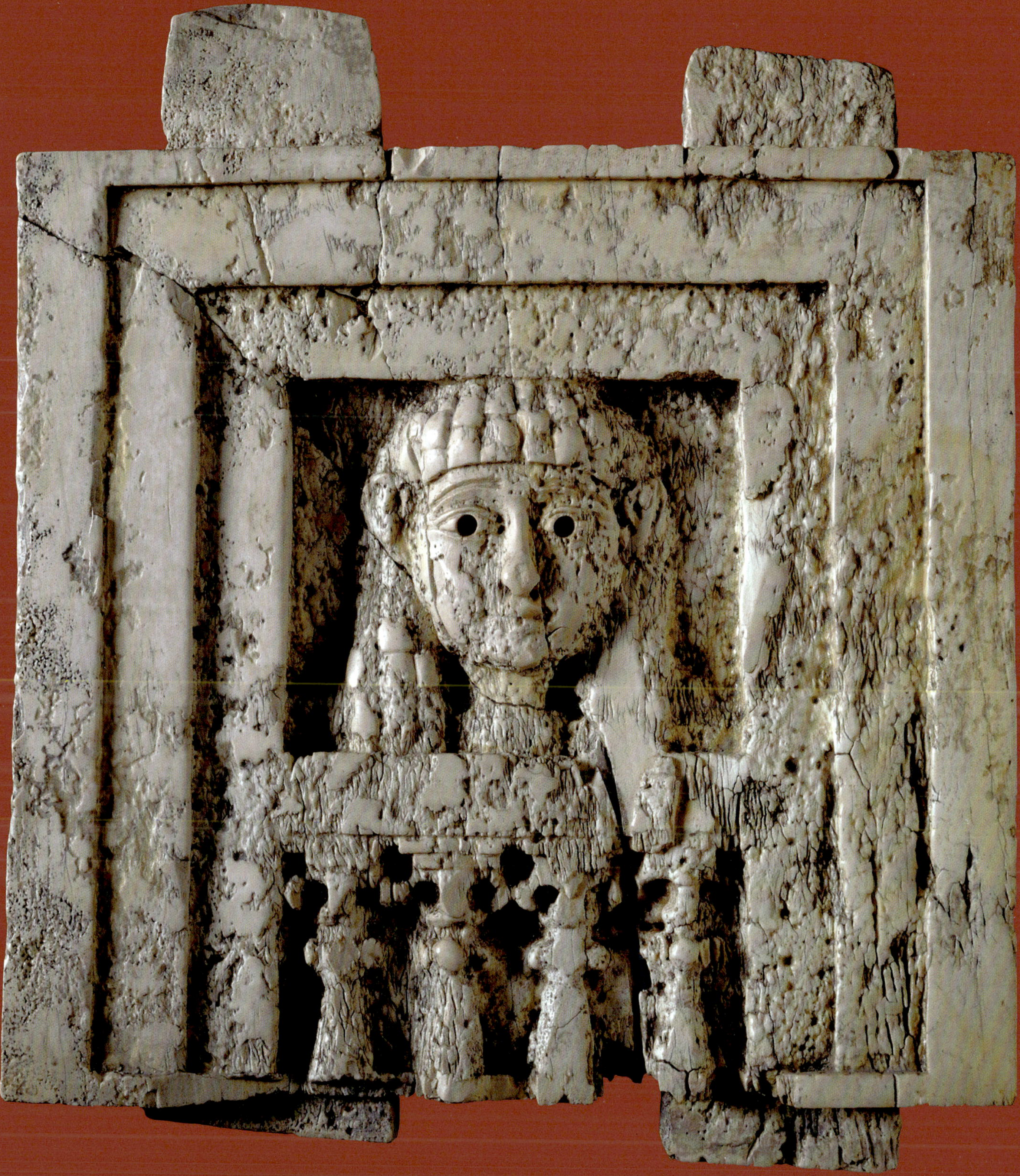

The origins of the window with a view as we know it today are not European but Middle Eastern. Indeed, the first European windows date to the early medieval period and were merely small vents intended to permit the movement of wind and smoke, a function that is reflected in the etymology of the word, derived from the Old Norse *vindauga* (from *vindr* 'wind' and *auga* 'eye').[9] These apertures permitted crucial ventilation and light to enter a building but differed from a more modern function of the window: to frame a view. The earliest evidence for windows with a view and window gazing are not textual but visual, and date centuries earlier to ancient Minoan-Mycenaean works representing a woman in a window. The so-called 'Ramp House' fresco fragments of c. 1450 BCE at Mycenae, for example, depict an architectural façade with female viewers shown in profile peering through window embrasures at the spectacle – bull-leaping – taking place beyond [fig. 1].[10] The earliest evidence for a window with a view, therefore, is also the first instance of the 'woman in the window' motif.[11] By depicting the women at a window, these early artists indicated that the windows were intended to facilitate a view but they also effectively framed the women within and put them on display, transforming them into a kind of spectacle for the viewer.[12]

The (fertility) goddess in the window

The sophisticated visual play between viewer and subject is underscored in slightly later Mycenaean and Phoenician works, such as a four-sided bronze stand of 1200–1050 BCE from Cyprus [fig. 2] and ivory relief of 900–700 BCE from Nimrud (modern-day Iraq) [cat. 1]. In these works, the women are oriented frontally at the window, adopting what was to become a long-standing convention of frontal representation in the ancient Middle East. In both cases, the women represented have been identified either as goddesses or as priestesses serving a particular cult. Unlike the passive observers represented in profile in the earlier work, these women are front-facing, active outward-looking figures within temple architecture.

This four-sided bronze stand probably served as an incense burner used for cult offerings to a deity in the temple in Cyprus where it was excavated. The stand represents a building, and each side includes two windows from which gaze two female heads with shoulder-length twisted plaits falling behind the ears. The women have been identified with the Great Goddess of Cyprus, known alternatively by her Assyro-Babylonian name Ishtar, her Phoenician incarnation as Astarte, or her later Greek name Aphrodite (or sometimes as Aphrodite *Parakyptousa*, 'Aphrodite the Peeper').[13] As this iconography spread across the ancient Middle East and Greece, the woman at the window also became identified with the Sumerian goddess Inanna, the Babylonian Ishtar and the Egyptian Isis, all goddesses associated with beauty, fertility, sexual love, and often also war.[14] Of these, Inanna-Ishtar had an explicitly sexual association and her many epithets include various allusions to her role as a sex worker sitting at a window waiting for clients.[15] Accordingly, the appearance of female figures at the window of a temple has led scholars to interpret them as 'sacred prostitutes' as described by Herodotus, a fifth-century BCE Greek scholar, of Cypriot and Sumerian practices in which women in the temple had sexual relations with strangers.[16] While the historian Strabo, writing in the first century BCE, also describes 'prostitution' in the temple of Aphrodite, the actual practice and historicity of this tradition continues to be debated.[17] Regardless of the precise identity of the woman and the nature of her role, the window may be read as a kind of portal between the secular and the sacred worlds. Further, as a spatial opening, the window was often linked to female sexuality and fertility more explicitly, becoming

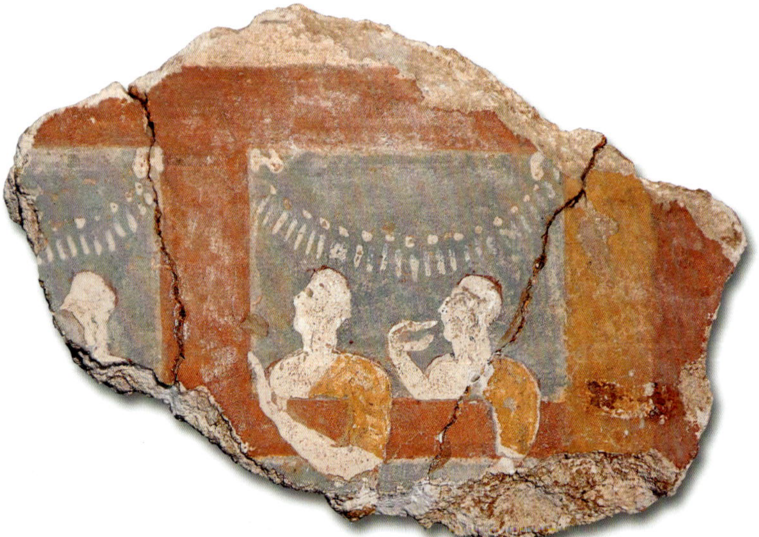

fig. 1
Mycenaean fresco wall painting of three women, Ramp House, Mycenae Acropolis, Greece, c. 1450 BCE

fig. 2
Bronze four-sided stand, Late Cypriot III, Cyprus, 1200–1050 BCE, bronze, 15.8 x 14 cm

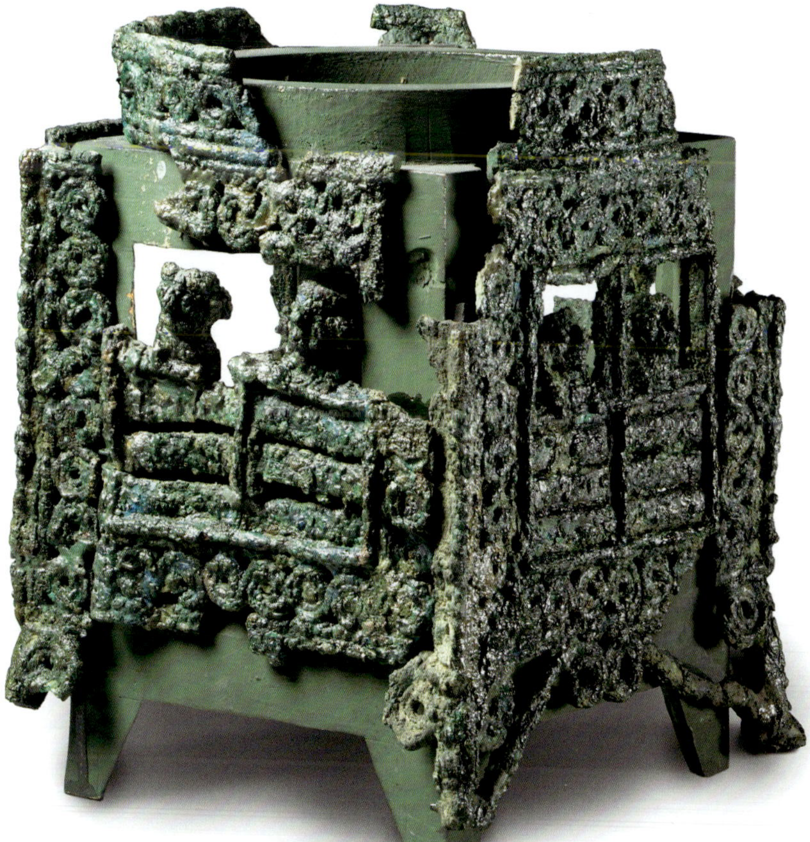

a kind of proxy for the female sexual organ itself.[18] This association was also made by the psychotherapist Sigmund Freud centuries later when he interpreted gates, doors, windows and other openings as possessing sexual symbolism and as suggesting an entrance to the womb.[19]

The composition was perhaps so well established by around 900–700 BCE, when the Phoenician ivory panel *Woman at the Window* [cat. 1] was carved, that the subject need not be directly tied to a cult object such as an incense burner.[20] Here the woman stares out directly at us from a window supported on the palm columns of a temple. This ivory carving originally served a decorative function, adorning a window frame or piece of furniture as seen, for example, on the legs of Ashurbanipal's couch in a banquet scene carved in relief from Nineveh in around 645–640 BCE.[21] By deliberately blending Phoenician, Assyrian and Egyptian styles, attributes and iconographies, this ivory could be traded across these regions and the woman would have formed one of a series, presented more as a patterned ornament than as a formidable cult goddess. Collected and presented this way, her presence may have been intended as a reflection of the power, control, wealth and far reach of the male whose palatial furniture she was meant to adorn.

Windows in the Hebrew Bible

While the precise meaning of the 'woman in the window' composition in these early Middle Eastern works may have varied according to their association with the local goddess, their explicit connection to polytheism and sexual cultic rituals ensured that monotheistic cultures with a different view of sexual practice viewed the motif with guardedness. In the Hebrew Bible, for example, the appearance of a woman in the window suggests someone who is both seductive and distrustful as in the accounts of Queen Jezebel (2 Kings 9:30), Rahab (2 Joshua) and the mother of Sisera (Judges 5: 28–30).[22] Interestingly, Sisera's mother is never named, despite being discussed at length in the biblical account, so her identity is entirely dependent on that of her son, the cruel chieftain of the Canaanite army. The Book of Judges, dated by biblical scholars to the late twelfth or eleventh centuries BCE, describes Sisera's mother at a window awaiting her son's delayed return from battle.[23] In the text, she recounts her joy in imagining his revelling in the spoils of war and in defiling female enemies in particular. Biblical commentators generally interpret this account as a revelation of the mother's cruel and sexually depraved character, of her role in nurturing Sisera's wicked ways and as an account of her failure, despite being queen, to save her son.[24] This 'failure' has also been interpreted more broadly to include the defeat of the Canaanite people. In this case, the 'woman at the window' becomes an emblem of vindictiveness, immorality and powerlessness.

The scene is rarely depicted in the history of art as artists have gravitated instead towards the later account of Sisera's violent end at the hands of Jael. A rare exception is Albert Joseph Moore's *The Mother of Sisera* (1861) [cat. 2], which appears to be a more empathetic interpretation of the biblical account.[25] In this work, the English Pre-Raphaelite artist seems to focus on the mother's anxiety in awaiting her son's return. This rendering also suggests a more positive reading of the tale, one which may follow a rabbinic tradition that focuses on her gaze out of the window and suggests that she had a glimpse of the future in which Sisera's descendants study and teach Torah in Jerusalem, with one of them even becoming the leading Jewish scholar and sage Rabbi Akiva (c. 50–135 CE).[26] Here Moore attempts what he must have believed was a kind of 'historical authenticity' through his inclusion of a kind of lattice or carved screen at the window and in his choice of model for Sisera's mother. The open screen upon which the woman

cat. 2
Albert Joseph Moore,
***The Mother of Sisera*, 1861,**
oil on canvas, 29.4 x 22.5 cm
Tullie House Museum, Carlisle

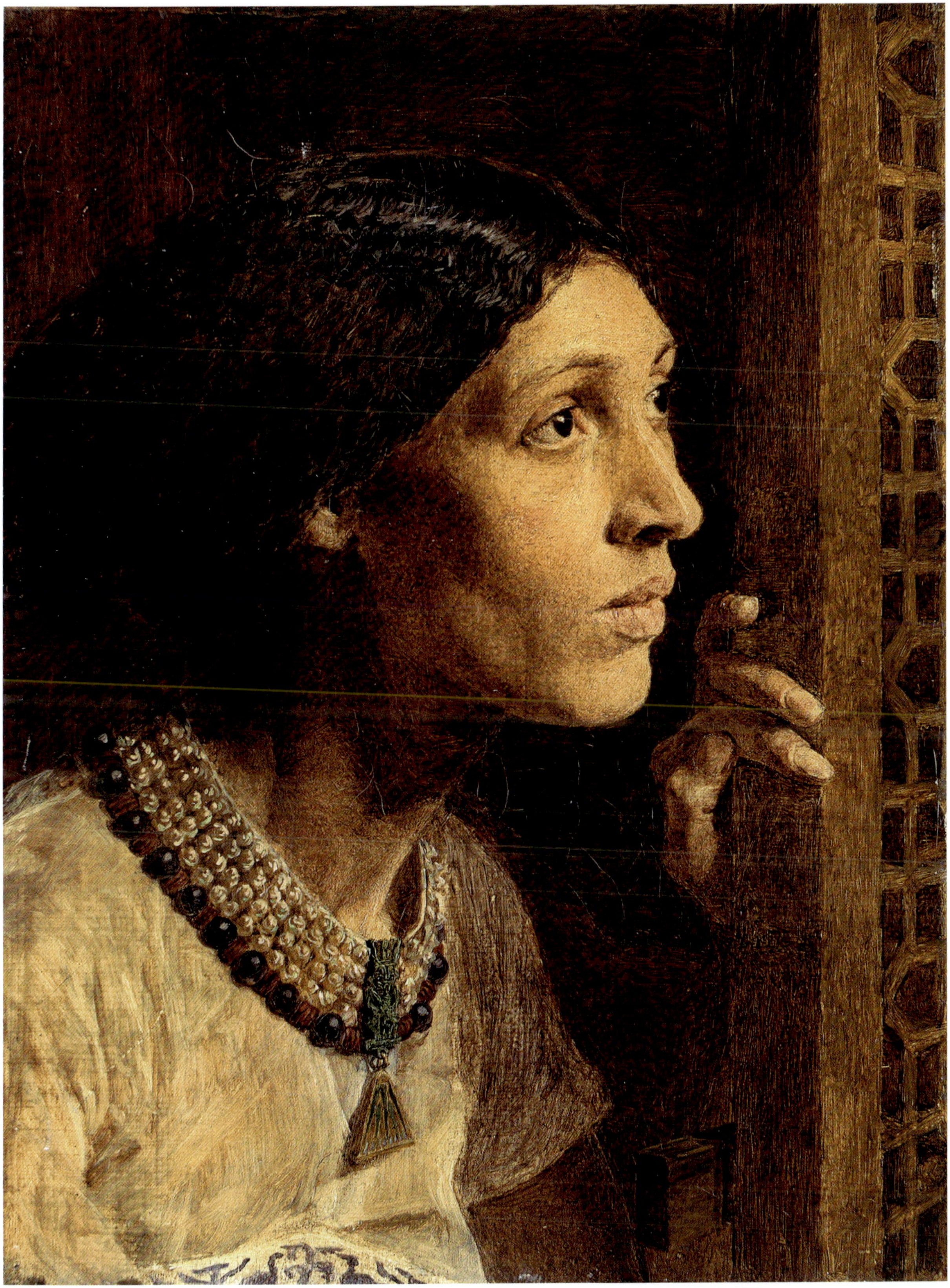

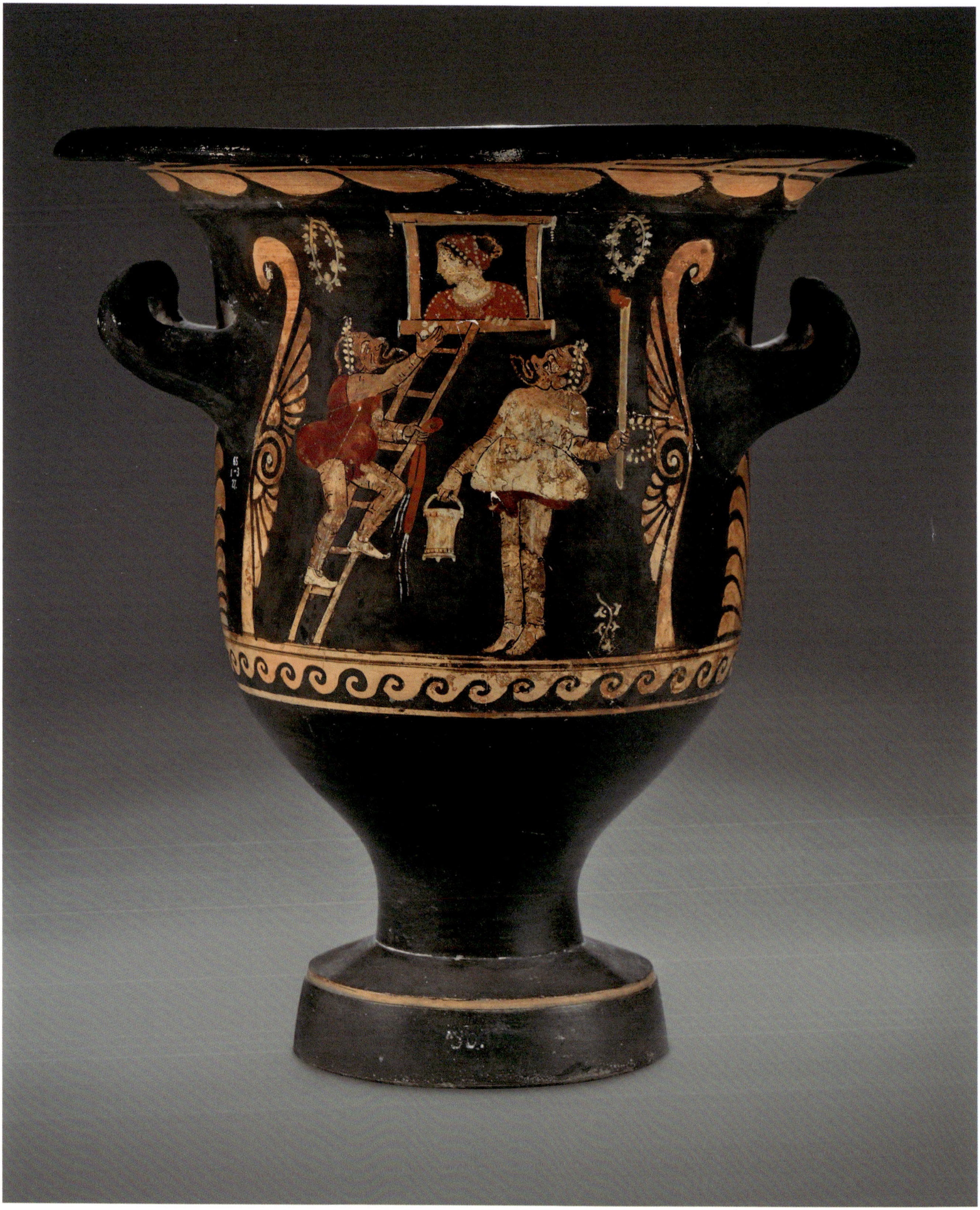

rests her left hand resembles an Indian *jali* [see cat. 26] or Arabic *mashrabiya*, devices traditionally used in areas of palaces or grand houses associated with women that were designed to allow light and air to circulate in hot climates and to allow the women to see out but remain unseen. Moore must have been familiar with this tradition and may even have seen similar carvings himself such as the *mashrabiya* collected by his contemporary Frederic Leighton and later installed in the so-called Arab Hall in his house in Holland Park, London. For his model here Moore turned to the Jamaican-born Fanny Eaton instead of the pale-skinned, blonde or red-headed models he commonly used.[27] Working for several members of the Pre-Raphaelite Brotherhood and their circle, Eaton was often chosen for her beauty, her darker complexion and distinctive features, which were used by artists to portray a variety of ethnicities and characters.

Windows in ancient Greece

Unlike the authors of the Hebrew Bible, the Greek authors of the classical period were not as concerned about the association of the 'woman in the window' with polytheistic worship. However, authors such as Herodotus and Aristophanes did criticize the veneration of women at windows as a lascivious practice of barbarians, suggesting that it was a custom that distinguished 'uncivilised' cultures from 'civilised' ones.[28] Nevertheless, the term *ópē*, often used by Greeks to refer to a window, also implies gazing, suggesting that the practice was prevalent. Artistic representations from the classical period onward – especially those painted on vases – imply however that window gazing was often seen as a questionable practice. A Greek red-figure bell-krater painted by the so-called Asteas painter of 360–340 BCE [cat. 3] uses the motif as part of a narrative, perhaps one taken from a specific play or comedy, which satirises male desire and female sex work.[29] On one side of the vessel, an old man is shown making a nocturnal, clandestine visit up a ladder to a *hetaera*, or highly educated courtesan, at a window. The old man's costume – a mask, padded stomach and a purple phallus – suggests that the scene derives from a comedy. With his arm extended, he offers apples up to the woman, a curious inclusion given that apples were associated with marriage in ancient Greece, where tossing a woman an apple was akin to a proposal and catching it, an acceptance. Rare and expensive, a single apple was usually shared by a bridal couple before going to bed and therefore may have sexual connotations or may refer to several famous Greek myths in which an apple is a portent of danger, marking the beginning of a war or a loss of virtue.[30] Here the offering of apples at the window may be both a proposition and a kind of visual cue for the beholder, a warning of the seductive power and potential danger of female beauty. The subject is particularly appropriate for a wine krater which was used for mixing wine and water and played a crucial part in the drinking, conversation, debates, music and dancing that took place at the Greek symposium. *Hetaerae*, but not wives, were also fixed presences at the symposium where they entertained men with their beauty, wit and conversation and sought out generous protectors.[31]

Roman views and windows in the afterlife

In dramatic contrast to the earlier Middle Eastern, Jewish and Greek traditions just discussed, the practice of gazing from windows in ancient Rome was seen as a more positive activity and was even supported by the law. Testifying to its popularity is the surviving architecture, which in addition to internal courtyards and atria, had outward-facing windows. In the Imperial period, in particular, the changing design of wealthier houses and villas reveals increased interest in the sight lines from a window.[32] Indeed, the window view became a sign of the power of a family over their dominions and

cat. 3
Bell Krater, Paestum (modern-day Italy), 360–340 BCE, pottery, 38 x 37.5 cm
British Museum, 1865,0103.27

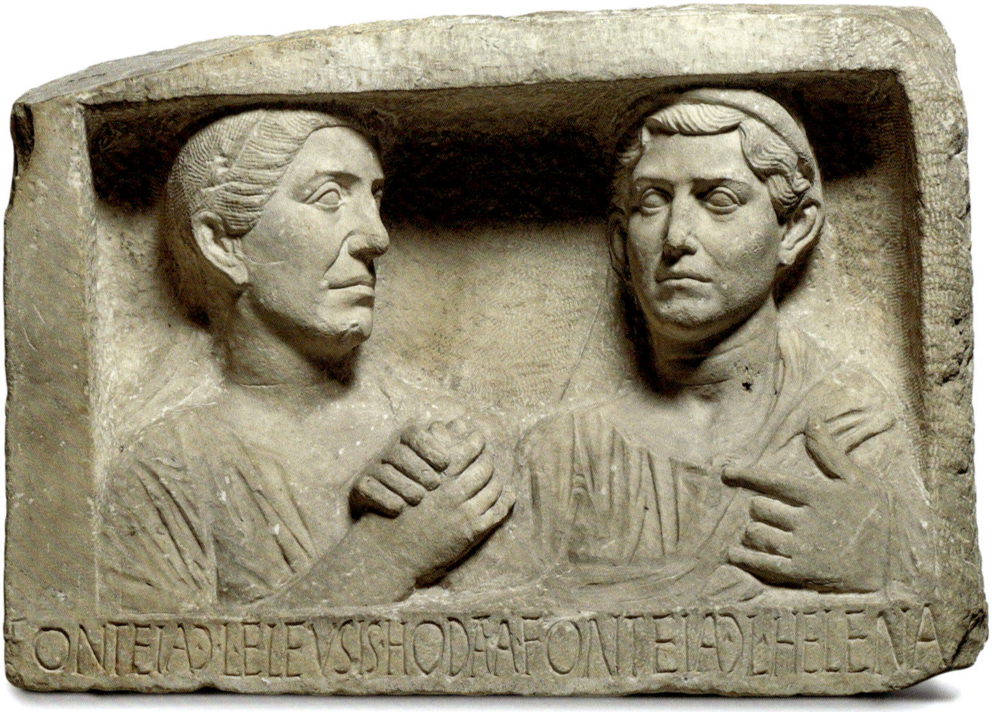

fig. 3
Marble sepulchral relief of two women, Roman, 1st century BCE (Augustan?), marble, 53.75 x 56.25 cm

over nature, a concept that came to be known as *prospectus*.[33] New laws were eventually introduced regulating people's claims regarding views, stipulating in particular that every homeowner had the right to three essential pleasures related to their windows: daylight (*lumen*), air (*aër*) and a view (*prospectus*) and that newer constructions could not obstruct the view of any pre-existing windows.[34] The language used in discussions and legal documents about *prospectus* indicates that they were largely the pride of male homeowners and landowners, suggesting that women's access to windows and their views were largely regulated by men.

This demand for, and interest in, windows extended not only to the dwellings of the living but also tombs of the dead. A funerary tradition developed towards the end of the late Republic and into the early Imperial period of representing the deceased as a carved stone or marble bust, as if looking out from a window. Known as the 'window-tomb' type, these carvings were originally set within the walls of a family mausoleum that was sometimes decorated like a house and included a *triclinium* (dining room) where descendants could eat commemorative meals with the deceased.[35] Traditionally, these 'window tombs' represented a wedded couple, making this relief showing two freedwomen, identified as Eleusis and Helena in the accompanying inscription, from the first century BCE, exceptionally rare [fig. 3].[36] Shown posthumously and perpetually at a window, the women demonstrate the strength of their bond in one life and the next, serving as a source of inspiration and hope not only for their immediate families but also for future generations. Considered within the funerary context for which it was made, the motif of the window takes on an additional meaning, functioning as a threshold between two realms, between this life and the afterlife.

Notes

9. On the etymology of this word see entry 'window (n.)', Online Etymology Dictionary, https://www.etymonline.com/word/window.

10. Maria C. Shaw, 'The Bull-Leaping Fresco from below the Ramp House at Mycenae: A Study in Iconography and Artistic Transmission', *The Annual of the British School at Athens*, vol. 91 (1996), pp. 167–90. See also Donald G. Kyle, *Sport and Spectacle in the Ancient World* (Hoboken: Wiley-Blackwell, 2014), especially p. 42.

11. The same theme was subsequently used to decorate objects such as the Mycenaean ware 'Window-Krater', a large clay bowl used for mixing wine, discovered in Cyprus, on which women are represented in profile again at windows and appear to be watching chariot races. These works identify the women represented as spectators of sporting entertainments to which they are given visual access from a discrete distance.

12. Scholars have suggested that while actual bull-leaping seems to have been practiced by the ancient Minoans at the Palace in Knossos, Crete, only the images and not the sport itself were exported elsewhere. Understood as a kind of demonstration of power, authority and bravura, the subject was adopted and reinterpreted for different locations. In the so-called Ramp House in Mycenae, therefore, the representation of the sport, with the addition of female spectators, may be understood as an importation and dramatisation of this assertion of power in a new context.

13. On this work as a representation of the Aphrodite Parakyptousa, see Rose Mary Washbourne, 'Aphrodite Parakyptousa "the Woman at the Window": The Cypriot Astarte-Aphrodite's Fertility Role in Sacred Prostitution and Rebirth', in *Report of the Department of Antiquities of Cyprus* (1999), pp. 163–77. On the iconography more broadly, see Carla Gottlieb, *The Window in Art: From the Window of God to the Vanity of Man: A Survey of Window Symbolism in Western Painting* (New York: Abaris, 1981), pp. 31–40, and Othmar Keel, Christoph Uehlinger, *Gods, Goddesses, and Images of God in Ancient Israel*, trans. Thomas H. Trapp (Minneapolis: Fortress Press, 1998), p. 201.

14. The combination/elision of the Innana-Ishtar-Astarte on the island of Cyprus has been traced to at least the thirteenth century BCE. For more on these goddesses and their associations, and the links between Middle Eastern and Greek goddesses, see Rose Mary Washbourne, 'Out of the Mouths of Pots: Towards an Interpretation of the Symbolic Meaning of Cypriot Bronze Age Funerary Artefacts Including Examples in the University of Canterbury's Logie Collection', *Studies in Mediterranean Archaeology and Literature, Pocketbook 158* (2000), p. 393, especially section 5.2: 'The Genealogy of Aphrodite: the transmission into ancient Greece of Near Eastern myth and ritual,' pp. 267–327.

15. Rose Mary Washbourne, *Aphrodite Parakyptousa, 'the Woman at the Window'. The Cypriot Aštarte-Aphrodite's fertility in sacred prostitution and rebirth*. Report of the Department of Antiquities, Cyprus: (1999), p. 164.

16. See Herodotus, *The Histories* (I, 199); Herodotus, a Greek historian, wrote that every Sumerian woman had to attend the temple of Ishtar/Inanna and agree to sex with any male that asked her. Once she performed this ritual, the male visitor gave her money to donate to the temple. Scholars have called this 'sacred prostitution', although the rite was essentially performed as a devotion or prayer to the goddess to ensure fertility. Given that he lived many centuries after the purported establishment of this practice, Herodotus' reliability is debated by scholars. See also Hellenistic author Athenaeus in his book *The Deipnosophists* ('The Sophists at Dinner'), 13.572 e–f, 573a. On the ivories see Richard David Barnett, *A Catalogue of the Nimrud Ivories: With Other Examples of Ancient Near Eastern Ivories in the British Museum* (London: British Museum Press, 1957). The first major study on this iconography was Wolfgang Fauth, *Aphrodite Parakyptus: Untersuchungen zum Erscheinungsbild der vorderasiatischen Dea Prospiciens* (Wiesbaden: Franz Steiner, 1967), pp. 331–437. On accounts of 'sacred prostitution' and its interpretations in the scholarship see Washbourne, *Aphrodite Parakyptousa*, pp. 163–177.

17. See *Strabo Geographica* (VIII. 6.20) In Pindar's eulogy for Xenophon of Corinth it is stated that Xenophon vowed to devote one hundred courtesans to the temple of Aphrodite at Corinth should he succeed in competition for the Olympic crown; see frag. 122 (Snell-Maehler), cited in Washbourne, *Aphrodite Parakyptousa*, p. 166.

18. See discussion on this topic in Nehama Aschkenasy, *Woman at the Window: Biblical Tales of Oppression and Escape* (Detroit: Wayne State University Press, 1998), especially p. 14.

19. Sigmund Freud, *The Complete Introductory Lectures on Psychoanalysis,* trans. and ed. James Strachey (London: Allen and Unwin, 1971).

20. Like the Mycenaeans, the Phoenicians also settled in Cyprus from about the tenth century BCE and the island served as a crucial meeting point between cultures.

21. This carved gypsum wall panel relief fragment is now held in the British Museum, inv. 124920.

22. Jezebel was the daughter of the Phoenician King Etbaal. She is often interpreted as an embodiment of evil in the Bible, having instituted the worship of a false God in Israel, engaged in a large number of brutal killings including Elijah and other prophets of Yahweh, and suffered a gruesome death by defenestration for her wicked acts (2 Kings 9:30). The account has been interpreted as an example of a woman flaunting her feminine and sexual powers, who interfered in the male world of politics and who effectively left her assigned position 'at the window' and was punished for it. On Jezebel see Aschkenasy, *Woman at the Window*, pp. 15–16. The story of Rahab at the window is told in 2 Joshua, which recounts how Rahab the harlot admitted two Israelite spies through the window of her house in the city walls of Jericho, where

she hid them for the night and then lowered them to safety through the window the next day. The breaching of this window-threshold by the spies in this account is what secures her protection but also marks the end of an old alliance and the establishment of a new one.

23. On these various datings, see W.F. Albright, 'Further Light on the History of Israel from Lachish and Megiddo', *Bulletin of the American Schools of Oriental Research*, no. 68 (1937), pp. 22–26; A.D. Mayes, 'The Historical Context of the Battle against Sisera', *Vetus Testamentum*, vol. 19, no. 3 (1969), pp. 353–60.

24. Don Seeman, 'The Watcher at the Window: Cultural Poetics of a Biblical Motif,' in *Prooftexts*, vol. 24, no. 1 (Winter 2004), pp. 1–50.

25. For the most recent discussion of this work see Peter Funnell, Charlotte Gere, Jan Marsh, Pamela Nunn, *Pre-Raphaelite Sisters* (London: National Portrait Gallery, 2019), p. 104, cat. 73.

26. On this tradition see Barbara Sofer, 'The Human Spirit: Sisera's mother,' *The Jerusalem Post*, 21 October 2011.

27. On Eaton see: Jan Marsh, *Black Victorians: Black People in British Art, 1800–1900*, exh. cat. (London: Lund Humphries, 2005), pp. 149, 160, 162.

28. See Gottlieb, *The Window in Art*, p. 41; and Fauth, *Aphrodite Parakyptusa*, pp. 356–57, 362.

29. Samuel Birch, Sir Charles Thomas Newton, *A Catalogue of the Greek and Etruscan Vases in the British Museum* (London: William Nichol, 1851); also Henry Beauchamp Walters, Edgar John Forsdyke, Cecil Harcourt Smith, *Catalogue of the Greek and Etruscan vases in the British Museum* I–IV (London: British Museum Press, 1893); A.H. Smith, F.N. Pryce, *Corpus Vasorum Antiquorum: Great Britain 2, British Museum 2* (London: British Museum Press, 1926), pl. 2, 1.

30. The apples may have been intended to call to mind myths such as the Golden Apples of the Garden of Hesperides, which conferred immortality and were given to Hera as a wedding present when she married Zeus or the story of Paris who presented the apple of discord to Aphrodite, inadvertently causing the start of the Trojan War. The fruits may have also called to mind the tale of the nymph Atalanta who paused to pick up apples during a foot race, causing her to lose both the race and her virginity. For the story of Paris see a brief allusion in Homer's *Iliad* (24.25–30); Ovid's *Heroides* 16.71ff, 149–152 and 5.35f; Lucian's *Dialogues of the Gods* 20; Pseudo-Apollodorus, *Bibliotheca*, E.3.2; and Hyginus' *Fabulae*, 92; the story of Atalanta's footrace is told in the Pseudo-Apollodorus, *Bibliotheca*, 3. 9. 2; Ovid, *Metamorphoses*, 10. 605; Servius on the *Aeneid*, 3. 113 and Hyginus' *Fabulae*, 185.

31. On *hetaerae* at the symposium, see Laura McClure, *Courtesans at Table: Gender and Greek Literary Culture in Athenaeus* (London: Routledge, 2003).

32. See Hans-Jürgen Horn, 'Respiciens per fenestras, prospiciens per cancellos: Zur Typologie des Fensters in der Antike', in *Jahrbuch für Antike und Christentum* 10 (1967), pp. 30–60, especially p. 32; Hans-Jürgen Horn, 'Fenster', in *Reallexikon für Antike und Christentum: Sachwörterbuch zur Auseinandersetzung des Christentums mit der Antiken Welt*, ed. Theodor Klauser et al., 25 vols. to date (Stuttgart, 1950–), col. 734; and Reinhard Herbig, 'Fensterstudien an antiken Wohnbauten in Italien', *Mitteilungen des Deutschen Archäologischen Instituts, Römische Abteilung*, no. 44 (1929), pp. 260–321, especially p. 296.

33. See Heinrich Drerup, 'Bildraum und Realraum in der römischen Architektur', *Mitteilungen des Deutschen Archäologischen Instituts, Römische Abteilung*, no. 66 (1959), pp. 147–74; also Zoja Pavlovskis, *Man in an Artificial Landscape: The Marvels of Civilization in Imperial Roman Literature* (Leiden: Brill, 1973), especially pp. 5–7, 14–16; and Hans-Jürgen Horn, 'Respiciens per fenestras, prospiciens per cancellos: zur Typologie des Fensters in der Antike', *Jahrbuch für Antike und Christentum*, no. 10 (1967), especially pp. 35–40.

34. Jütte, p. 619.

35. John E. Stambaugh, *The Ancient Roman City* (Baltimore: Johns Hopkins University Press, 1998) p. 195.

36. The women are shown clasping their right hands in the *dextrarum iunctio* gesture which traditionally symbolised a marriage bond which cannot be the case here. Fascinatingly, the relief was recut, probably in late antiquity, to alter the image so that the figures more closely resembled this married couple type. Indeed, the figure on the left now resembles a man, a feat achieved in part by cutting most of the woman's original veil or head covering away. A wedding ring was also added to the fourth finger of the left hand of the woman on the right. Once freed, enslaved people commissioned these kinds of *libertini* sculptures as substitutes for the kind of ancestor portraits that non-enslaved people had. The two women in this relief were *conlibertae* as the inscription makes clear but they might also have been mother and daughter. They may have proudly commissioned this work as a means of asserting their new status and, in selecting this particularly charged gesture, may have sought to express a new familial bond or kinship or to reaffirm their blood relationship in new visual terms. On the *dextrarum iunctio* gesture see Reinhard Stupperich, 'Zur dextrarum iunctio auf frühen römischen Grabreliefs', *Boreas 6*, (1983) pp. 143–50; also Glenys Davies, 'The Significance of the Handshake Motif in Classical Funerary Art', *American Journal of Archaeology*, vol. 89, no. 4 (October 1985), pp. 627–40. On freed slave reliefs see Paul Zanker, 'Grabreliefs römischer Freigelassener', *JdI*, vol. 90 (1975), pp. 267–315; on the identities of these women see Davies (1985), Keegan (2003) and Walker (1981) who favour either a mother-daughter relationship, a '*conliberta*' (female slave belonging to the same collective social unit), or a relative of the second woman. Others, such as D'Angelo (1990) and Brooten (1998), have seen the two women as partners/lovers.

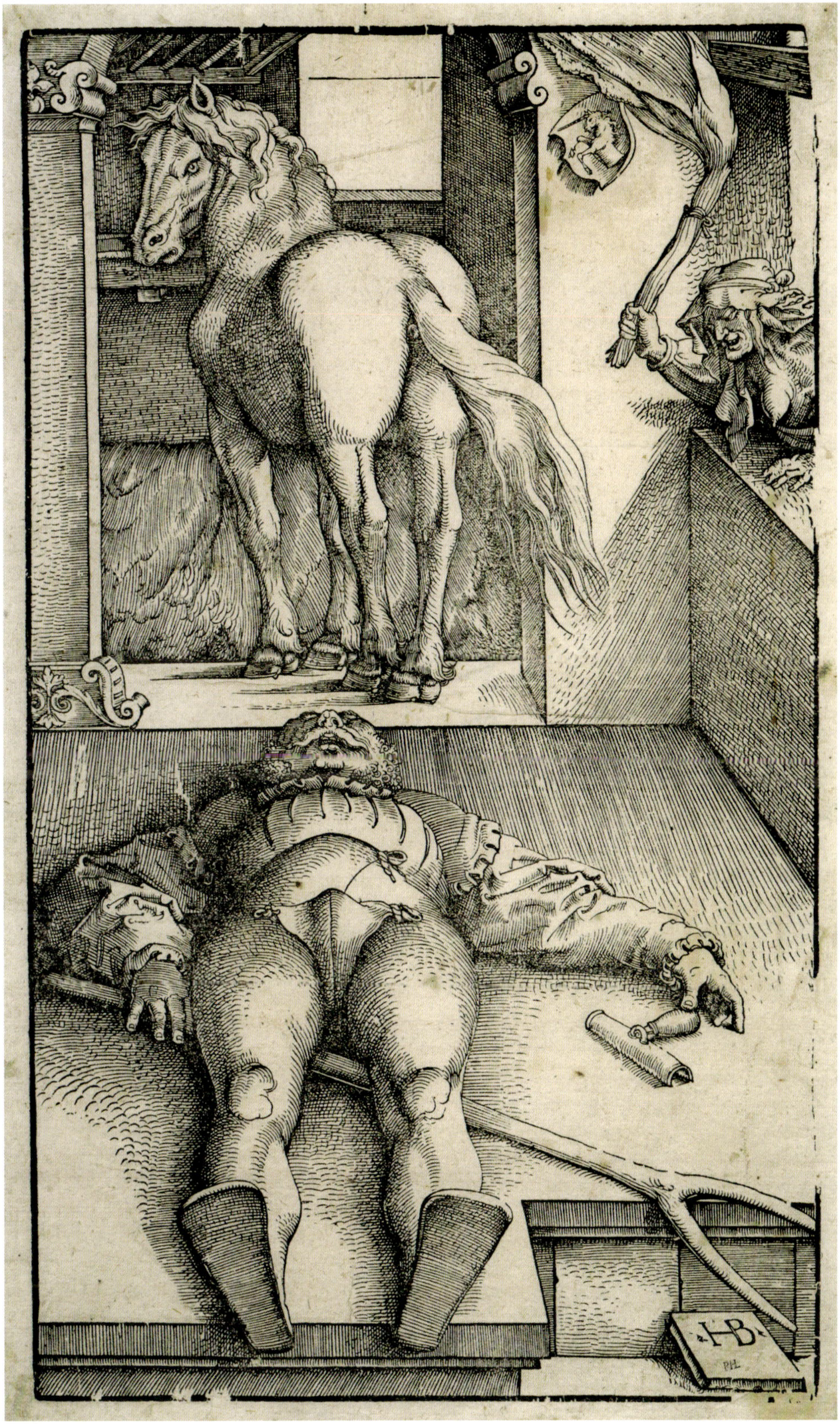
HB

print is known was given at a later date, and the precise interpretation of the scene is still a subject of debate. Here we see the interior of an elegant stable in which the groom, rendered in extreme foreshortening, is curiously stretched out on the ground while his horse appears agitated in its stall. The scene is observed by a bare-breasted old woman who leans through the window at the right, brandishing a flaming torch. There is an overall sense of disquiet, which has led scholars to propose several interpretations, all centring on the woman, often called a hag, witch or sorceress. It has been suggested that she has just worked her magic on the horse who has somehow rendered the groom unconscious. Accordingly, she may embody the 'triumph of women' theme, in which the dangerous or misappropriated power of women is presented as a kind of parody (and warning) of a world turned upside down. The prone groom might represent the artist himself, given that he bears a resemblance to Baldung, whose coat of arms also appears at the upper right of the composition. While attempts have been made to associate this print with a contemporary fascination with witchery, a particular narrative from German folk tales, or to interpret the whole as an allegory or warning against anger or lust, its interpretation remains elusive. A new possible identity for the woman, one associated with contemporary beliefs about gazes is advanced here. The old woman's appearance, her long, sagging breasts, gap-toothed smile and wild hair associate her with stereotypical images of witches from this period but, more precisely, seem to refer back to a personification of the vice of envy.[49] Baldung may have been drawing on a late fifteenth-century print showing *A Battle of Sea Gods* by Andrea Mantegna in which Envy (identified by the Latin inscription *Invidia*) is represented as a naked hag with sagging breasts astride a sea monster. Mantegna's figure swiftly inspired a host of artists including Albrecht Dürer (Baldung's master), suggesting that Baldung could have easily known the composition either directly or indirectly.[50] The term *Invidia* derives from the verb *invidere*, meaning 'to look too closely', and traditionally this was the vice most associated with witches and their magic as they were believed to possess the power to cast a curse with a malevolent glare, known as the Evil Eye. This type of gaze reflects the ancient belief, as described in the writings of Ovid, Virgil and others, that envy originates from the eyes and it is through the gaze that one can cast a spell or 'bewitch'.[51] If Baldung's witch is a personification of *Invidia* then we might read the print on two complementary levels. On one, the witch, lacking her traditional beastly mount, may be seen as envying the groom's horse and, having bewitched the groom through her gaze, be preparing to take his steed. On a second, meta-level, we might understand the print as a kind of allegory of looking, in which the witch's envious gaze embodies that of Baldung's artistic rivals and the groom, whose coat of arms and likeness associate him with the artist, is cast as a victim of such malicious envy. Cleverly, the artist implicates the viewer of this print in this game of 'close looking' as we effectively take up the position of the woman at the window and become aware of the power of our own gaze. Although the groom/artist appears to be the victim of *Invidia*'s spell here, he also transcends it as, ultimately, it is the viewer who is most bewitched by Baldung's skill in rendering this dramatic perspective and enigmatic subject matter.

Spiritual seeing

Given the concerns about different kinds of gazes and window 'peeping' in the Medieval and early Renaissance periods, it is unsurprising that scenes depicting people looking out from windows are relatively scarce. Those that do exist often represent a kind of internal looking

fig. 5
Fol. 14 v from the
Hours of Mary of Burgundy,
1470–79, 22.5 x 16.3 cm

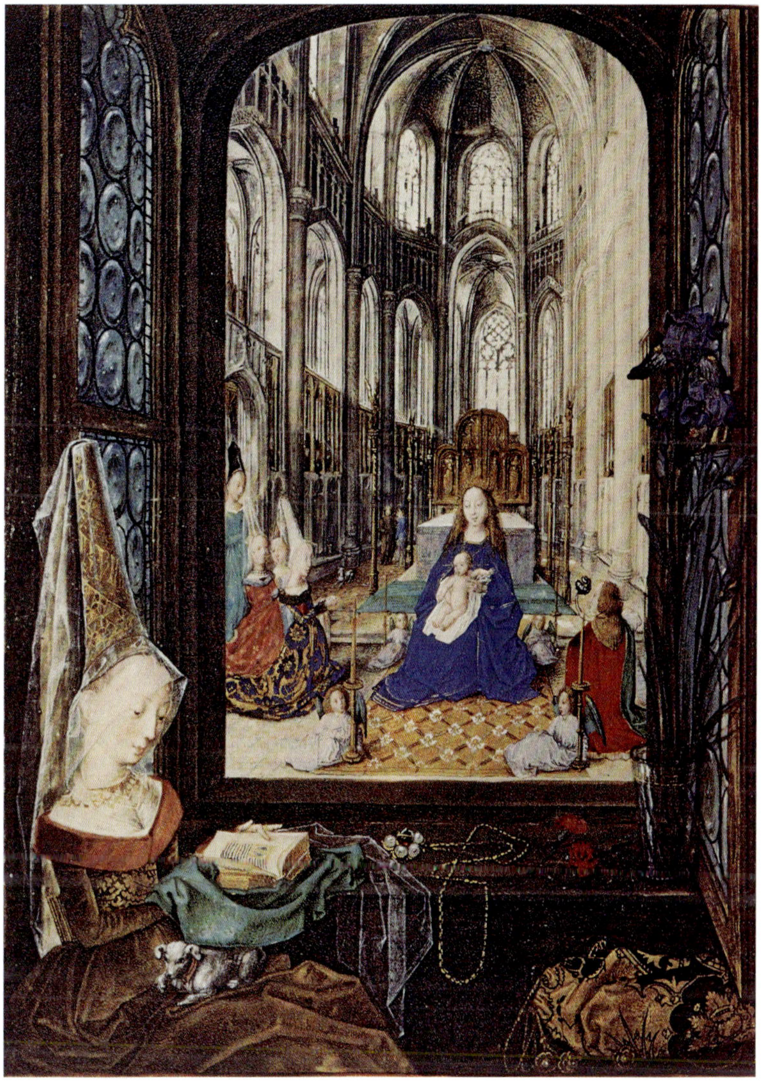

or 'spiritual seeing' that occurs, for example, when a figure experiences a sacred vision, as in the case of an illumination of 1470–79 in which Mary of Burgundy is shown sitting at a window and reading from a book of hours. [fig. 5][52] The reward for her sustained prayers is revealed through the window as a vision of the Virgin and Child enthroned within a medieval church. In this complex composition, Mary of Burgundy's domestic interior opens up, through a window, onto another interior scene, one modelled on ecclesiastical architecture but which is clearly otherworldly.

Similarly, Renaissance painters such as Paolo Veronese used the window as a way of representing a spiritual vision, experienced by the figure in their mind but revealed to the viewer through a window. In *The Dream of Saint Helena* (c. 1570) [fig. 6], for example, Veronese represents the mother of Emperor Constantine asleep at a windowsill while the events taking place outside the window are understood as the vision she experienced in a dream.[53] Through the window frame, we see winged angels bearing the cross upon which Christ was crucified and revealing the location of the True Cross in the Holy Land to Helena. Veronese seems to have devised this artistic solution from a print by Marcantonio Raimondi [cat. 5] who in turn borrowed it from a drawing by Raphael.[54] The painting, print and drawing all show a woman, sitting with one foot up on a stone bench in a window alcove with her head resting in her hand and her elbow on the window ledge. However, while Marcantonio's print probably represents Helena, the woman's identity in the Raphael drawing remains unknown as there is no view to provide any further clues, leading some scholars to suggest that she represents the Greek princess Danaë instead. The motif of the 'woman in the window' was one that particularly appealed to artists' sensibilities and which they often adopted after seeing it used by another artist and transformed

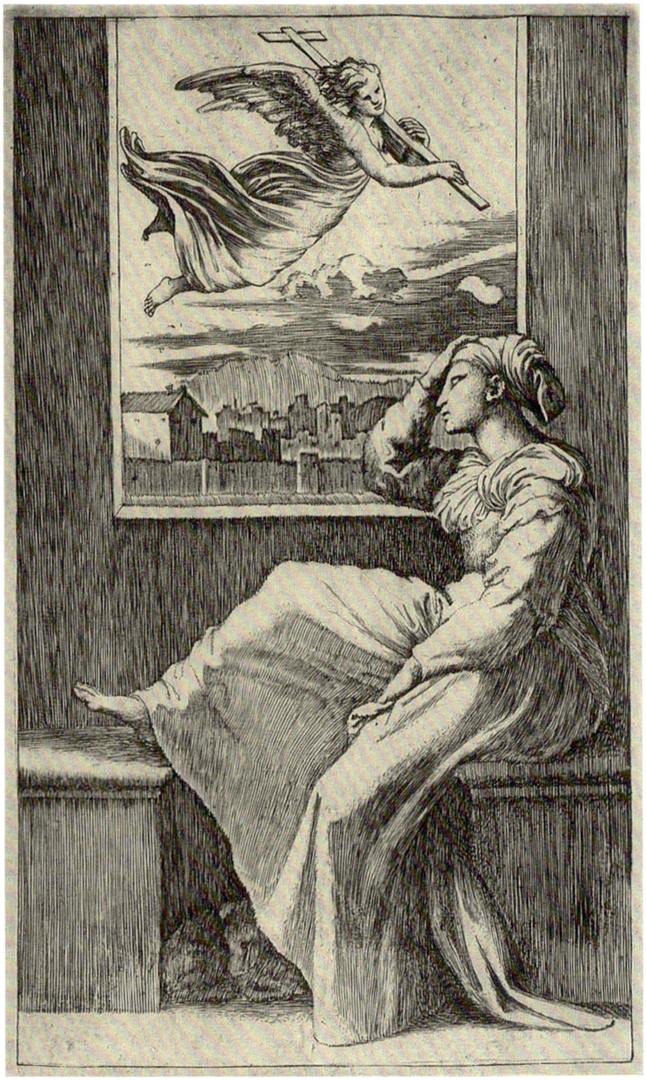

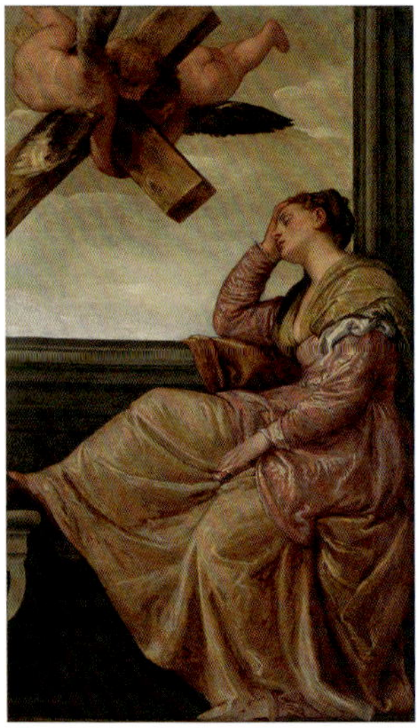

above, cat. 5
Marcantonio Raimondi,
***A Woman by a Window*, c. 1510–20,**
engraving, 16.4 x 10 cm
The Royal Collection / HM Queen Elizabeth II

right, fig. 6
Paolo Veronese, *The Dream of Saint Helena*, c. 1570, oil on canvas, 197.5 x 115.6 cm

to serve their own artistic needs. In this case, Veronese seems to have given the composition an additional, witty association as the canvas probably served as the outside shutter of a church organ. Accordingly, the woman's somnolent posture at the window suggests not only a vision but also a moment of quiet during which the organ was not in use.

The Virgin Mary as the window of heaven

Dirk Bouts' *The Virgin and Child* (c. 1465) [cat. 6] exemplifies the medieval exegetical tradition of interpreting the Virgin Mary as the 'window of heaven' (*fenestra coeli*) and as the 'crystal clear window' (*fenestra crystallina*).[55] Here the Virgin is shown at a window with the Christ Child seated on a cushion and white cloth in front of her on the sill. The white fabric below the Child, suggestive of both swaddling clothes and his future winding sheet, was probably painted over the (now missing) original frame as if unfurling outside of the painting. This detail would have further underscored how, together, the window and frame bridge the world of the beholder and that of the sacred figures. Indeed, the window here serves several functions: to present the sacred figures in a manner akin to the way royals presented themselves to their subjects, as an allegory of the Virgin and as a kind of picture frame. Strikingly and rather unusually for this kind of composition, Bouts also includes a second window in the background of his picture, through which we see a landscape and the spires of a medieval city.

In representing the Virgin at a window, the artist seems to have been drawing on several textual traditions that liken her to a *fenestra coeli*. The earliest of these derives from a medieval Christian interpretation of the Song of Songs in the Hebrew Bible.[56] In the Song, the Bridegroom describes glimpsing his Bride, who Christians associated with the Virgin, through a window.[57] Such allegorical associations are subsequently found in a sermon attributed to Saint Augustine and several medieval hymns that extol Mary as a 'window of Heaven'.[58] Further, Petrarch's description of the Virgin as '*fenestra del Ciel lucente altera*' ('a noble and bright window of heaven') in his fourteenth-century *Canzoniere* attests to the sustained currency of this epithet.[59]

Bouts' *Virgin and Child* is a particularly distinct visualisation of this textual tradition as he places the Virgin between two windows to underscore her role as mediatrix, a figure who mediates between the earthly and celestial realms, and an intercessor who commends the viewer and their prayers to Christ. Read against the window behind her, which is clear or open below but set with coloured glass at the top, she may also be identified with the *fenestra crystallina* as, like a piece of clear glass, the divine light of God passed through her, endowing the world with light. This metaphor is intended to remind the viewer of Mary's role as the mother of God, that is, through whom he was incarnated and became fully human, and that through her intercession the faithful might approach paradise. In setting her against a rich brocade cloth, known as a cloth of honour, in the manner of medieval royalty, we are also reminded of her role as Queen of Heaven. Despite the long textual and popular history of describing the Virgin as a window, artists seem to have only begun visualising the metaphor in the fifteenth century and the tradition appears to originate with Bouts and his Netherlandish contemporaries, with the subject only becoming prevalent in paintings made south of the Alps several decades later.[60]

The scale, subject and medium of Antonio Rizzo's *Virgin and Child*, dating to the second half of the fifteenth century [cat. 7], suggest it was intended for private devotion. Originally installed within a domestic interior at a height that suggested an actual window, it may have

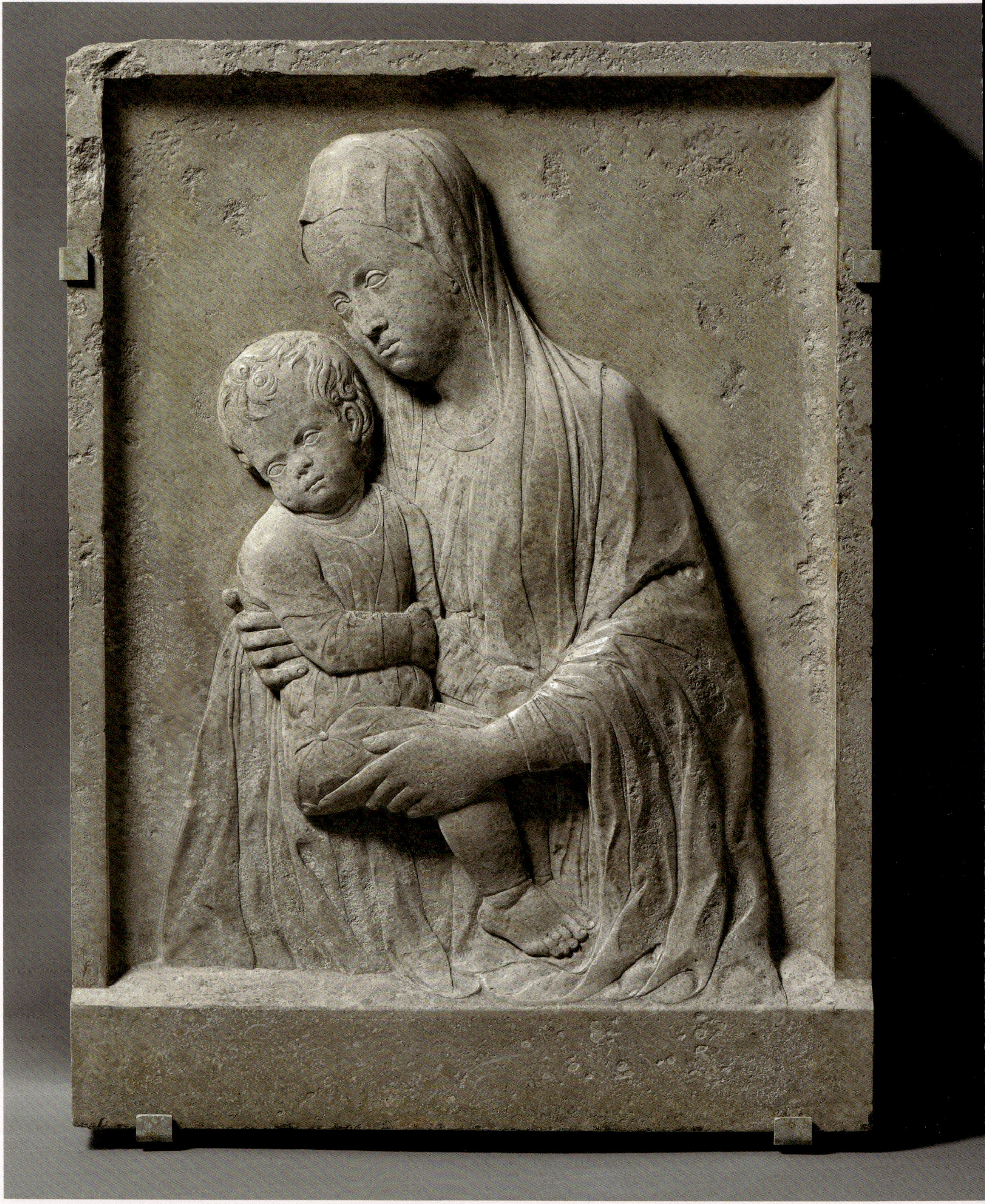

seemed as if the Virgin and Child had miraculously appeared in response to the devotee's prayers. This work draws on an earlier sculptural tradition established by Donatello in his *Pazzi Madonna* of c. 1420 which was probably produced for the private devotions of the Pazzi family within their Florentine palazzo [fig. 7].[61] Donatello's marble relief is often described as the first appearance in Renaissance art of a perspectival window frame that mediates between the beholder and the image within. Copies after Donatello's work were swiftly produced both in sculpted form and in paint, testifying to both the dissemination and popularity of this theme beyond Florence.[62] Nevertheless, Rizzo's *Virgin and Child* is a distinctive and particularly solemn reinterpretation of the more familiar Florentine models sometimes referred to as 'window ledge Madonnas'.[63] Here, for example, Mother and Child are not locked in a tender embrace, nor do they even look at each other or engage the viewer directly but instead gaze obliquely out of the window frame as if preoccupied with foreknowledge of events to come. Indeed, Rizzo makes several sophisticated visual arguments through his interpretation of the motif: the window becomes an allegory of the Virgin, a kind of boundary delimiting two realms, a means of suggesting a visionary experience and, as an allusion to the way royals presented themselves to their subjects, an evocation of the Kingdom of Heaven.

Sacred encounters at the window

Given the frequency with which many Early Modern viewers saw the Virgin Mary at a window, they may at first have mistaken the beautiful and serene figure of Saint Avia for the mother of Jesus [cat. 8]. Avia's window, however, is one of incarceration and is often barred, given that she was jailed for refusing to marry, consecrating herself instead to God. While the dates and details of Avia's life vary according to different legends, all

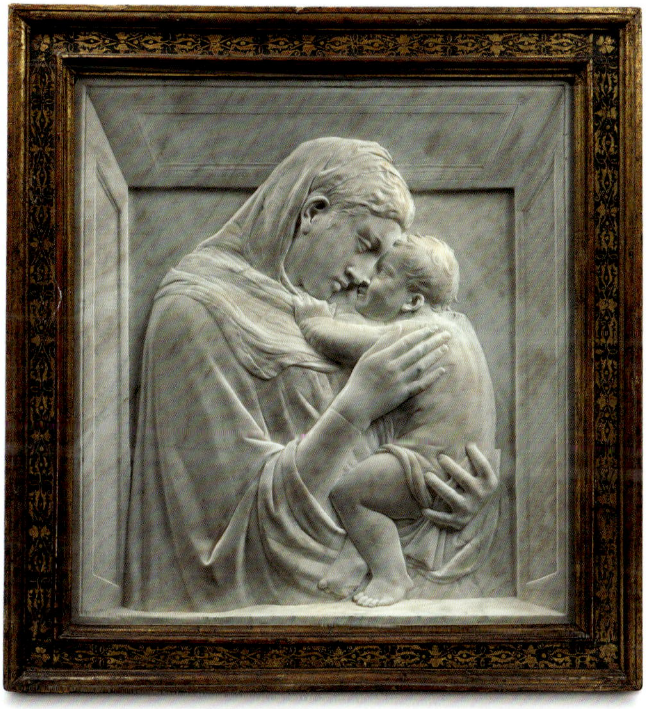

opposite, cat. 7
Antonio Rizzo, *Virgin and Child*,
second half of the 15th century,
Pietra di Nanto, 63.7 x 48.5 x 5 cm
Courtesy of Daniel Katz Gallery, London

above, fig. 7
Donatello, *Pazzi Madonna*,
c. 1420, marble, 74.5 x 69.5 cm

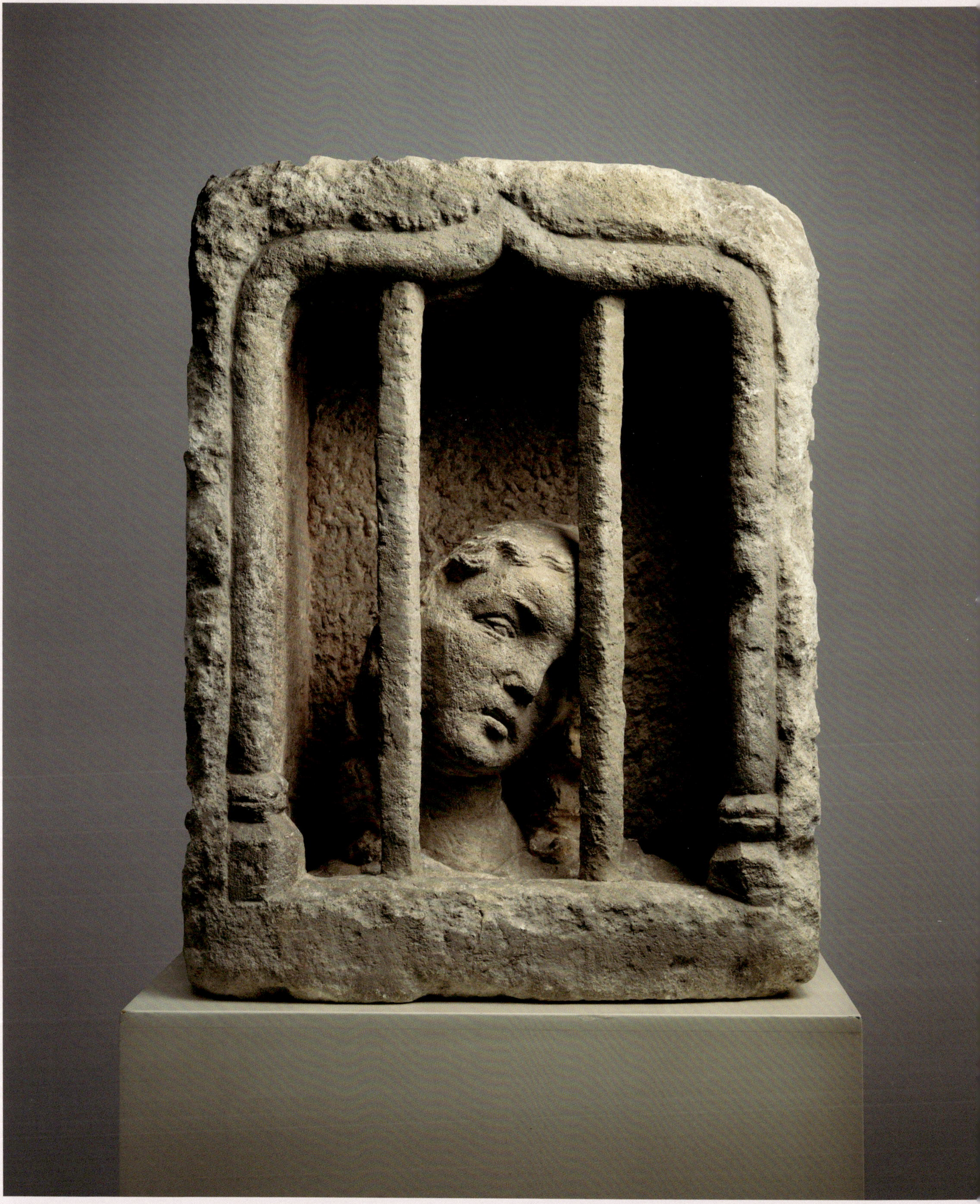

accounts agree that she was imprisoned for adhering to her Christian beliefs and, accordingly, her primary identifying characteristic is her incarcerated appearance at a window. Differing accounts suggest that she was either a third- or fifth-century Christian martyr originally from Sicily (where she is known as Avia) or that she was from or travelled to Cornwall (where she is venerated as Saint Ewe), to Cologne and finally to Boulogne-sur-Mer, France (where she is known as Avoye or Auré).[64] Most of the surviving representations of the saint are of Flemish or northern French origin, suggesting her cult was particularly strong in those areas. One version of the legend describes her as a young woman of extraordinary beauty who, having consecrated herself to God, prayed to have her beauty taken away so as not to attract the attention of suitors. Her prayers unanswered, she elected to live a life of seclusion instead. Nonetheless, in Cologne she attracted the attention of a barbarian chieftain who imprisoned her without food after she refused to marry him. She was sustained by the Virgin Mary who, every week, brought her bread (or the Eucharist) 'kneaded by angels'. Most of the known representations of the saint are contained in small manuscript illuminations such as this page from a French book of hours which includes an intercessory prayer, an appeal for assistance addressed to the saint [fig. 8]. A similar prayer may have been used by the faithful to address Avia in this rare, life-sized, bust-length sculpture which was probably originally set within an external wall of a French church or chapel [cat. 8]. In this context, visitors could have approached and communicated with her as if she were a living woman, effectively taking up the Virgin's traditional position outside her window. The saint was intended to serve as a model of chastity and courage for the faithful, and young women in particular, and this sculpture must have served as a powerful agent of prayer and petition in the life of the religious community of the building it once adorned.

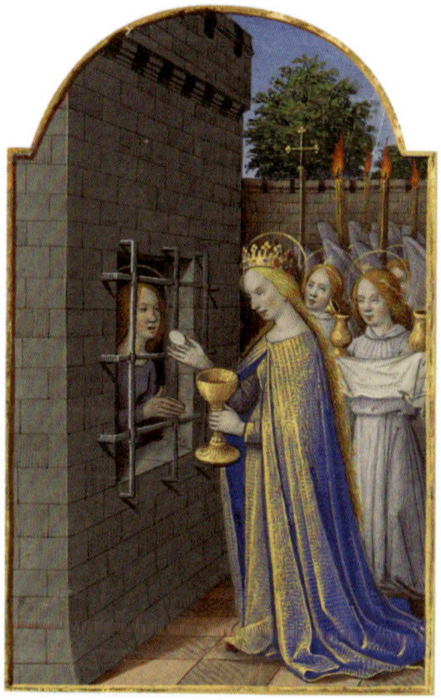

opposite, cat. 8
***Saint Avia (The Jailed Woman)*, northern France, c. 1450–1500, limestone with traces of polychromy, 69 x 53 x 23 cm**
Private Collection

left, fig. 8
Jean Bourdichon, *Saint Avia in Prison Receiving Communion from the Virgin*, (detail), c. 1480–85, tempera colours, gold, and ink on parchment, 16.4 x 11.6 cm

Notes

37. Jütte, p. 620.
38. See Diane Shaw, 'The Construction of the Private in Medieval London', *Journal of Medieval and Early Modern Studies*, vol. 26 (Autumn 1996), pp. 447–66, especially pp. 450, 455; and Christine Schedensack, *Nachbarn im Konflikt: Zur Entstehung und Beilegung von Rechtsstreitigkeiten um Haus und Hof im frühneuzeitlichen Münster* (Münster: Aschendorff, 2007).
39. Shaw, 'The Construction of the Private in Medieval London', pp. 452–57.
40. See Petrus Pancratius Crausius, *Disputatio Juridica, De Jure Fenestrarum = Vom Fenster-Recht: In Illustri Academia Jenensi Anno MDCLXIX. Habita* (Halae Magdeburgicae : Hendel, 1740), pp. 8–9; also Shaw, 'The Construction of the Private in Medieval London', pp. 454–55; Schedensack, pp. 32, 155; Mary Thomas Crane, 'Illicit Privacy and Outdoor Spaces in Early Modern England', *Journal of Early Modern Cultural Studies*, vol. 9, no. 1 (Spring–Summer 2009), pp. 10–11; and Lena Cowen Orlin, 'Boundary Disputes in Early Modern London', in Lena Cowen Orlin (ed.), *Material London, c. 1600* (Philadelphia: University of Pennsylvania Press, 2000), p. 361.
41. There is a huge body of literature on these frescoes but an accessible overview can be found in Diana Norman, *Painting in Late Medieval and Renaissance Siena (1260–1555)* (New Haven: Yale University Press, 2003); for more detailed discussions, see Jack Greenstein, 'The Vision of Peace; Meaning and Representation in Ambrogio Lorenzetti's Sala Della Pace Cityscapes', *Art History*, vol. 4, no. 11 (1988), pp. 500–03; and Quentin Skinner, 'Ambrogio Lorenzetti's Buon Governo Frescoes: Two Old Questions, Two New Answers', *Journal of the Warburg and Courtauld Institutes*, vol. 62 (1999), pp. 1–28.
42. Nazareno Orlandi (ed.), *Bernardine of Siena: Sermons*, trans. Helen Josephine Robins (Siena: Tipografia Sociale, 1920), p. 140.
43. Michael P. Foley (ed.), *Augustine: Confessions*, trans. F.J. Sheed (Indianapolis: Hackett, 2006), pp. 220, 219, 221.
44. Ibid. On the *concupiscentia oculorum* see also 1 John 2:16.
45. Jerome, *Select Letters of St. Jerome*, trans. F.A. Wright (Cambridge, MA: Harvard University Press, 1933), p. 113. On the importance of windows as sites of interaction for women, see Daniel Jütte, 'Das Fenster als Ort sozialer Interaktion: Zu einer Alltagsgeschichte des Hauses im vormodernen Europa', in Inken Schmidt-Voges, Joachim Eibach (eds.), *Das Haus in der Geschichte Europa: Sozialer Raum, Identitätsort, Ordnungskonzepts* (Berlin: De Gruyter Oldenbourg, 2015), pp. 467–83.
46. Richard Sennett, *The Conscience of the Eye: The Design and Social Life of Cities* (New York: Alfred A. Knopf, 1992), p. 11. See also Gudrun Schleusener-Eichholz, *Das Auge im Mittelalter*, vol. 2 (Munich: W. Fink, 1985), pp. 803–15; Achatz von Müller, 'Der Politiker am Fenster: Zur historischen Ikonographie eines "lebenden Bildes"', in Gottfried Boehm (ed.), *Homo Pictor* (Leipzig: De Gruyter, 2001), pp. 323–38, especially pp. 323–24; and Gerd Blum,

'Epikureische Aufmerksamkeit und euklidische Abstraktion: Alberti, Lukrez und das Fenster als Bild gebendes Dispositiv', in Horst Bredekamp, Christiane Kruse, Pablo Schneider (eds.), *Imagination und Repräsentation: Zwei Bildsphären der frühen Neuzeit* (Leiden: Brill, 2010), p. 82.

47. *Anchoritic Spirituality: Ancrene Wisse and Associated Works*, trans. Anne Savage, Nicholas Watson (New York: Paulist Press, 1991), pp. 66–67. See also Joy A. Schroeder, 'The Rape of Dinah: Luther's Interpretation of a Biblical Narrative', *Sixteenth Century Journal*, vol. 28, no. 3 (Autumn 1997), pp. 777–78.

48. The literature on this particular print is vast but for the most recent account (and for support of the earlier dating) see Holger Jacob-Friesen, Julia Carrasco, Johanna Scherer (eds.), *Hans Baldung Grien: heilig / unheilig*, exh. cat. (Berlin and Munich: Deutscher Kunstverlag, 2019) pp. 466–68. See also Dale Hoak, 'Art, Culture, and Mentality in Renaissance Society: The Meaning of Hans Baldung Grien's *Bewitched Groom* (1544)', in *Renaissance Quarterly*, vol. 38, no. 3 (1985), pp. 488–510; Giulia Bartrum, *German Renaissance Prints 1490–1550* (London: British Museum Press, 1995) and more recently Giulia Bartrum, *Albrecht Dürer and his Legacy* (London: British Museum Press, 2002), p. 231.

49. Witches are portrayed in this way, for example, by Baldung's contemporaries such as Albrecht Dürer, Jacopo de' Barbari, Salvator Rosa and Rosso Fiorentino, among others. These works all attest to an increased interest in witches, magic and the occult in sixteenth-century Europe.

50. Mantegna's celebrated print swiftly inspired a host of artists including Dürer, who took up the Italian artist's allegorical *Invidia* and transformed her into a screeching hag riding a goat backwards in his print of 1500. Dürer's rival de' Barbari also adopted the figure in one of his prints and showed her riding a hippocamp-triton hybrid. On these prints see Patricia Simons, 'Mantegna's Battle of the Sea Gods: The Material and Thematic Interaction of Print and Sculpture', in Suzanne Karr Schmidt, Ed Wouk (eds.), *Prints in Translation, 1450–1750: Image, Materiality, Space* (London: Routledge, 2017), pp. 89–135.

51. On the evil eye, see Hans Peter Broedel, *The 'Malleus Maleficarum' and the Construction of Witchcraft: Theology and Popular Belief* (Manchester: Manchester University Press, 2003). For ancient accounts see Ovid's *Amores* 1.8.15–16; Virgil: Eclogues 3.102–1.

52. For more on this illumination see Erik Inglis, *The Hours of Mary of Burgundy: Codex Vindobonensis 1857, Vienna, Osterreichische Nationalbibliothek* (London: H. Miller, 1995).

53. Nicholas Penny, *The Sixteenth-Century Italian Paintings. National Gallery Catalogues: Volume II: Venice 1540–1600*, National Gallery London, 2008, pp. 388–395.

54. The Raphael drawing c. 1514 is now in the Uffizi, Florence (inv. 1973 F).

55. On Bouts, see Catheline Périer-D'Ieteren, *Dieric Bouts: The Complete Works* (Brussels: Mercatorfonds, 2006), p. 161; on the Virgin as *fenestra coeli* see Eileen Reeves, *Painting the Heavens: Art and Science in the Age of Galileo* (Princeton: Princeton University Press, 1997), pp. 144–47; Gottlieb, *The Window in Art*, pp. 67–71; Hana Hlavackova, Hana Seifertova, 'La Madone de Most: Imitation et symbole', *Revue de l'Art*, vol. 67 (1985), pp. 59–65.

56. Song of Songs 2:9.

57. By the twelfth century the Bride and Bridegroom in the Song of Songs were interpreted by Christian theologians as representing the mystical marriage of the Virgin Mary and Jesus Christ. For a discussion of Christian interpretations of the Song of Songs see Anne Matter, *The Voice of My Beloved: The Song of Songs in Western Medieval Christianity* (University of Pennsylvania Press, 2011), especially p. 201.

58. In the tenth book of his *De Laudibus Beatae Mariae Virginis*, Albertus Magnus offered two rhymes, the second of which he attributes to Saint Augustine describing the Virgin as the '*porta coeli*' and the '*porta crystalline*'. See also Anselm Salzer, *Sinnbilder und Beiworte Mariens in der deutschen Literatur und lateinischen Hymnenpoesie des Mittelalters* (Darmstadt: Wissenschaftliche Buchgesellschaft, 1967), especially pp. 71–76.

59. See Francesco Petrarch, 'Vergine bella che di sol vestita', no. 366 in Piero Cudini (ed.), *Canzoniere* (Milan: Grandi Libri Garzanti, 1974), p. 473.

60. Note that earlier works such as the *Annunciation* attributed to the Master of Flémalle and dated to the 1420s (Musées Royaux des Beaux-Arts, Brussels) features windows in the background that have been convincingly associated with the *fenestra coeli* tradition, Bouts' work of 1465 appears to be one of the earliest works to explicitly set the Virgin at a window and to imply that she herself should be understood as the window of Heaven.

61. There is an extensive body of literature on Donatello and the *Pazzi Madonna*, but for the most recent see Beatrice Paolozzi Strozzi, Marc Bormand (eds.), *La Primavera del Rinascimento: La Scultura e le Arti a Firenze 1400–1460*, exh. cat. (Florence: Mandragora, 2013).

62. It has been argued however, that Rizzo, a Venetian, also spent time in Florence around 1470 and may have observed this popular Florentine subject first-hand. For more on the artist, see Anne Markham Schulz, *Antonio Rizzo Sculptor and Architect* (Princeton, Princeton University Press, 1983).

63. This type was recently discussed, for example in Andrea De Marchi, Francesco Caglioti (eds.), *Verrocchio, il Maestro di Leonardo*, exh. cat. (Florence: Mandragora, 2019).

64. On the Saint, see the compilation of accounts brought together by an unknown author in *Notes and Queries* (Oxford: Oxford University Press, 1869), pp. 78, 139; Nicholas Orme, *The Saints of Cornwall* (Oxford: Oxford University Press, 2000), pp. 120–21; Sabine Baring-Gould, John Fisher, The Lives of the British Saints: The Saints of Wales and Cornwall and Such Irish Saints as Have Dedications in Britain, vol. 2 (1908), pp. 475–76.

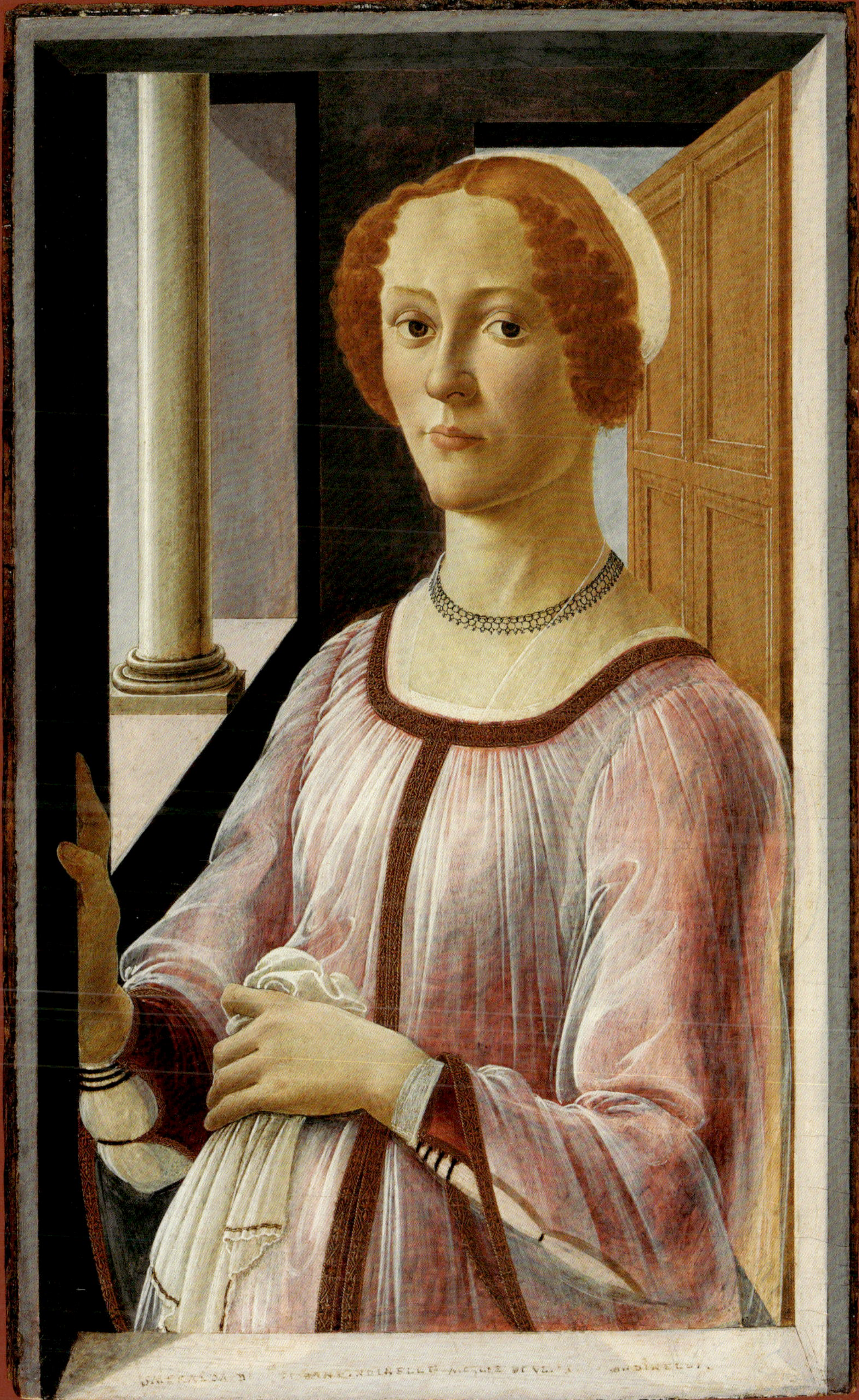

Curiously, two opposing attitudes toward gazing from windows prevailed in pre-modern Europe. While Church authorities continued to warn against gazing from windows as a practice believed to encourage sin and lust, surviving architecture attests to increased attention to window design, particularly in government buildings and family palaces. Architects in Renaissance Italy, in particular, elevated windows to the status of independent elements, as in, for example, Michelangelo's window additions to the Palazzo Farnese in Rome, the magnificent appearance of which became a marker of prestige.[65] It is worth noting that most windows in this period were glass-less and covered with wooden shutters, hinged in several places to regulate the light and air. Some even contained wooden frames stretched with a membrane of oiled linen, known as *impannate*, which enabled the inhabitants of the house to control the amount of air and light passing through this porous skin.[66]

The tension between the pleasure and potential danger of window gazing is also reflected in the writings of the celebrated architect, humanist and painter Leon Battista Alberti in his treatises *De pictura* (On Painting, 1435) and *De re aedificatoria* (On Architecture, 1452). In *De pictura* Alberti famously recommended that artists should paint their subjects as if viewed through an open window. He instructs his reader: 'Let me tell you what I do when I am painting. First of all, on the surface on which I am going to paint, I draw a rectangle of whatever size I want, which I read as an open window through which the subject to be painted is seen.'[67] Alberti's promotion of the window as an artistic device has dominated theories and discussions on painting, perspective, architecture and even moving-image media ever since.[68] In his *De re aedificatoria* however, Alberti stipulated that private houses should 'avoid having windows and doors opening out'.[69] Here the author cites security as a primary concern but, in another treatise on the family, he expresses his concern for the potential distraction or immoral activity occurring at the window, cautioning women not to 'spend all day sitting idly with [their] elbows on the windowsill, like some lazy wives who always hold their sewing in their hands for an excuse, but their sewing never gets done'.[70]

The life of women in Renaissance Florence was not particularly easy, and indeed it has been argued that the city was among the most unlucky places in Western Europe to be born a woman.[71] While elsewhere women could inherit wealth and a measure of power with their noble blood, Florentine inheritance was through the male line only and women were largely excluded from public life and remained sequestered in the home to ensure the 'purity' of the blood line through which the family property descended.[72] The degree to which Florentine women, especially those of noble birth or high social standing, remained indoors is further testified by a report by a French traveller to the city in 1610 who commented that 'women are more enclosed [here] than in any other part of Italy: they see the world only from the small openings in their windows'.[73] Accordingly, even a glimpse of a woman at the window may have been a rare occurrence.

Dante Alighieri's *Donna Della Finestra*

If catching sight of an elegant woman at a window was rare, it was also likely to have been thrilling and perhaps even romantic. Indeed, this is suggested in Dante Alighieri's poetic account in *La Vita Nuova* (The New Life; 1290s) of mourning the loss of his beloved Beatrice and finding comfort in the gaze of an unnamed woman that he spied at a window.[74] The *Vita*, a kind of idealised diary recounting his love for Beatrice, centres paradoxically on her death. Here the woman in the window is a kind of ideal feminine figure who, in some ways, becomes a surrogate for Dante's lost beloved. It is through the poet's interaction with the woman at the window that he both falls in love and recovers his dedication to the memory of Beatrice.

Indeed, the poem seems to establish a kind of leitmotif of the unexpected view of a beautiful woman at the window who becomes an embodiment of empathy, longing and love. It is the enduring appeal of this medieval poem in the Renaissance, combined with Alberti's recommendation to artists to paint as if seeing through a window, that seems to have encouraged artists to take up the 'woman in the window' as a model for female portraiture.

Portraits of women at the window

One of the earliest examples of the Florentine visual tradition of representing the woman in the window is Fra Filippo Lippi's *Portrait of a Woman with a Man at a Casement* (c. 1440) [fig. 9]. Crucially, this work is the first to place the female sitter at a window within a notional interior, and the first to include a landscape background as visible through a second window.[75] This unusual composition dramatises the amatory gaze of the primary intended beholder, the suitor-husband, of his beloved for the admiration of the viewer. This innovation notwithstanding, the work also demonstrates many of the key conventions for female portraiture at the time. The profile format, the enclosure within the casement window, the embroidery of the motto '*lealta*' (loyalty) on the cuff of her sleeve and the inclusion of the Scolari family coat of arms all situate the woman within the context of more traditional marriage portraiture, portraying her like a beautiful object to be possessed and protected by her husband. In the case of works such as this, the woman's otherwise unusual or possibly indecorous appearance at the window is sanctioned through marriage and by the fact that she is clearly represented for the benefit of her husband, who probably commissioned the work.

Sandro Botticelli's *Portrait of a Lady known as Smeralda Bandinelli* (c. 1470–80) [cat. 9] demonstrates a key moment in the development of the motif and of female portraiture more broadly.[76] Botticelli modifies the more traditional profile format for a female sitter – one that made her a passive recipient of the beholder's gaze – to a three-quarter turn, so that the woman's eyes are raised and oriented towards the viewer. This dramatic shift combined with the figure's active gesture – her right hand rests casually on the window frame – creates a dynamic interaction between sitter and viewer. The painting has long been considered a portrait of Smeralda Bandinelli and, although this identification is spurious, the woman represented must be a member of the Florentine upper class.[77] Behind her, a column supporting a kind of loggia may be interpreted as a symbol of fortitude while the window shutter behind her suggests the cloistered existence of aristocratic women in contemporary Florentine society. Accordingly, Botticelli here frames his woman at a window while maintaining a sense of decorum through the suggestion that this view is a privileged one created for the pleasure of its intended viewer, the woman's husband.

Both Botticelli's portrait and the poetic works of Dante were profoundly important to the English Pre-Raphaelite artist Dante Gabriel Rossetti who acquired Botticelli's *Woman at a Window* in 1869.[78] The artist took up the composition himself in many of his works in which he frequently represented his wife or mistresses as the beloved at the window. When his wife Elizabeth Siddal died not long after they were married, Rossetti represented his lover Jane Morris at a window in *La Donna Della Finestra* (also known as *The Lady of Pity*, 1871) [cat. 10], paralleling the poet Dante's experience in being consoled in Beatrice's death by the unnamed woman at the window in *La Vita Nuova*.[79] Rossetti even inscribes his work with a passage from Dante's text, in which he describes the 'woman in the window' as she looks down upon the poet-protagonist, on a scroll on the windowsill: '*Color d'amore e di pietà sembiante*' (colour of love and air of sympathy).[80] Rossetti juxtaposes the scroll with a sprig of ivy, an evergreen, alluding to both Rossetti

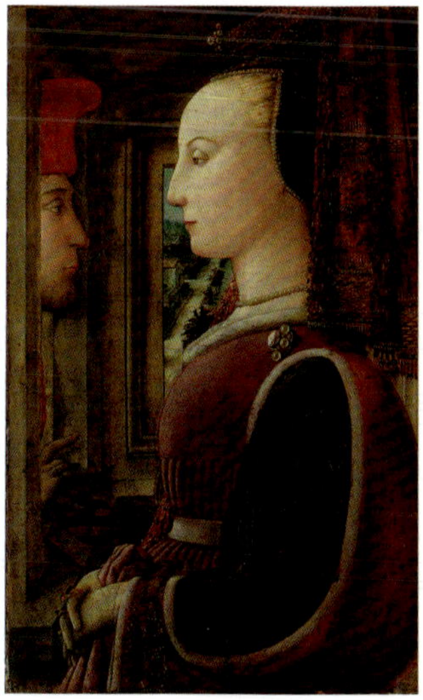

fig. 9
Fra Filippo Lippi, *Portrait of a Woman with a Man at a Casement*, c. 1440, tempera on wood, 64.1 x 41.9 cm

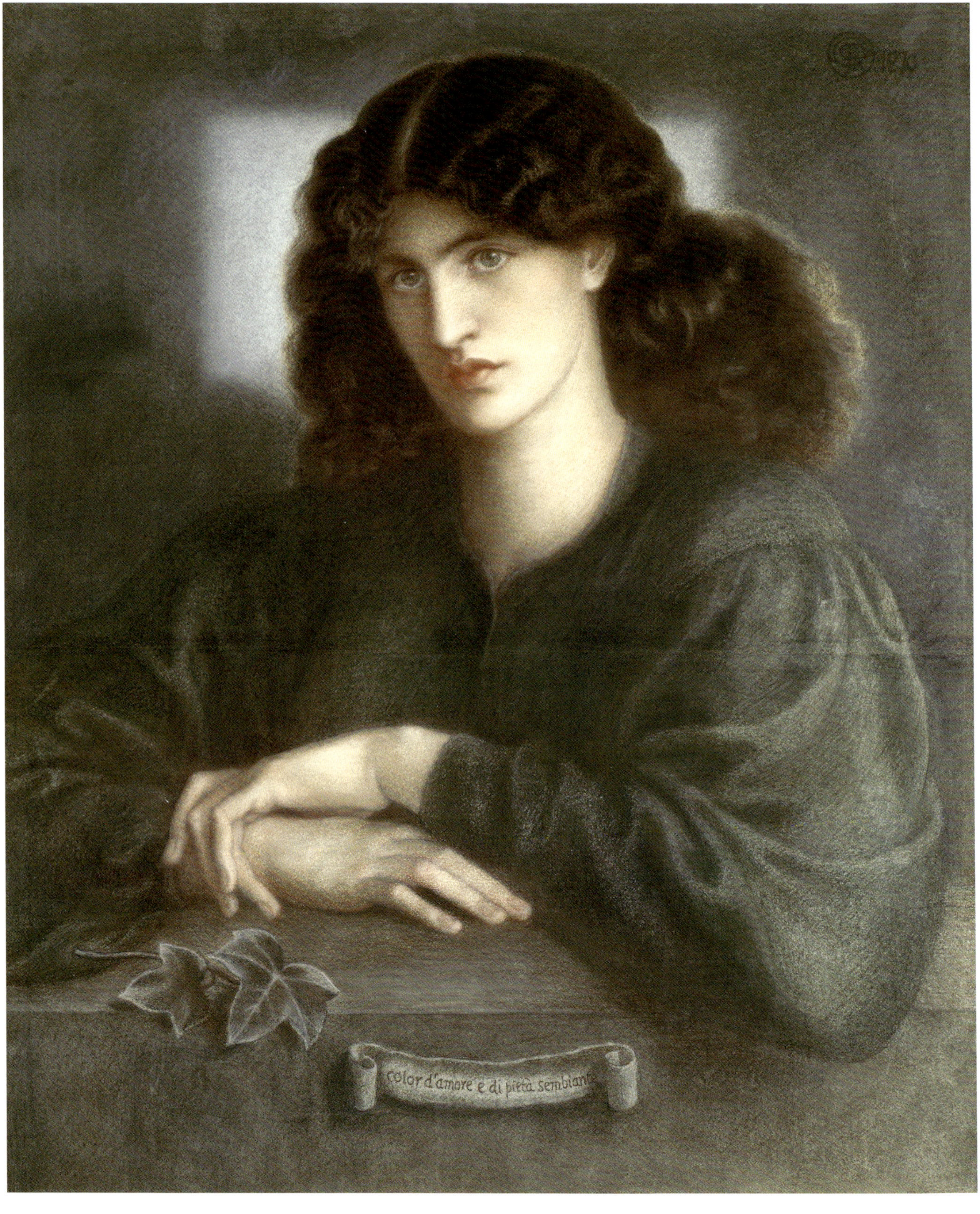
color d'amore e di pietà sembiante

and Dante's enduring love for their absent partners and to the immortality of their memory.

Framing his woman at a window parapet like so many Renaissance Madonnas [see section on *fenestra coeli*, pp. 19, 25–27], Rossetti also underscores the almost 'saintly' status he accords to the *Donna Della Finestra* by the way the light passing through the window illuminates the wall behind her, creating a halo-like effect. It has also been suggested that Rossetti's 'women at the window' compositions evoke Phoenician ivories of the same subject [see cat. 1] which had been recently excavated, brought to London and displayed at the British Museum where their appearance was met with great enthusiasm from the London public.[81]

Subverting tradition

The Florentine tradition of representing women at a window exemplified by Lippi and Botticelli and taken up by Rossetti, among other members of the Pre-Raphaelite brotherhood, also appears in a playful and somewhat transgressive guise in a frontispiece to a collection of carnival songs composed by Lorenzo de' Medici, the *de facto* ruler of Florence, and his circle around 1500 [cat. 11].[82] Here Lorenzo stands at the corner of a palace, possibly his family's own, before a group of masked carnival performers whose singing has attracted the attention of a host of young women who had assembled at the palace windows. Evidently, during carnival, all traditional rules for decorous behaviour were flaunted or ignored so that rulers mixed with street performers and aristocratic ladies, normally hidden away in the domestic interior, were visible at windows. The carnival performers exploited the double-entendre and innuendo-laden lyrics of their songs and offered the women at the window *confortini*, doughnut-like sweets, perhaps intended to suggest the female anatomy. The appearance of the women here may be read in parallel as a kind of breach of both architectural and sexual boundaries.[83]

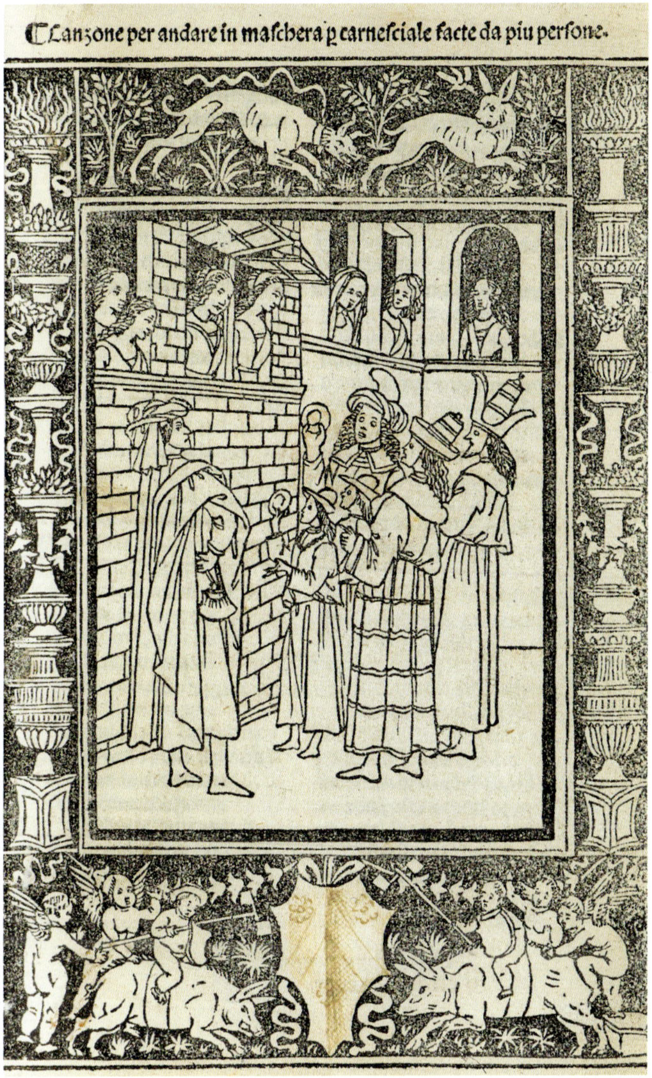

opposite, cat. 10
Dante Gabriel Rossetti, *La Donna Della Finestra, Lady of Pity*, 1871, chalk on paper, 84.7 x 72 cm
Bradford District Museums and Galleries, CBMDC

above, cat. 11
Lorenzo de' Medici, Woodcut frontispiece from *Canzone per andarre in Maschera (A Song to be sung masked during Carnival)*, 1515
The British Library, C.8.g.9

Notes

65. On Michelangelo's contribution to Palazzo Farnese see Emanuela Ferretti, 'Palazzo Farnese', in Mauro Mussolin (ed.), *Michelangelo, architetto a Roma* (Cinisello Balsamo: Silvana Editoriale, 2009), pp. 158–69.
66. Friedberg, p. 104.
67. Leon Battista Alberti, *On Painting and On Sculpture: The Latin Texts of De Pictura and De Statua*, trans. Cecil Grayson (London: Phaidon, 1972), p. 55.
68. As testified by Friedberg, 2006.
69. Leon Battista Alberti, *On the Art of Building in Ten Books*, trans. Joseph Rykwert, Neil Leach, Robert Tavernor (Cambridge, MA: The MIT Press, 1991) pp. 119–20.
70. Leon Battista Alberti, *I libri della famiglia* (Turin: G. Einaudi, 1994), p. 249; trans. Renée Neu Watkins, under the title *The Family in Renaissance Florence* (Long Grove, IL: Waveland Press, 2004), p. 222.
71. Dale Kent, 'Women in Renaissance Florence', in David Alan Brown, *Virtue and Beauty: Leonardo's Ginevra de' Benci and Renaissance Portraits of Women*, (Princeton: Princeton University Press, 2001), pp. 25–47.
72. On Florentine society and values, see Kent, 'Women in Renaissance Florence', pp. 25–47; and Gene Brucker, *Renaissance Florence* (New York: Wiley, 1969); on women's roles within the Florentine family, F.W. Kent, *Household and Lineage in Renaissance Florence: The Family Life of the Capponi, Ginori and Rucellai* (Princeton: Princeton University Press, 1977); F. W. Kent, 'La famiglia patrizia florentina nel quattrocento. Nuovi orientamenti nella storiografia recente,' in Daniela Lamberini (ed.), *Palazzo Strozzi: Meta Millenio 1480–1080* (Rome, 1991), pp. 70–91; Christiane Klapisch-Zuber, *Women, Family and Ritual in Renaissance Italy: Collected Essays*, trans. Lydia G. Cochrane (Chicago: University of Chicago Press, 1985); Christiane Klapisch-Zuber, 'Images without Memory: Women's Identity and Family Consciousness in Renaissance Florence', in Hilliard T. Goldfarb (ed.), *Fenway Court: Imaging the Self in Renaissance Italy* (Boston, MA: Isabella Stewart Gardner Museum), pp. 37–44; Thomas Kuehn, *Law, Family and Women: Towards a Legal Anthropology in Renaissance Italy* (Chicago: University of Chicago Press, 1993).
73. Quoted in Natalie Tomas, *A Positive Novelty: Women and Public Life in Renaissance Florence* (Clayton: Monash University Publications in History, 1992), p. 67.
74. For a good English translation of the poem, see *Dante Alighieri, Vita nuova*, trans. Mark Musa (Bloomington: Indiana University Press, 1973).
75. Brown, *Virtue and Beauty*, pp. 106–08.
76. For a good summary of the main arguments and history of interpretation of this work, see Brown, *Virtue and Beauty*, pp. 17[illegible]–71; see also Mark Evans, Stefan Weppelmann, *Botticelli Reimagined*, exh. cat. (London: Abrams and Chronicle, 2016).
77. The purported identity of Botticelli's sitter derives from an inscription that postdates 1530, may date much later, and is almost certainly false. The inscription may have been part of a campaign by the Florentine sculptor Baccio Bandinelli to increase his social status by writing an autobiographical *Memoriale* as well as appropriating this woman and her portrait into his family genealogy. See Joanna Woods-Marsden, *Renaissance Self-Portraiture: The Visual Construction of Identity and the Social Status of the Artist* (New Haven: Yale University Press, 1998) and Patricia L. Rubin, Alison Wright (eds.), *Renaissance Florence: The Art of the 1470s*, exh cat. (London: National Gallery Publications, 1999). Botticelli's fashionably dressed, palace-dwelling, patrician lady cannot represent the Florentine sculptor Baccio Bandinelli's grandmother Smeralda because his grandfather was a blacksmith, and only the upper classes had their features recorded in fifteenth-century Italy.
78. Gail S. Weinberg, 'D.G. Rossetti's ownership of Botticelli's "Smeralda Brandini" [sic]', *Burlington Magazine*, vol. 146, no. 1210 (January 2004), pp. 20–26.
79. Julian Treuherz, Elizabeth Prettejohn and Edwin Becker (eds.), *Dante Gabriel Rossetti*, exh. cat. (London: Thames and Hudson, 2003) pp. 208–09 (no. 144); Debra N. Mancoff, *Jane Morris: The Pre-Raphaelite Model of Beauty* (San Francisco: Pomegranate, 2000), pp. 77–78.
80. The passage is taken from sonnet XXXVI 4–5 of *La Vita Nuova*.
81. Rossetti's earlier *Bocca Bacciata* (Lips that Have Been Kissed; 1859; Museum of Fine Arts, Boston, MA) is a particularly sensual example of his 'woman in the window' compositions, and the frontality, framing, jewellery and hair of the woman are all reminiscent of the Phoenician reliefs; for a discussion of these similarities, see Bahrani, Zainab. *Women of Babylon: Gender and representation in Mesopotamia*. London and New York: Routledge, 2001, pp. 166–169.
82. For the carnival songs and print, see Bernardo Giambullari, *Canzone per andare in maschera carnesciale facte da piu persone* (Florence: Bartolomeo dei Libri, c. 1515); on the songs and performances see Adrian Randolph, *Engaging Symbols: Gender, Politics, and Public Art in Fifteenth-Century Florence* (New Haven: Yale University Press, 2002) pp. 102–103.
83. Patrick Paul Macey, *Bonfire Songs: Savonarola's Musical Legacy* (Oxford: Clarendon Press, 1998), pp. 35–37; also Marco Eggenter, *L'amor 'Scortese' – Morale e sessualità nel Medioevo Cristiano* (Iseo: Universitas Ysei, 2018).

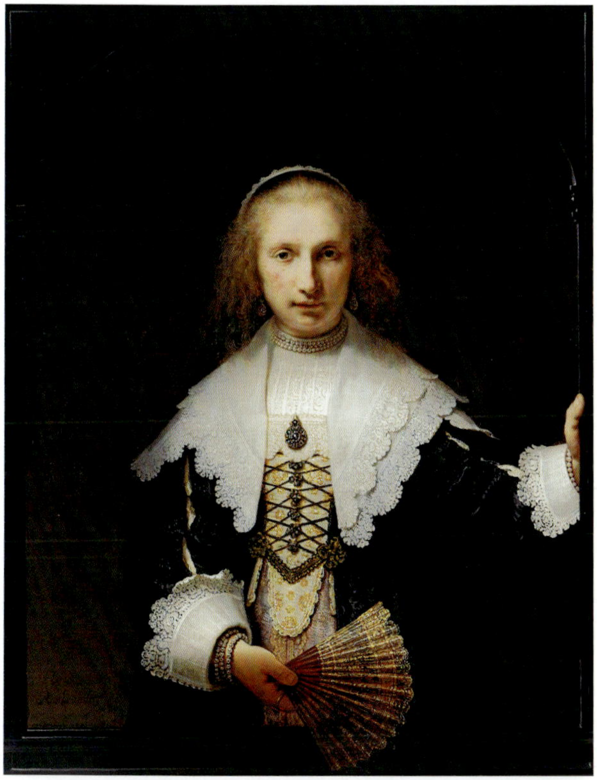

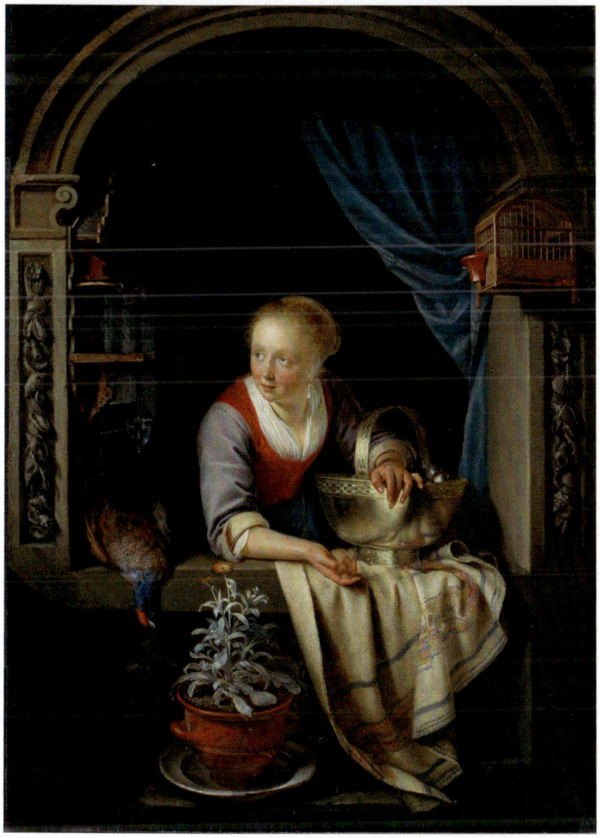

Considered altogether, all three of these works by Rembrandt demonstrate how he skilfully exploited the window/frame device to different ends, alternatively engaging, arresting or even tricking the eye of the beholder. The success of this composition encouraged Rembrandt's students, such as Gerrit Dou, to adopt it for their own needs and soon it was also taken up by Gabriel Metsu [cat. 14] (who was taught by Dou) and Johannes Vermeer [fig. 11], among others.

Learning directly from the master, Dou adopted the composition and made it a signature motif, becoming especially known for these trompe-l'oeil 'niche' paintings as in his *Woman at a Window with a Copper Bowl of Apples and a Cock Pheasant* (1663) [fig. 12] and *Old Woman at a Window with a Candle* (1671) [cat. 13]. In the earlier work, Dou highlights the illusory aspect of the window through the inclusion of a blue velvet curtain that appears to have been pulled back to allow the beholder a more penetrating view into the darkened interior. The young woman leaning out of the window may be a kitchen maid, albeit an elegantly dressed one, and recalls similar works by Dou showing women selling poultry, fish and other wares at the window. This genre of painting seems to reflect contemporary Dutch comedic literature, which may represent actual practice, in which women had a reputation for entertaining male visitors at the window. Dou translated these female types into paint, including highly detailed animals and objects at the window that often had erotic and symbolic associations based on play-on-words or contemporary emblem books or proverbs. Frequently, the presence of a dead fowl or a birdcage on or near the windowsill is read as an allusion to the Dutch word for bird (*vogel*), which was also a slang term for 'copulation'.[89] The interpretations, however, are varied. A caged bird may be seen as a metaphor for love's sweet entrapment, while an absent bird or a bird freed from its cage may refer to the loss

fig. 10
Rembrandt van Rijn, *Agatha Bas (1611–1658)*, 1641, oil on canvas, 105.4 x 83.9 cm

fig. 12
Gerrit Dou, *Woman at a Window with a Copper Bowl of Apples and a Cock Pheasant*, 1663, oil on panel, 38.5 x 27.7 cm

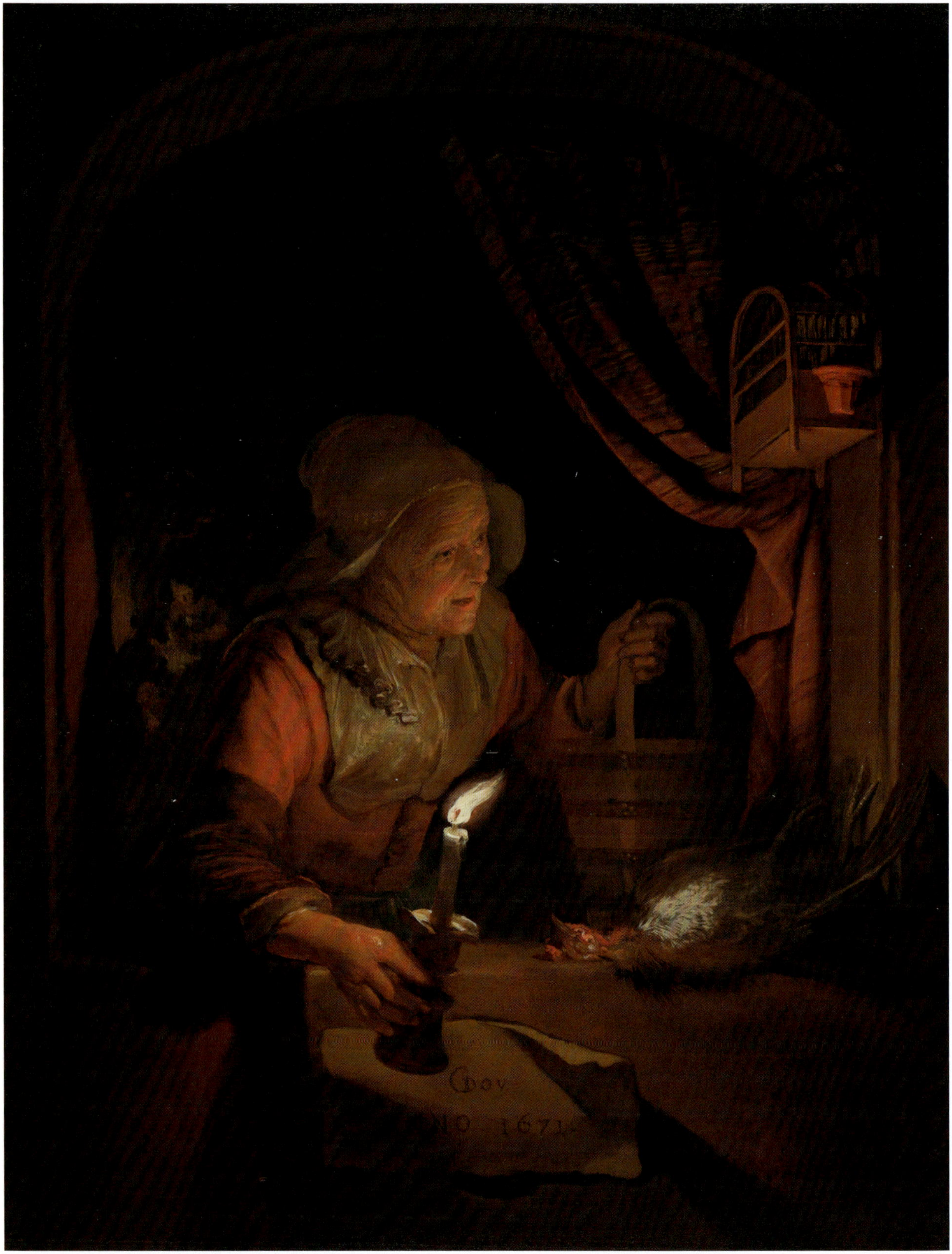
GDov
NO 1671

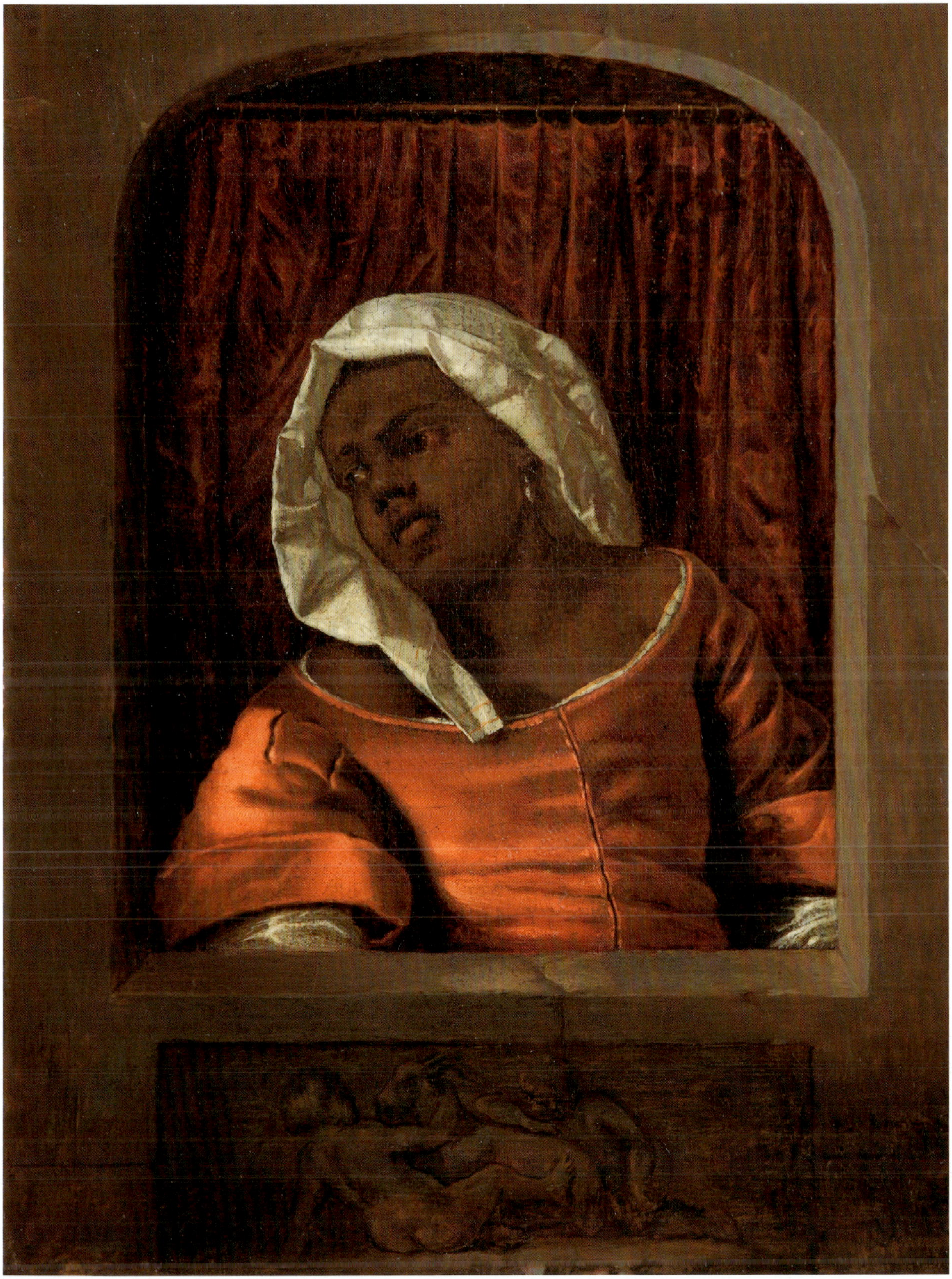

of innocence, chastity or virtue. Dou's later *Old Woman at a Window with a Candle* (1671) [cat. 13], represents a rare example of an older female figure at a window, a type which scholars have tended to interpret as 'withered hags' whose countenance have been shrivelled by lust and avarice.[90] In this work, the unoccupied birdcage, the dead bird on the windowsill and the empty pail held in the woman's hand seem to allude to a departed beauty and innocence and perhaps even the approach of death. Accordingly, the woman seems to be an embodiment of 'old age' and is deliberately juxtaposed with the cosy couple in the left background who may represent 'young love'.[91]

The great demand for Dou's trompe-l'oeil 'stone window-surround' compositions created a market for similar works such as *Woman in a Red Dress* (c. 1660–69) [cat. 14], attributed to Gabriel Metsu who studied with Dou in Leiden. While Dou's women often appear as more generic 'types', Metsu's woman seems to be modelled on a real person, though her identity remains unknown. Her appearance here is particularly striking as figures of African descent are rare in Dutch seventeenth-century painting and when they are represented it is most often as male, attendant figures in portraits or minor biblical roles. Portraits of Black women as subjects in their own right are exceptionally rare, and this unidentified woman may reflect the presence of enslaved Africans in the Netherlands in this period.[92] However, her elegant red dress resembles that worn by Metsu's wife in a contemporary portrait and, considered together with her pearl earring, suggests she is a valued part of a relatively wealthy household.[93]

Here Metsu also takes up another of Dou's favourite motifs, a simulated bas-relief beneath the window reminiscent of the Flemish sculptor François Duquesnoy's marble frieze of putti carousing with a theatrical mask and a goat (1626, Galleria Doria Pamphilj, Rome).[94] This subject, painted several times by Dou, has been assigned various meanings, with most scholars associating it with the deceitfulness of appearances (as represented by the mask) inspired by lust (embodied by the goat).[95] It is not entirely clear how the relief relates to the woman here, but it may provide a clue as to how she is to be interpreted. Interestingly, the figure was painted on a piece of canvas which was subsequently attached to the panel onto which the stone window surround was painted. This curious kind of construction is not unheard of in this period as some artists are known to have extended and adapted their works in this way though we cannot exclude the possibility that the canvas was added to the panel and transformed into a 'woman in the window' at a later date. However, if the composition is original, as seems likely, the allusion to Duquesnoy, an artistic hero of Metsu's, together with the dress redolent of one worn by Metsu's wife, suggests that this 'woman in the window' may have been a part of the artist's intimate inner circle.[96]

A window onto the domestic interior

A composition related to the trompe-l'oeil 'niche' type also developed in this period and presented a woman as if viewed through a passageway, usually just beyond an arched door or curtained room, at a window. This structure was adopted by Dou, for example, in his *A Woman Playing a Clavichord* (c. 1665) [cat. 15] but was perhaps made most famous by Johannes Vermeer in his *Girl Reading a Letter at an Open Window* (1657) [fig. 11] which appears to have been directly inspired by Dou.[97] As both works make evident, the use of transparent leaded glass panes in wooden frames and casement hinges had become customary in wealthier secular domestic spaces by this time. Represented open or closed, these types of windows had the potential

page 40, cat. 13
Gerrit Dou, *Old Woman at a Window with a Candle*, 1671, oil on panel, 26.5 x 20.5 cm
The Leiden Collection, New York

page 41, cat. 14
Attributed to Gabriel Metsu, *Woman in a Red Dress*, c. 1660–69, oil on canvas and panel, 22.9 x 17.8 cm
National Trust Collections, Polesden Lacey (The McEwan Collection)

opposite, cat. 15
Gerrit Dou, *A Woman Playing a Clavichord*, c. 1665, oil on oak panel, 37.7 x 29.9 cm
Dulwich Picture Gallery, London

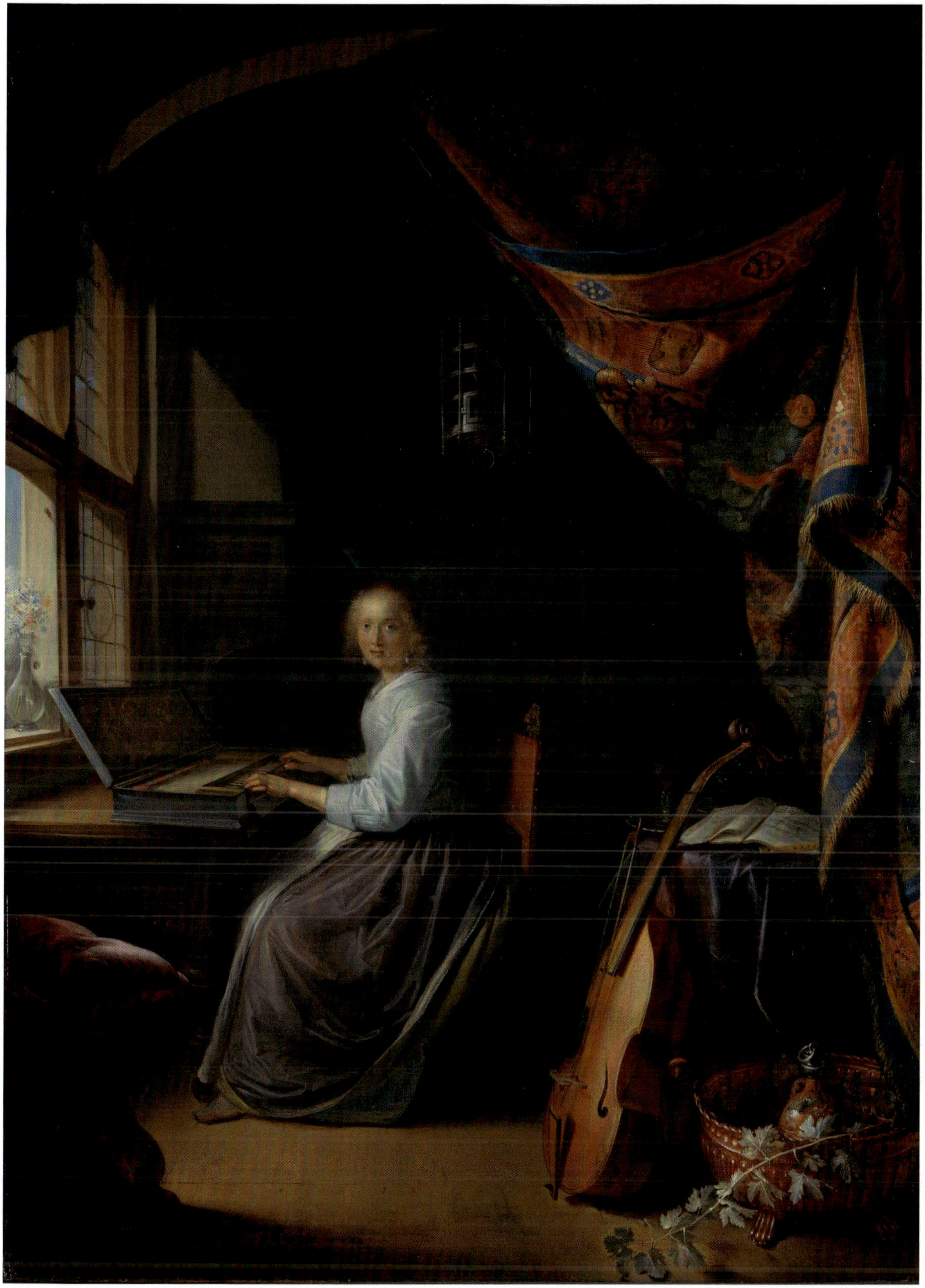

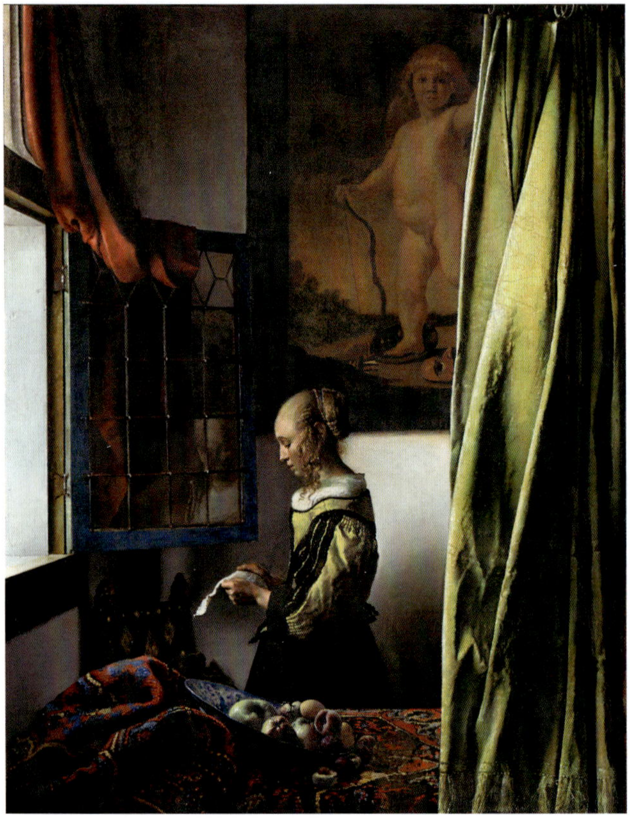

to add further symbolic or allegorical dimensions to a painting. In Dou's composition, a hanging tapestry is pulled back to reveal a sumptuous interior with a woman, illuminated by the bright light pouring in from an open window, seated at her clavichord below an empty metal birdcage. Small 'cabinet' paintings, like these, often depicted music-playing, letter-writing or reading as allusions to romantic love. Similarly, the light here seems to illuminate furniture and objects that help us reconstruct a romantic narrative around the woman at the window. At the right, a viola da gamba, a flute resting on a musical score and a half-drunk glass of wine appear temporarily abandoned. These objects, combined with the inviting velvet-cushioned seat at the left, seem to cast the viewer as the woman's music-playing lover who has just arrived and caught her attention.

In Vermeer's *Girl Reading a Letter at an Open Window* the letter is often interpreted as a missive from the woman's absent lover and, again, the motif of the empty chair in the corner seems to reinforce this reading. The recent cleaning of the work also seems to support this interpretation because a painting of Cupid, the god of love, now appears on the wall behind the woman.[98] Her position before the open window has been interpreted as suggesting her longing to move beyond the domestic sphere and societal constraints while the overturned bowl of fruit on the table in the foreground has been described as a possible allusion to extramarital relations.[99] Like so many of Vermeer's works, however, a single precise meaning is elusive and the composition seems to invite interpretation.

Artistic adoptions and adaptations

The enduring fascination of Vermeer's *Girl Reading a Letter at an Open Window* is attested by Tom Hunter's photograph *Woman Reading Possession Order* (1997) [cat. 16] which both acknowledges and transforms the historic work into a contemporary event.[100] In Hunter's composition, the sumptuous interior of Vermeer's painting has been replaced by a squatter's residence in Hackney, east London and the love letter substituted with an eviction notice, a copy of which accompanies the photograph, asserting the harsh reality behind this carefully staged composition. Interpreted alongside the Vermeer, we may understand the baby on the table in Hunter's photograph as the result of the actions of Cupid upon the woman at the window and as a fruitful manifestation of the abundant produce in the Dutch painting. In contrast to the Vermeer, the window here is closed, suggesting a more fixed outcome or certain finality to the situation. The light passing through the window, however, illuminating the woman's resigned face and the child's head, suggests there may be hope beyond these dire circumstances.

above, fig. 11
Johannes Vermeer, *Girl Reading a Letter at an Open Window*, c. 1657–59, oil on canvas, 83 x 64.5 cm

opposite, cat. 16
Tom Hunter, *Woman Reading Possession Order*, 1997, from the series 'Persons Unknown', dye destruction print, 59.1 x 49.2 cm
Victoria and Albert Museum. Purchased through the Cecil Beaton Royalties Fund

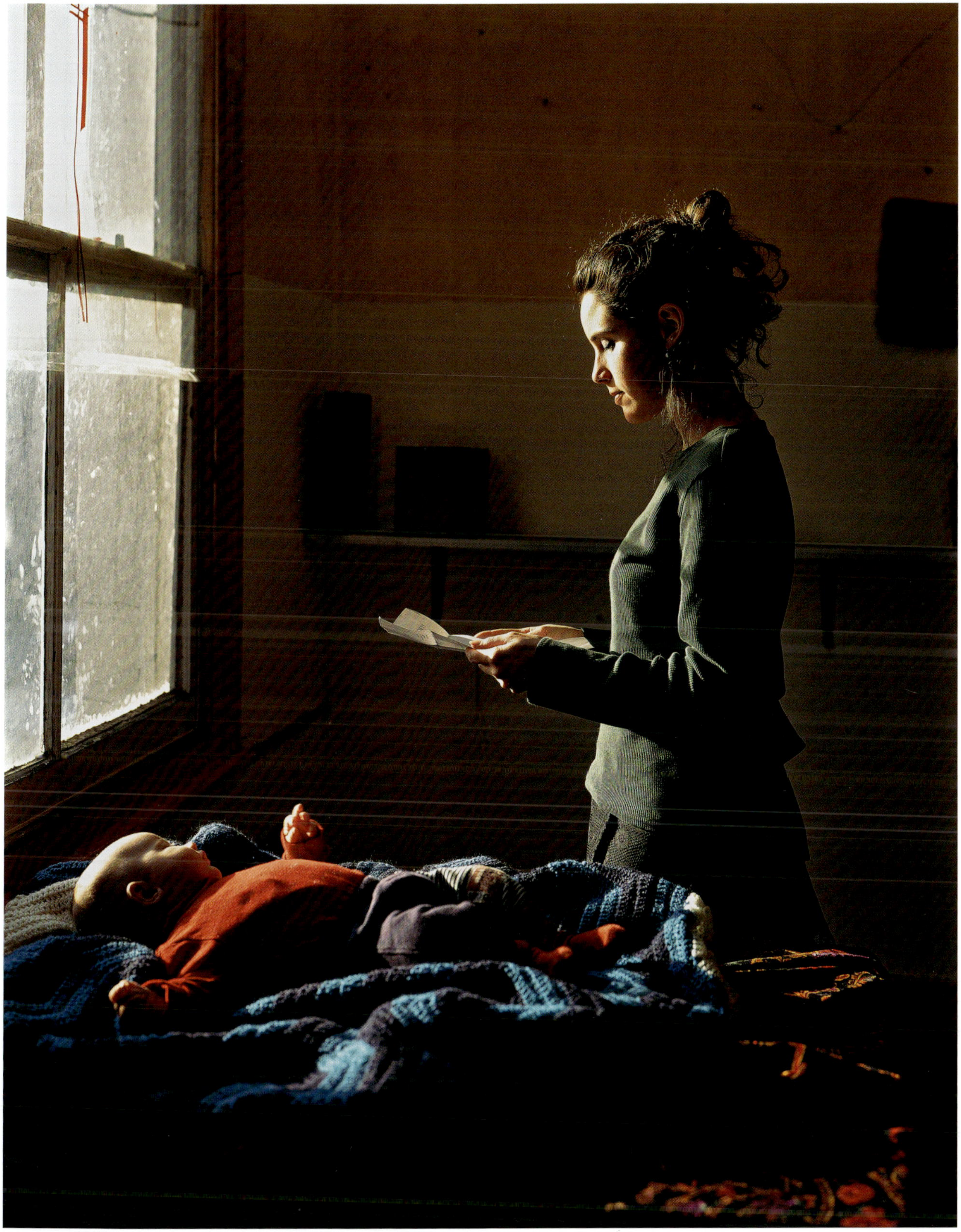

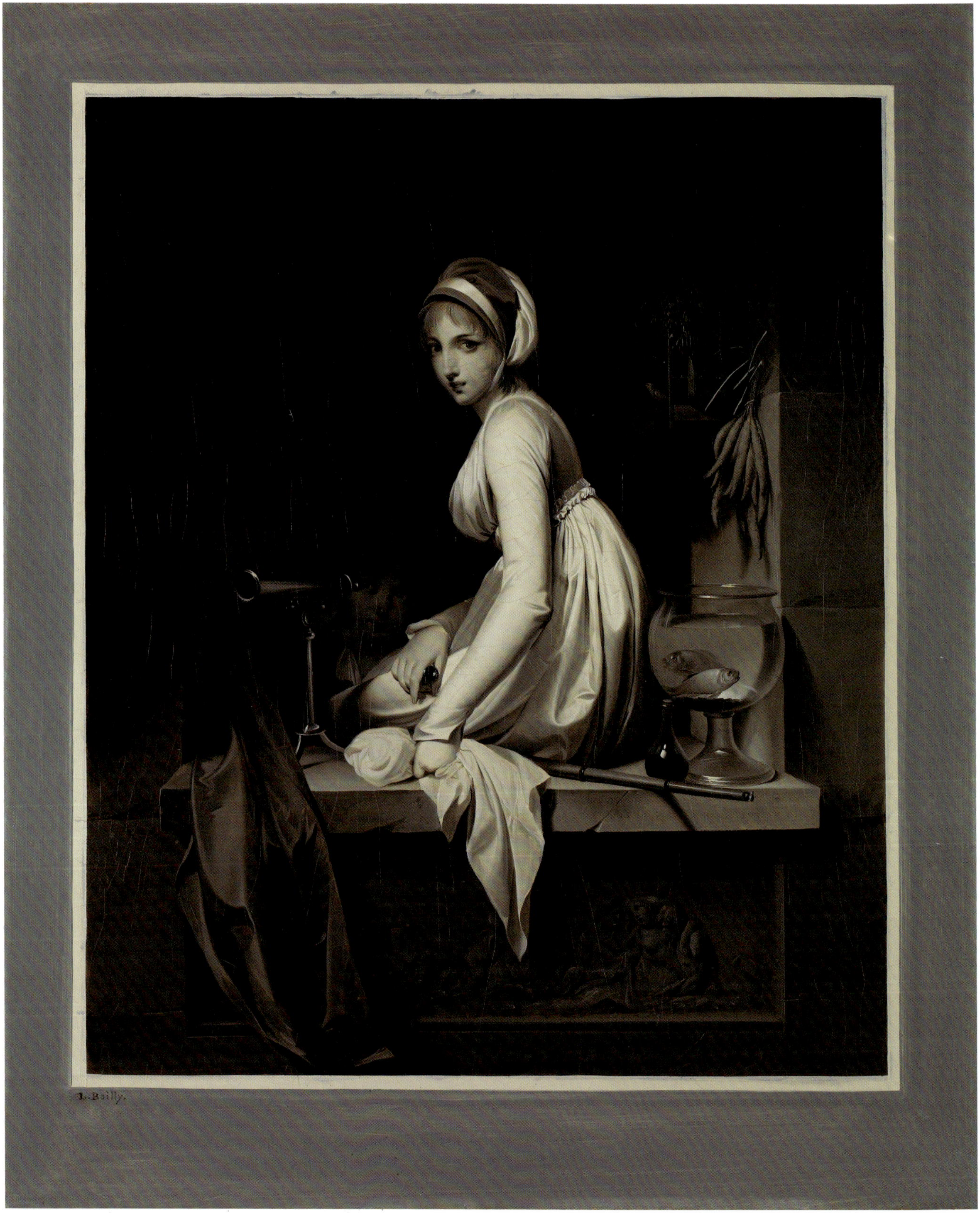
L. Boilly.

As Hunter's work testifies, the legacy of this Northern Baroque 'woman in the window' type is long-lived. The composition was adopted by French artists in the early eighteenth century, especially those who came to know Rembrandt's *Girl at a Window* in France as part of the collection of Roger de Piles, an influential theorist who also gave lectures on the work at the Académie royale in Paris.[101] French artists also looked to the Dutch *fijnschilders* (fine painters) such as Dou, as is the case in Louis Léopold Boilly's *A Girl at a Window* (after 1799) [cat. 17].[102] Boilly had a particular fascination with optics and this composition, representing a girl holding an eyeglass while sitting on a stone window ledge and looking out at the beholder, may be understood as a meditation on seeing and perception. Beside the girl on the ledge is a telescope, a goldfish bowl and a small bottle, each of these objects facilitating, manipulating or reflecting vision respectively. Just behind the girl, in the shadows, a young boy looks through a second telescope. This painting makes the viewer acutely aware of their position in front of the work, especially given the seductive outward gaze of the young girl. While the composition is filled with optical instruments and references to different kinds of 'sight', the work itself is a manipulation of the beholder's perception in that it imitates in paint a work, perhaps a mezzotint, printed on paper. Accordingly, Boilly's painting uses the motif of the 'woman in the window' to draw attention to the different means by which artists manipulate the viewer's perception and consequently also the reception of their works.

Like Boilly, the Austrian artist Oskar Kokoschka seems to have been directly inspired by the compositions if not the techniques of the *fijnschilders* in his *Woman at a Window* postcard of 1908 [cat. 18].[103] Here the print technique, bright colour palette, crisp black decorative lines and Art Nouveau style are all distinctive of the Wiener Werkstätte (Viennese Workshops, a co-operative pioneering modern design) where Kokoschka worked between 1906 and 1908. The simple composition is defined by geometric forms and strong verticals which articulate the ironwork in the balcony enclosure and the bars of the bird cage, suggesting that the woman and bird are similarly confined. Beyond the window, these rectilinear shapes give way to the curving, organic forms of the slightly unsettling moonlit landscape beyond. Aspects of this small early work seem to anticipate the artist's later highly expressive and psychologically charged compositions. As a postcard, Kokoschka's 'woman in the window' composition would be distributed around the world, fulfilling the Werkstätte's mission to make good design accessible to all.

The visual legacy of the Dutch Baroque 'woman in the window', along with several associated details such as birds, birdcages, curtains and vessels, persisted across Europe in the centuries that followed. Fascinatingly, the tradition endures to this day as evidenced by the Cameroonian artist Ajarb Bernard Ategwa's *Posing with my Parrot* (2021) [cat. 19]. Contrasting with the smaller, darker Baroque works in which the woman appears enveloped within the domestic setting, in Ategwa's large-scale, brightly coloured work the woman dominates the interior and commands our attention with her confident but relaxed pose. Filling the entire span of the window, this woman effectively takes its place, with only a small patch of blue and a suggestion of the cross bar remaining visible above her head. The curtains follow the contours of her body and appear drawn back as if to accommodate or reveal her, rather than the window. She is at once a portrait of a stylish Cameroonian model/influencer and a kind of African 'everywoman' as her skin, executed in Ategwa's

cat. 17
Louis Léopold Boilly, *A Girl at a Window*, after 1799, oil on canvas, 55.2 x 45.7 cm
The National Gallery, London. Presented by Emilie Yznaga, 1945

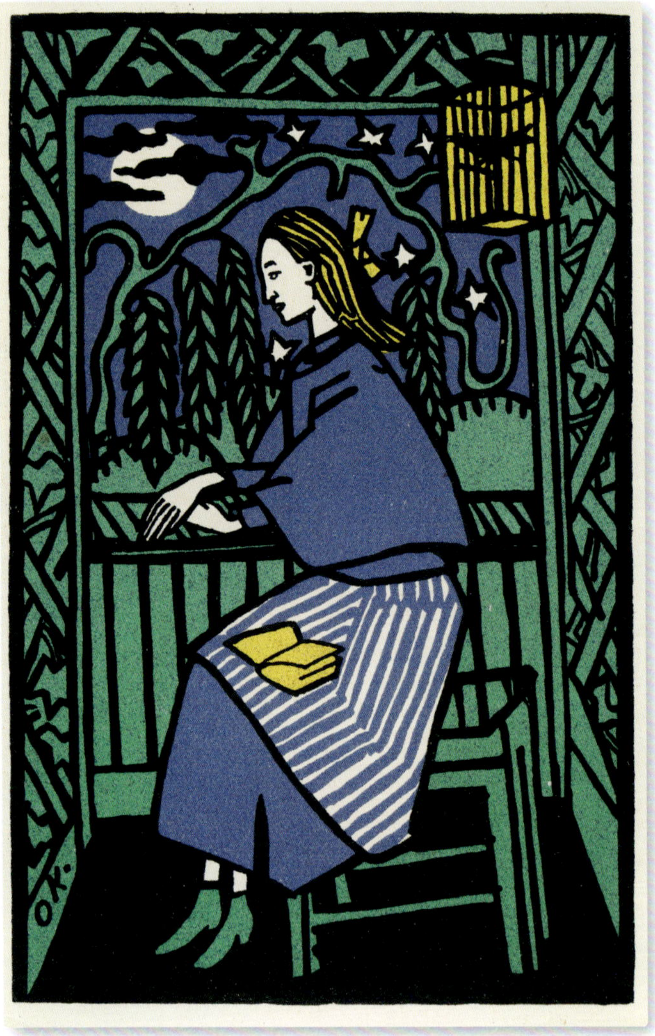

left, cat. 18
Oskar Kokoschka, *Woman at a Window*, 1908, lithographic postcard, 14 x 9 cm
Victoria and Albert Museum

opposite, cat. 19
Ajarb Bernard Ategwa, *Posing with my Parrot*, 2021, acrylic on canvas, 237 x 199 cm
Private Collection, USA

characteristic rainbow palette of colours, is intended to represent all Black African women.[104] The angle of her head suggests she is addressing her parrot who seems less out of place here than in the many seventeenth-century portraits that feature parrots as exotic pets, usually imported from Africa and the Amazon, as part of the vast trade network of the Dutch Republic.[105] In historic portraits, the type of parrot, its characteristics and its relationship to the sitter were all ways painters alluded to the woman's character and status.[106] In Ategwa's work, we are similarly invited to read the parrot in relation to the woman – perhaps as a symbol of communication given the bird's ability to imitate human speech – as it is clearly part of the image that this 'influencer' would like to present to the world. One of the most striking features of this painting is the textiles evoked, a feature in many of Ategwa's works. The fabric of the woman's shirt appears to be executed in the wax-print technique, a method developed by the Dutch and imported to Africa in the late nineteenth century. While West and Central Africa soon became the largest markets for this kind of fabric, it was predominantly manufactured in Europe until the 1960s when it became increasingly African-designed and produced. Beyond their aesthetic appeal, the subject matter, colours and names of many of these printed fabrics are imbued with local and cultural meaning, providing a way for the wearer to communicate something about her feelings, aspirations and identity.[107] Accordingly, the woman's powerful presence – her posture, clothes and the way she fills the composition – seems to subvert traditional interpretations of the Dutch compositions and, as suggested by the title, reads instead as a deliberate 'pose' and a powerful presentation of female African identity.

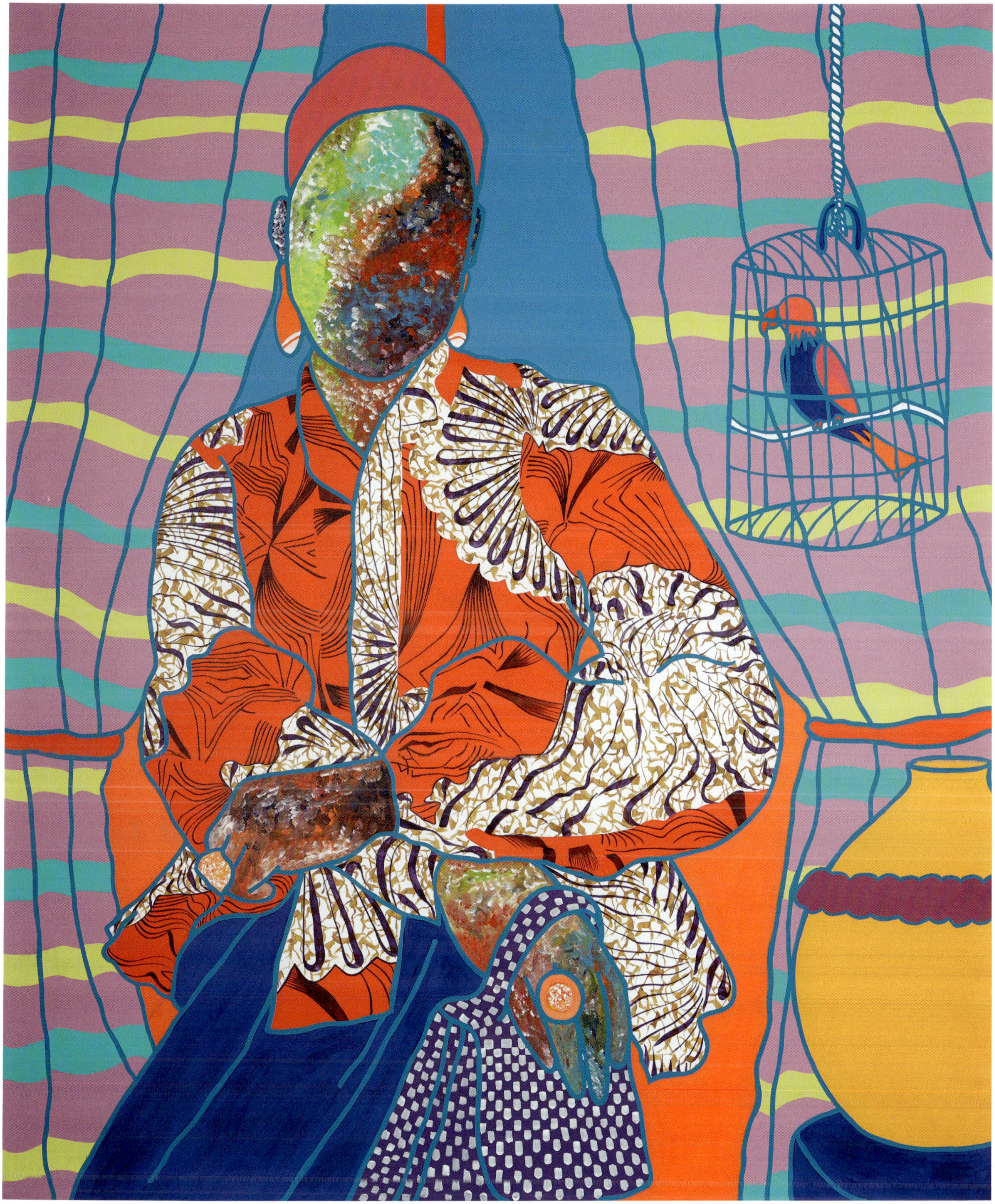

Notes

84. Jütte, p. 631.
85. Martin Luther, *Briefwechsel*, 5:531; Martin Luther, *Eine einfältige Weise zu beten, für einen guten Freund* (A Simple Way to Pray) (1535), *Werke*, 38:360, both cited in Jütte, p. 641, n. 101.
86. Christopher Boyd Brown, Jaroslav Pelikan, Helmut T. Lehmann (eds., trans.), *Luther's Works*, 55 vols. (St. Louis, MO: Concordia Press, 1957–86), vol. 1, pp. 202, 203.
87. C. Hofstede de Groote, *A Catalogue Raisonné of the Works of the Most Eminent Dutch Painters of the Seventeenth Century*, 10 vols. (London, Stuttgart, Paris, 1907–26), no. 327; A. Bredius (revised by H. Gerson), *Rembrandt: The Complete Edition of the Paintings* (London, 1971), no. 368; C. White in *Rembrandt's Girl at a Window*, exh. cat., (London: Dulwich Picture Gallery, 1993), no. 1; *Corpus of Rembrandt Paintings 1982–2015*, (Dordrecht, Boston, Lancaster: Nijhoff, Springer, 1982–ongoing) vol. 4 (2005), pp. 263, 392, 407–08 (discussed in relation to 'Rembrandt leaning on a windowsill' Cincinnati, Ohio, The Taft Museum).
88. Note that both the London and Stockholm paintings derive from a study from life now in The Courtauld Gallery. See Rembrandt's study for the painting *A Girl at a Window*, 1645, black chalk touched with white, 6.5 cm x 8.3 cm, Seilern bequest, 1978, D.1978.PG.192.
89. On the motifs of the bird and the bird cage see Eddy De Jongh (ed.), T*ot Lering en Vermaak: Betekenissen van Hollandse genrevoorstellingen uit de zeventiende eeuw*, exh. cat. (Amsterdam: Rijksmuseum, 1976), pp. 226–27; also Eric Jan Sluijter, 'Een stuck waerin een jufr: voor de spiegel van Gerrit Douw', *Antiek*, vol. 23 (October 1988), p. 159; and Elaine Shefer, 'The Bird in the Cage in the History of Sexuality: Sir John Everett Millais and William Holman Hunt', *Journal of the History of Sexuality*, vol. 1, no. 3 (January 1991), pp. 446–80.
90. On these figures see Simon Schama, 'Wives and Wantons: Versions of Womanhood in 17th Century Dutch Art', *Oxford Art Journal*, vol. 3, no. 1, Women in Art (April 1980), pp. 5–13, especially p. 7.
91. For the most up to date scholarship on this work, see the online catalogue entry: Dominique Surh, 'Old Woman at a Window with a Candle', in Arthur K. Wheelock Jr. (ed.), *The Leiden Collection Catalogue*: https://www.theleidencollection.com/archive/. See also Dennis P. Weller, *Small Treasures: Rembrandt, Vermeer, Hals, and Their Contemporaries*, exh. cat. (Raleigh, NC: North Carolina Museum of Art, 2014), pp. 81–83.
92. For more information on the Black presence in seventeenth-century Holland, see Dienke Hondius, 'Black Africans in Seventeenth-Century Amsterdam', *Renaissance and Reformation/Renaissance et Réforme*, vol. 31, no. 2 (Spring 2008), pp. 87–105.
93. Metsu's portrait of his wife Isabella de Wolff is known as *Young Woman Seated in an Interior, Reading a Letter*, c. 1658–6, oil on panel, 25.8 x 21 cm, The Leiden Collection, GM-103; for more on this work see Blaise Ducos, Lara Yeager-Crasselt (eds.), *Rembrandt, Vermeer and the Dutch Golden Age: Masterpieces from The Leiden Collection and the Musée du Louvre*, exh. cat. (Louvre Abu Dhabi, London: Saqi Books, 2019), p. 154, no. 74.
94. Many casts, sculpted copies and pictorial records of the original circulated in European studios as noted by Lydie Hadermann-Misguich in *Dictionary of Art*, 1996, vol. 9, p. 409.
95. On Dou's use of the relief see Ronni Baer, with contributions by Arthur K. Wheelock, Jr., Annetje Boersma, *Gerrit Dou 1613–1675: Master Painter in the Age of Rembrandt*, exh. cat. (Washington, London, The Hague, 2000), pp. 104, 140 no. 5.
96. Metsu's admiration for Duquesnoy is underscored by his inclusion of a bust by the sculptor in his own self-portrait in now in the Royal Collection Trust, see Gabriel Metsu, *A Self-Portrait*, c. 1655–58, oil on panel, 37.7 x 31.4 cm, RCIN 405943.
97. On the Dou see Baer, Wheelock, Jr., Boersma, cat. 30., pp. 124–25; on the Vermeer, see Walter A. Liedtke, *Vermeer and the Delft School* (New York: Metropolitan Museum of Art, 2001), pp. 153–56.
98. The figure of Cupid within this painting was painted over in the late eighteenth century so that the wall appeared blank but its presence has been known about since 1979 through the analysis of x-ray images made of the work. The overpainting was reversed by a restoration project conducted by the Staatliche Kunstsammlungen Dresden from 2018 to 2021 and is discussed in the catalogue accompanying the current exhibition: Stephan Koja, Uta Neidhardt, Arthur K. Wheelock Jr., *Johannes Vermeer: Vom Innehalten*, exh. cat. (Dresden: Staatliche Kunstsammlungen, 2021).
99. Norbert Schneider, *Vermeer, 1632–1675: Veiled Emotions* (Cologne: Taschen, 2016), p. 49.
100. On the work, see Tracey Chevalier, Colin Wiggins, *Tom Hunter: Living in Hell and Other Stories*, exh. cat. (London: National Gallery Publications, 2005), pp. 40–41.
101. On the French eighteenth-century interest in Rembrandt's *Girl in the Window* and for the composition more broadly see John Chu, 'Windows of Opportunity: The Fantasy Figure and the Spirit of Enterprise in the Early Eighteenth Century', in Melissa Percival, Muriel Adrien (eds.), *Fancy in Eighteenth-Century Visual Culture*, Oxford University Studies in the Enlightenment (Liverpool: Voltaire Foundation, 2020), pp. 49–67.
102. Susan L. Siegfried, *The Art of Louis-Léopold Boilly: Modern Life in Napoleonic France* (New Haven: Yale University Press, 1995), pp. 167ff; also Lelia Packer, Jennifer Sliwka, *Monochrome: Painting in Black and White*, exh. cat. (London: National Gallery Publications, 2017), pp. 165–67; Francesca Whitlum Cooper (ed.), *Boilly: Scenes of Parisian Life*, exh. cat. (London: National Gallery Publications, 2019).
103. Alice Strobl, Alfred Weidinger (eds.), *Oskar Kokoschka, Works on Paper: The Early Years, 1897–1917*, exh. cat. (New York: Solomon R. Guggenheim Museum, 1994), p. 18.
104. I'd like to thank the artist for providing me with this information (personal correspondence, August, 2021).
105. Dutch paintings of women with parrots include, for example, Caspar Netscher, *A Woman Feeding a Parrot, with a Page*, 1666, oil on panel, National Gallery of Art, Washington, 2016.118.1; Gerrit Dou, *Woman with a Parrot*, c.1660–65, oil on panel, The Leiden Collection, New York, GD-105; Frans van Mieris, *The Duet*, 1658, oil on panel, Staatliches Museum Schwerin; Frans van Mieris, *Woman Feeding a Parrot*, 1663, oil on panel, The Leiden Collection, New York, FM-112.
106. Compositions featuring women with parrots have been widely interpreted. Wayne E. Franits emphasizes the domestic significance of these 'demure maidens' in *Paragons of Virtue: Women and Domesticity in Seventeenth-Century Dutch Art* (Cambridge, UK, 1993), p. 205, while Eddy de Jongh places significant emphasis on eroticism in his reading of the parrot as well as other birds in 'A Bird's-Eye View of Erotica: Double Entendre in a Series of Seventeenth-Century Genre Scenes', in E. de Jongh, *Questions of Meaning: Theme and Motif in Dutch Seventeenth-Century Painting*. Michael Hoyle (trans. and ed.) (Leiden: Primavera, 2000), pp. 22–46; Richard Verdi has discussed how the parrot can stand in for a person, play the role of a woman's surrogate lover, or mocks and comments on the follies of human behaviour in *The Parrot in Art: From Dürer to Elizabeth Butterworth* (London: Scala Publishers in association with the Barber Institute of Fine Arts, The University of Birmingham, 2007).
107. For more on these fabrics, their history and cultural significance see John Gillow, *African Textiles: Colour and Creativity across a Continent* (London: Thames and Hudson, 2003); Anne Grosfilley, *African Wax Print Textiles* (London: Prestel, 2018).

interior and bright landscape, has encouraged several metaphorical interpretations of the work as a reflection on the nature of life and death, the earthly and the heavenly, or the confinement and dependency of a woman bound to her house and husband.[115]

An interesting counterpoint to Friedrich's composition is found in Danish artist Catherine Caroline Cathinka Engelhart's *The Artist in her Studio* (1894) [cat. 20].[116] Engelhart's composition invites the beholder to enter her private world – in this case, her studio in London. In addition to her neat arrangement of brushes, palettes and easels, Engelhart showcases one of her most critical artistic tools – the window and the light it affords. Here, as in Friedrich's studio, the light through the window is carefully monitored and controlled although this time through a series of veils and curtains rather than shutters. The artist has drawn a curtain at the lower level allowing the light to enter only from above, while a second sail-like curtain perpendicular to the wall appears to have been pulled back to reveal the window but perhaps also to contain or direct the light within this part of the studio. The manipulation of the light at the window is only one preparatory step of many as detected from the open cupboard door, the drawing of a female nude pinned to the easel and the paints that the artist appears to be mixing on her palette. Shown leaning with her back to the window, the artist seems to turn away from the outside world, already fully absorbed in her work.

Contrasting interior and exterior worlds

In compositions of women at a window in which the exterior view is visible to the beholder, the artist seems to set up a deliberate contrast between exterior and interior worlds, inviting the viewer to consider both literal and figurative relationships between the two. Often these works have an allegorical or psychological dimension in which each space might reveal something of the figure

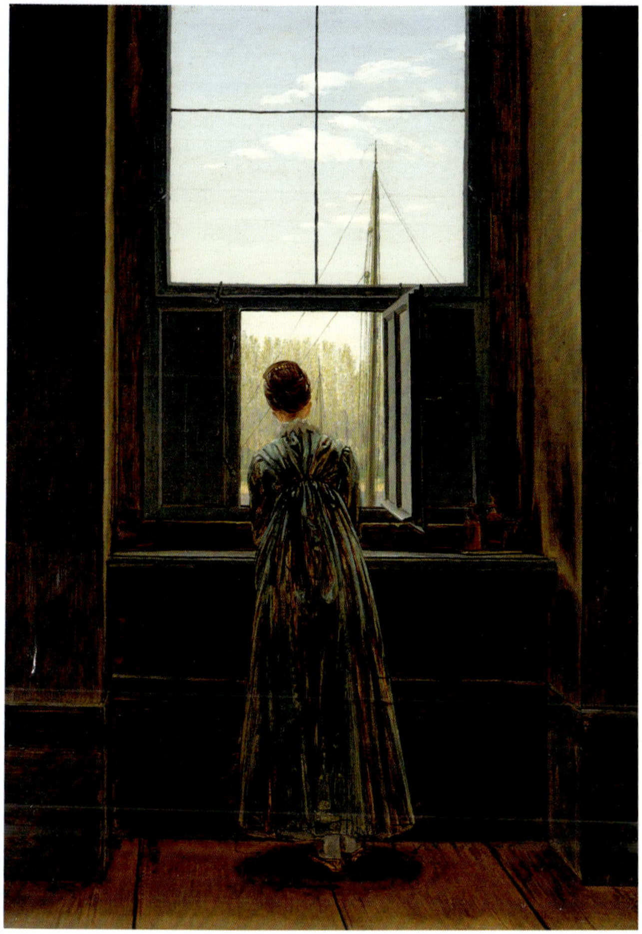

fig. 13
Caspar David Friedrich, *Woman at a Window*, 1822, oil on canvas, 73 x 44.1 cm

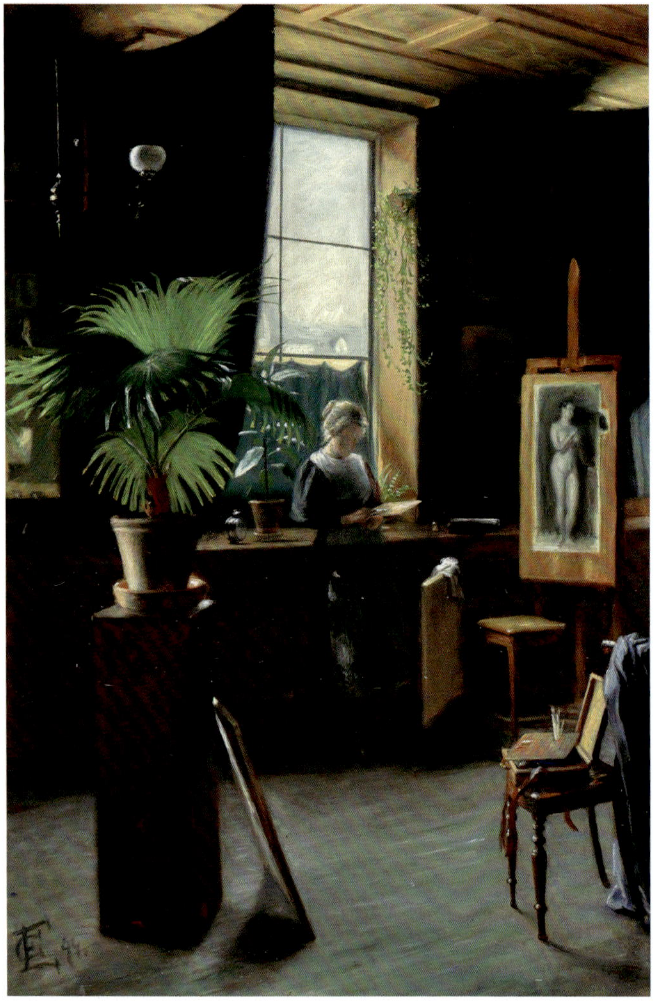

left, cat. 20
Catherine Caroline Cathinka Engelhart, *The Artist in her Studio*, 1894, oil on canvas, 79 x 55 cm
Katrin Bellinger Collection

opposite, cat. 21
Isabel Codrington, *The Kitchen*, 1927, oil on canvas, 100.5 x 67.2 cm
On loan from the Russell-Cotes Art Gallery & Museum, Bournemouth

portrayed. In Isabel Codrington's *The Kitchen* (1927) [cat. 21] the woman, wearing an apron and with her sleeves rolled up as if ready to work, instead turns her back to the kitchen and stares out of the window onto a bare garden. Executed in a period of renewed interest in painting after raising her children, the painter carved out a new artistic identity for herself, asking to be known simply as 'Codrington'. Having trained at the Royal Academy School in London, Codrington was also immersed in the art world both through her first husband, a famous art critic, and her second, a partner in the Bond Street art dealers Colnaghi & Co.[117] Described in the press as 'in the forefront of the movement' to secure recognition for women in the fine arts, Codrington's work nevertheless looks back to nineteenth-century images of women enclosed within the domestic interior and to earlier Dutch and Flemish still-life paintings containing sexual allusions, religious morals or witty play-on-words.[118] For example, the dead fowl, with its limp head falling over the kitchen table in Codrington's composition, particularly recalls Netherlandish works in which the appearance of the bird often alludes to the woman's romantic status [see discussion of these on pp. 39–42]. Further, the unsettling dead bird, knife and half-empty bottle on the table all suggest anticipation of an arrival or contemplation of the absence of another, figure, presumably male, as implied by the vacant chair on the left. Codrington creates a tension here between contemplation and action, and a deliberate ambiguity as to whether the woman is longing to escape the confines of her kitchen and abandon her assigned role at the table or anxiously awaiting the return of her husband. The interior and exterior of the composition may be read more broadly still, with the near-barren garden and dead tree suggesting a longing for springtime, or a period of renewal or regeneration that will provide

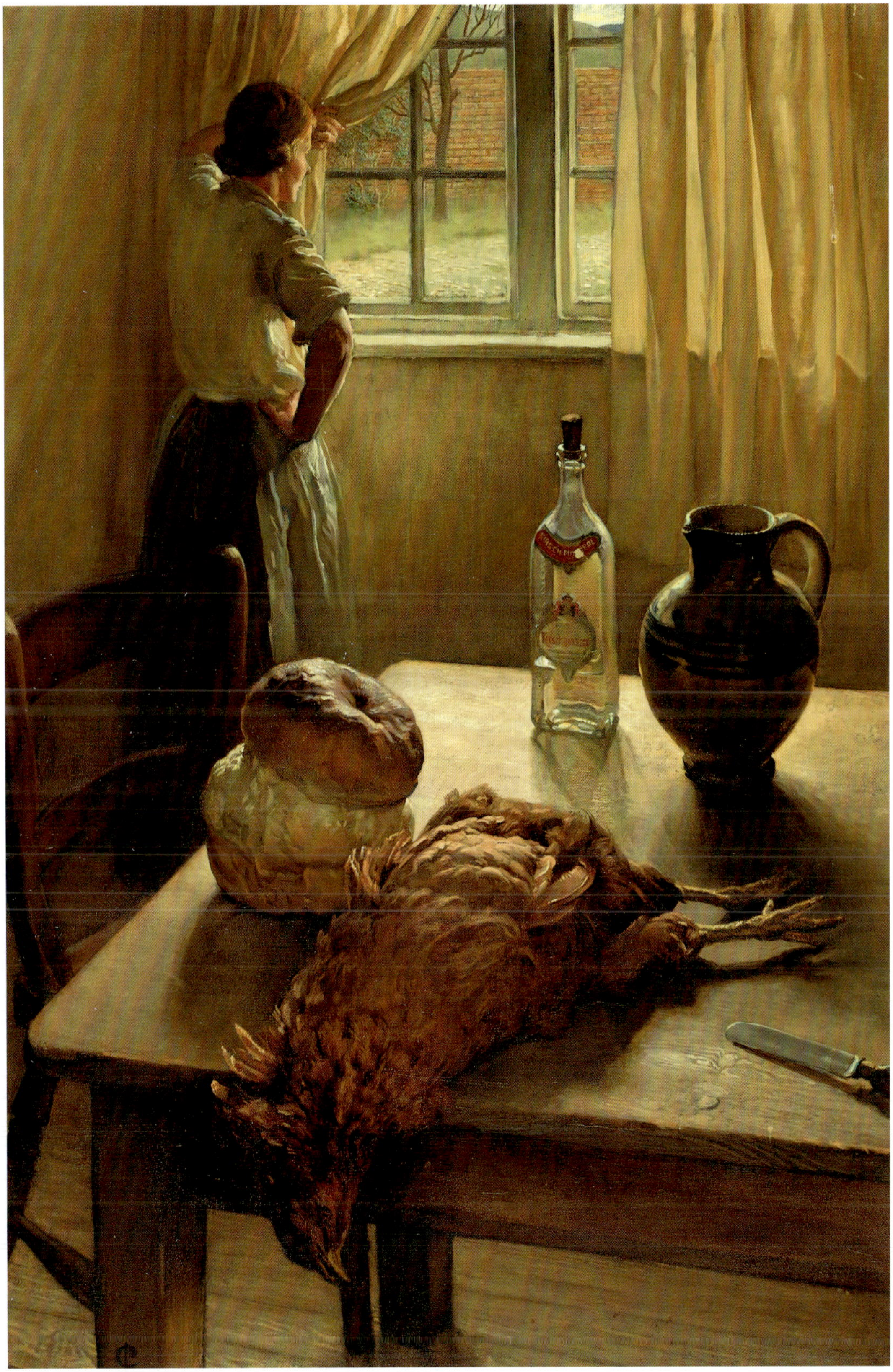

the woman, perhaps a kind of self-portrait of the artist, with a restored sense of ambition and purpose.

Another artist who raised the profile of women in the arts in this period was Vanessa Bell who, together with her sister Virginia Woolf, belonged to a group of English writers, intellectuals, philosophers and artists known as the Bloomsbury Group after the area of central London in which they lived and worked in the first half of the twentieth century. Unlike Codrington's historic visual sources and more Victorian approach, Bell was part of the vanguard of progressive ideas in British art and by 1914 she had almost entirely turned to working in abstraction.[119] While figurative, Bell's *Woman in a Red Hat* (1915) [cat. 22] includes more abstract passages that anticipate her later works and features one of her favourite compositional elements, the window.[120] Here the window takes up almost half of the picture plane and reveals a flattened, almost geometric view of horizontally banded grass, zigzagging paths and a wall. The grey planes of the windowsill are given depth by the large vase of flowers which act as a kind of 'bridge' between the natural world outside the window and the domestic world inside. The woman's reclining body is parallel to the picture plane and fills the lower tier of the composition. She appears to have just turned her eyes from the outside view towards the beholder whose arrival has caught her attention. The domestic setting, sunny flowers, inviting view, open fan and relaxed body language of the sitter suggest a peaceful enclave away from the chaos and violence of the First World War. However, this sense of calm seems at odds with the sitter's seemingly tense, almost confrontational, facial expression.
As Bell fled London before the outbreak of the war, this work, painted in the spring of 1915, must have been made while she was sharing a studio near the Chichester Estuary with her lover Duncan Grant. Indeed, Grant even painted the artist, as seen from behind, seated

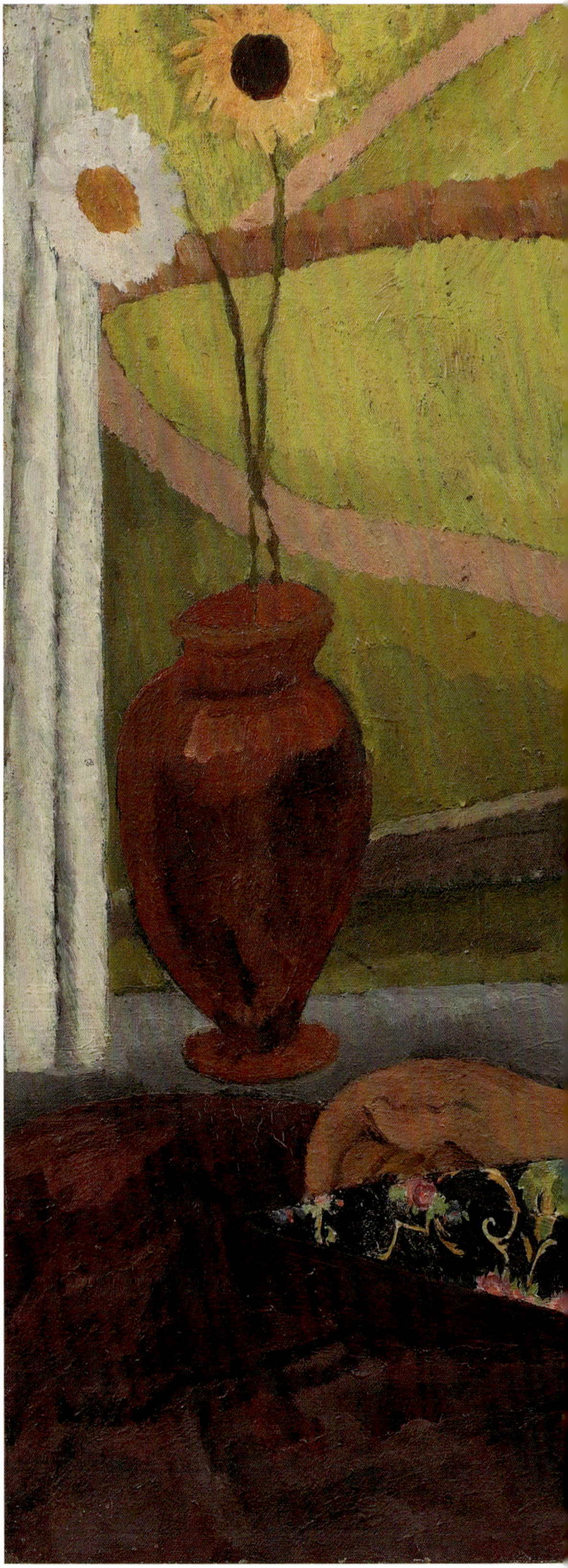

cat. 22
Vanessa Bell, *Woman in a Red Hat*, 1915, oil on canvas, 76 x 102 cm
Private Collection courtesy of PIANO NOBILE, Robert Travers (Works of Art) Ltd.

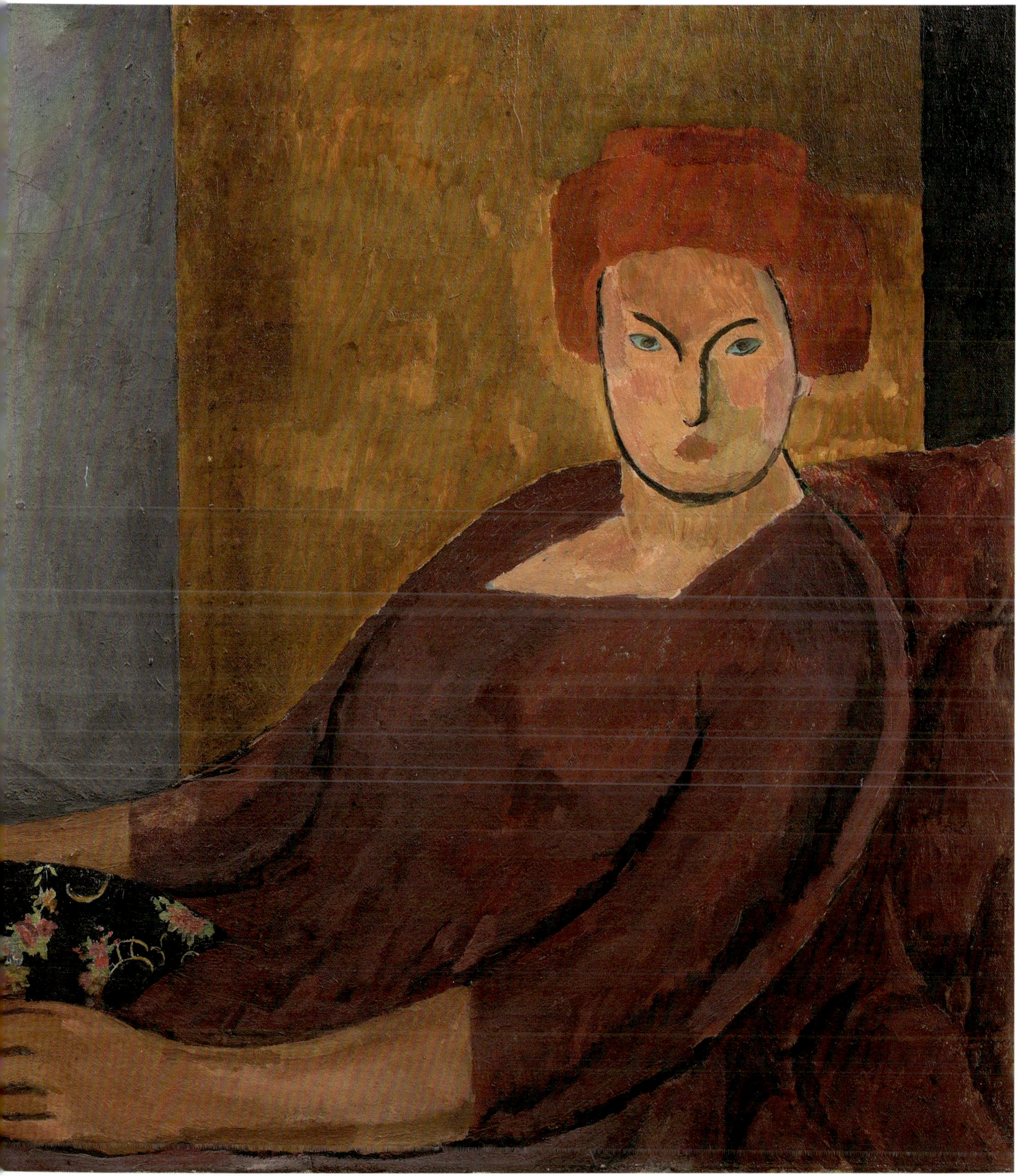

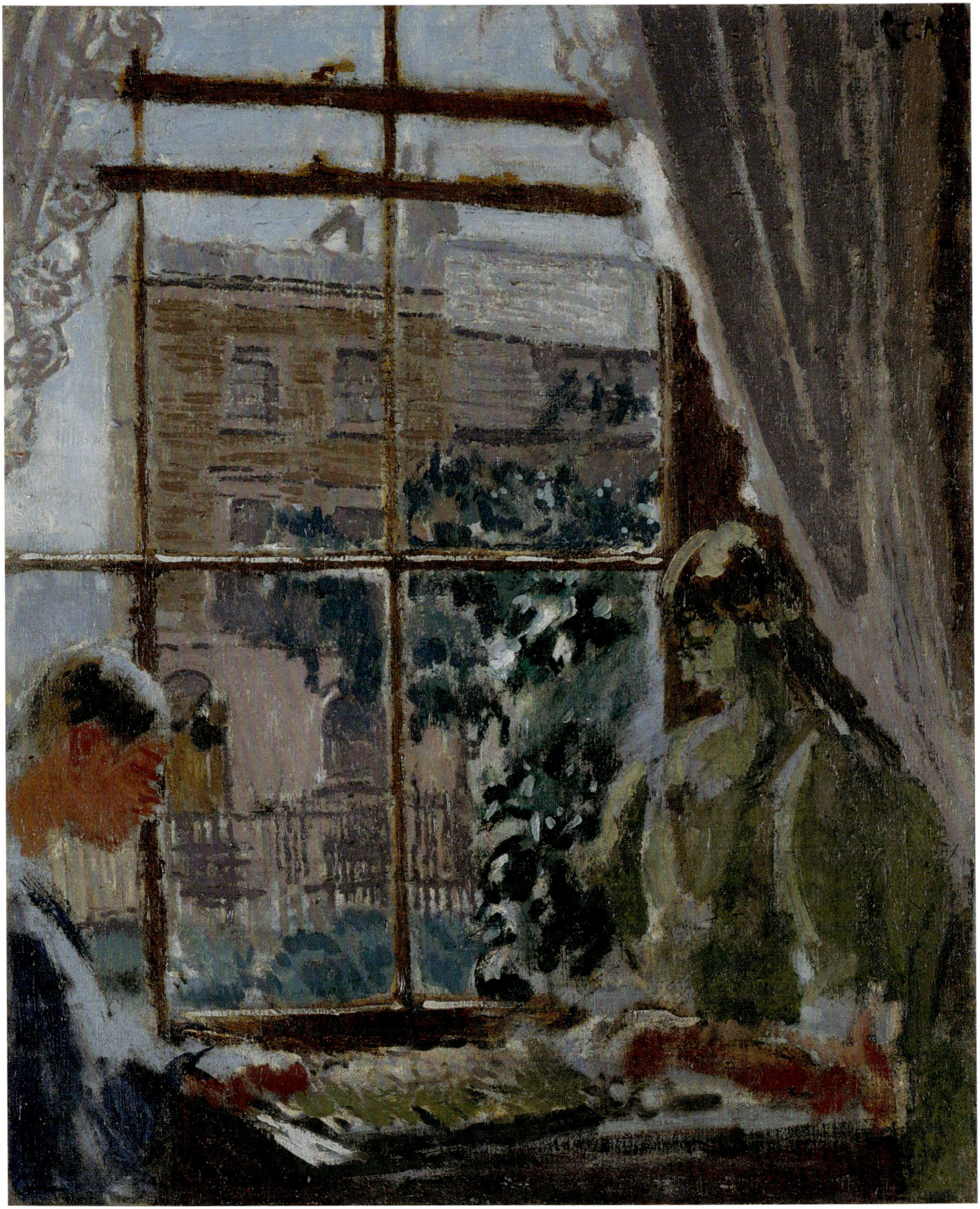

before a window, painting this work at an easel. Bell seems to have been dissatisfied with her composition, however, as the canvas was re-purposed by Grant who subsequently painted two men on a beach on its reverse. The work is a fascinating example of both intimacy and reserve, of psychological intensity and a certain ambiguity. The low 'close-up' viewpoint, together with the outward stare of the sitter, suggests the viewer has intruded on her tranquil space and distracted her from her contemplations at the window.

The English artist Walter Sickert also turned to the theme of the 'woman in the window' in the first decades of the twentieth century. His interest in this composition, however, seems to derive from the French Impressionist Edgar Degas [see cats. 28 and 29], whose work Sickert owned and admired. Indeed, the motif would become one that Sickert would return to regularly throughout his career. *Laylock and Thunderplump* (1924) [cat. 23], is one of Sickert's later iterations and here the artist portrays two female figures in profile against a window in the small front parlour room of his studio on Noel Street (now Noel Road) in Islington, north London.[121] The figures are Sickert's landlady (on the left) and her daughter (on the right) and the title of this work derives from his affectionate nicknames for them. Here shown working at their sewing by a sunlit window that fills the composition, this scene of quiet domesticity reminds the viewer that from the late nineteenth-century onwards sewing was considered a crucial female skill and was taught by mothers to their daughters, both of whom would sew regularly as part of their household duties.[122] The home was considered the proper place for women and their 'feminine' activities helped define their place within it. The female figures shown here are positioned at the window to take advantage of the bright light that facilitates their detailed handiwork. Absorbed in their duties, they ignore the view of the houses and the tree-lined street visible through the window, a view that seems reserved instead for the artist and beholder of this picture.

A sense of quiet domesticity also pervades Canadian artist Jeff Wall's monumental photograph *A View from an Apartment* (2004–05) [cat. 24], which also shows two female occupants absorbed in their respective activities with their backs to a large, rectangular window with an expansive city view beyond. This complex work sets up a strong contrast between interior and exterior worlds and explores the simultaneously absorptive and performative modes of the women.[123] In creating this work, Wall deliberately sought an interior space that included an outside view. After finding this apartment, he invited a woman to furnish and live in it for a few months during which time he set up a camera to film and photograph her as she went about her daily life. She and her friend are therefore both absorbed in their activities, ironing and reading a magazine respectively, and not posing but nevertheless aware that they are being watched or that, in some senses, they are 'performing' for the camera. Wall then composed this single picture by digitally combining and adjusting a multitude of photographic images shot at different times at this location. He was able to give the work an otherwise impossible clarity and consistency of detail and light in both the interior and exterior portions of the composition. The overall effect gives this everyday scene an almost hyperreality, a sense that all the precisely rendered details might provide clues to the identities of the women – as they often do in Dutch seventeenth-century paintings – or to their role in a wider narrative.

On one level the scene evokes the comfortable silence and familiarity between old friends. On another, the lack of interaction between the figures and their failure to engage with the view through the window might suggest something about the increasing detachedness of modern life. Outside we see an urban panorama, the port of Vancouver, including ships, a row of industrial cranes,

cat. 23
Walter Sickert, *Laylock and Thunderplump*, 1924, oil on canvas, 76 x 63.5 cm
Government Art Collection

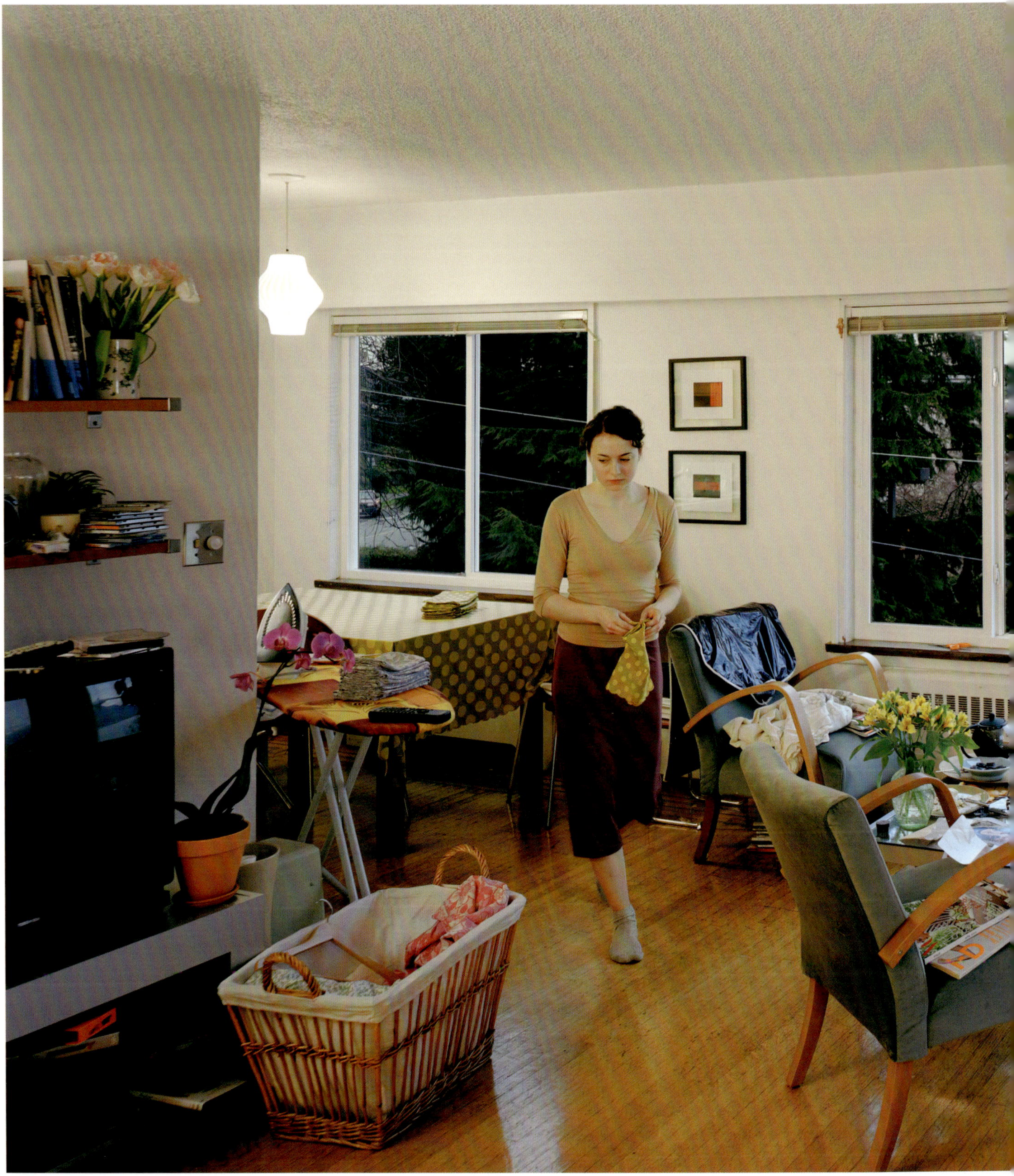

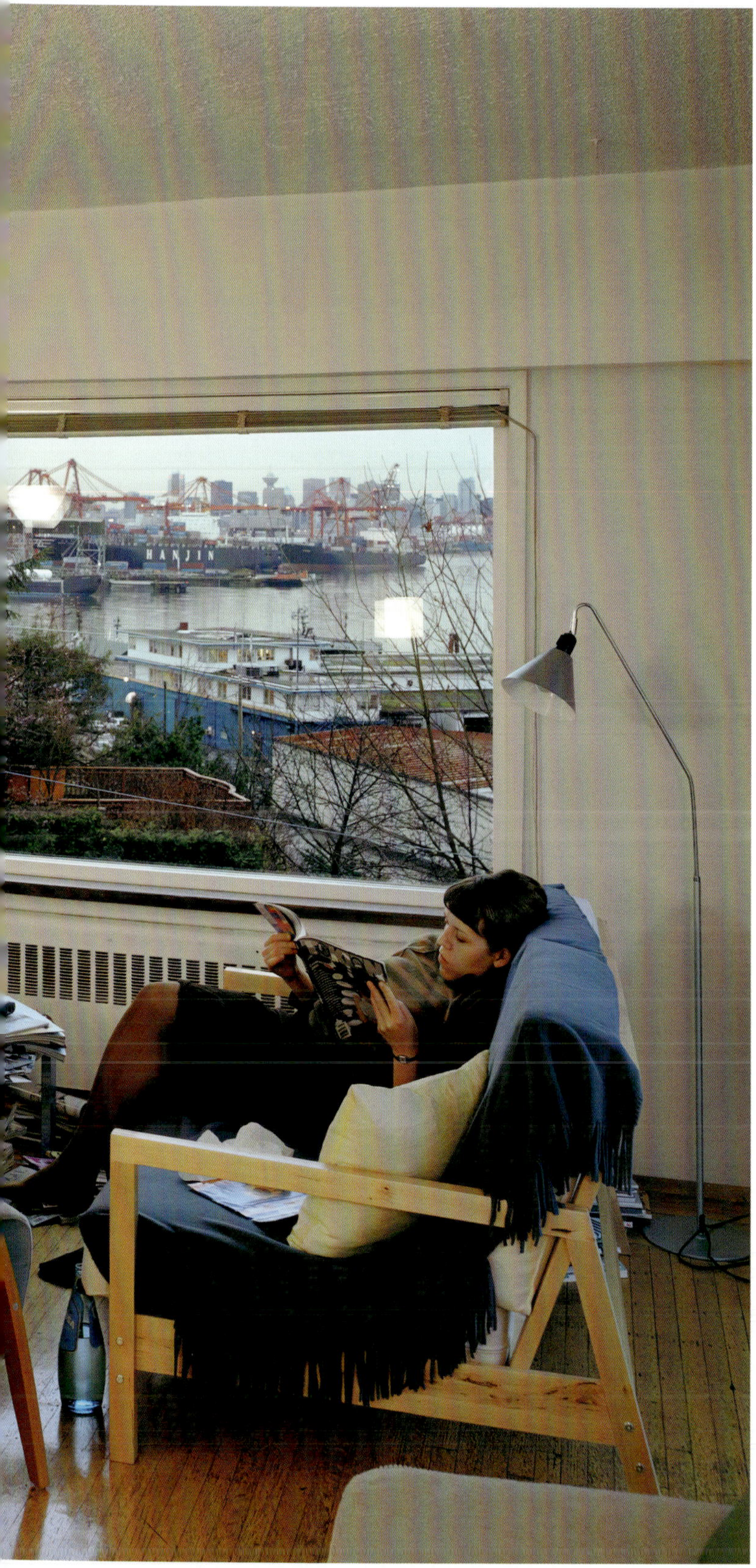

cat. 24
Jeff Wall, *A View from an Apartment*, 2004–05, transparency on lightbox, 167 x 244 cm
Tate: Purchased with assistance from the American Fund for the Tate Gallery and Tate Members 2006

telephone poles and electrical lines with the tall buildings of the city skyline in the far distance. This work seems to invite us to consider the women and the quiet, cosy domestic interior they inhabit in contrast to the implied noise and activity of the wintery industrial landscape outside. This work is arguably as much a view of an apartment as a view from an apartment (the given title). The fact that the view is ignored by the women, however, makes it exclusive to the beholder of this photograph. Further, the photographic medium, the large scale of the work and the 'everydayness' of the subject matter all seem to provide the beholder with privileged and intimate access to the women's interior world, as if they are somehow present but unobserved. As a composite work, this photograph also reminds us of the ability of works of art to take us beyond mere representation and invites us to reconsider our perception of the people and the world around us.

Screens as windows in Asian, Indo-Islamic and Arabic contexts

While the Western world has long understood windows as transparent architectural features offering a view, in the East, historically, light and air were regulated in buildings through the use of screens, which provided translucency, a diffused light or open latticework to facilitate the circulation of air.[124] In China and Japan, for example, window screens served multiple functions as doors, windows or room dividers in traditional architecture.[125] Scholars have traced the practice of using simple, carved window screens as far back as 1000 BCE based on representations of these on bronzes and ceramics found in ancient Chinese tombs. The earliest surviving window screens in China have been dated to the third century BCE by which time the lattice already included translucent paper and mica (a mineral crystal) panels. The patterns of these lattice windows grew increasingly complex over the centuries and, in many ways, their visual appearance and effect are their primary functions while the admission of light, air and any kind of view are secondary. In Japan, screens known as *shōji* [fig. 14] commonly consisted of translucent sheets, usually of paper, on simple grid-like lattice frames, which could be moved on sliders or removed altogether to suit the needs of the homeowner. Unlike Western windows, these Chinese and Japanese screens do not create sharp boundaries between interior and exterior and are prized for their ability to block the wind but allow air circulation, and to provide privacy but suggest what lies beyond through shadow and sound, encouraging inhabitants to speak softly and move gracefully through space. The use of glass in these screens was only introduced in the late 1800s and, even then, usually only comprised small panels within the larger screen. While the motif of the 'woman in the window' in these traditions exists, it should be approached with an understanding of these local architectural traditions.

A particularly charming Japanese example is found in a house-shaped, eighteenth- or nineteenth-century *inrō* [cat. 25] showing a woman seen through an oval-shaped window. Invented towards the end of the sixteenth century, *inrō* are small, portable stacks of nested boxes that were worn suspended by a cord from a waist sash (*obi*) and secured by a *netsuke*, a carved, button-like fastener that secured the cord at the top of the sash. *Inrō* were worn by Japanese men to hold items such as medicines and identity seals (*inrō* roughly translates as 'seal basket') because traditional Japanese robes lacked pockets.[126] Over time, *inrō* developed from more utilitarian objects into works of especially high artistic quality and craftsmanship and were worn to demonstrate one's status and wealth. They were decorated with a variety of subjects, most commonly with animals or landscapes but also with figures performing dance, music or plays. Given that the owner would wear an *inrō* regularly and that it

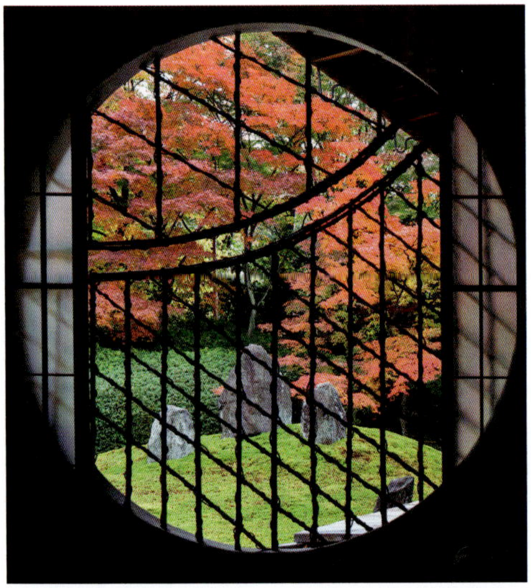

fig. 14
Tofuku-ji, Kyoto, Japan. The gardens of the zen temple of Komyo-in in autumn, seen through a round window

contained his personal seal – a kind of signature that he pressed onto documents to confirm authenticity and authority – the decoration of these objects must have been chosen carefully. This house-shaped *inrō* in which the top lid (known as a *ten*) is shaped like a thatched roof is relatively rare. The window, unscreened to render the woman visible, reveals her seated beside a lamp with an unfurled scroll across her lap. She appears to have just looked up from her reading as if interrupted by the viewer. Raising one hand, still wrapped in the folds of her kimono, she seems to wipe away a tear from her face, perhaps in response to something she has just read. Considered in relation to the object she decorates and to the owner who carried her, the woman becomes the keeper and protector of his identity and health in the form of the seal and medicines contained within. Rather than a portrait, she may represent a courtesan or a kind of ideal, patient and vigilant woman waiting to welcome the *inrō* wearer home safely.

In Indo-Islamic and Arabic countries screens, typically carved in stone and set into architecture, were often used as windows. In India, these perforated stone or latticed screens are known as *jali* and are usually carved with geometric, floral or arabesque patterns. *Jali*, such as this seventeenth-century carved and pierced, double-sided red sandstone example from Mughal India, were designed to filter the bright light and allow breezes to pass through but also to provide privacy for the inhabitants within [cat. 26 and fig. 15]. Traditionally, these types of windows, in this case with a central, geometric design of interlocking hexagons and six-pointed stars, decorated Indian palaces and, although the specific origins of this kind of screen work remain unclear, for Muslim and Hindu communities practicing *purdah*, *jali* played a crucial role in screening women from men or strangers.[127] Historically, *jali* screens and *jharokha* – projecting stone windows like enclosed balconies usually screened by *jali* –

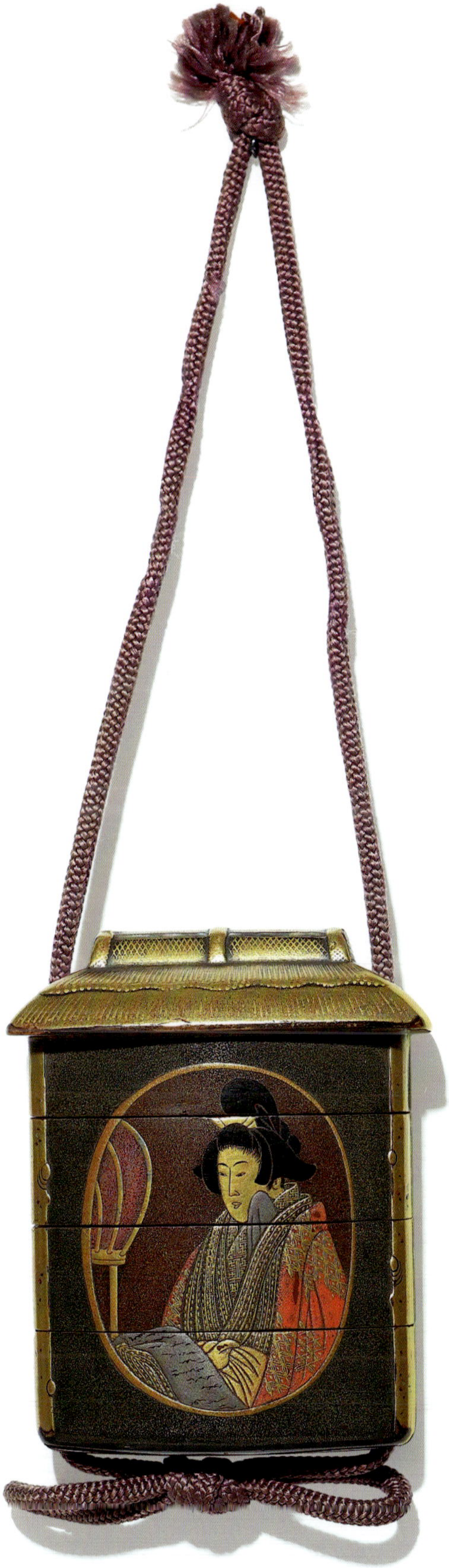

cat. 25
Inrō shaped as a house, with a woman seen through a window, Japan, 18th–19th century, wood covered in roiro lacquer, with fundame decoration, gold, silver, red, dark green and black hiramaki-e and aogai inlay, 6.2 x 5.1 x 2.4 cm
The Ashmolean Museum, University of Oxford. EAX.616

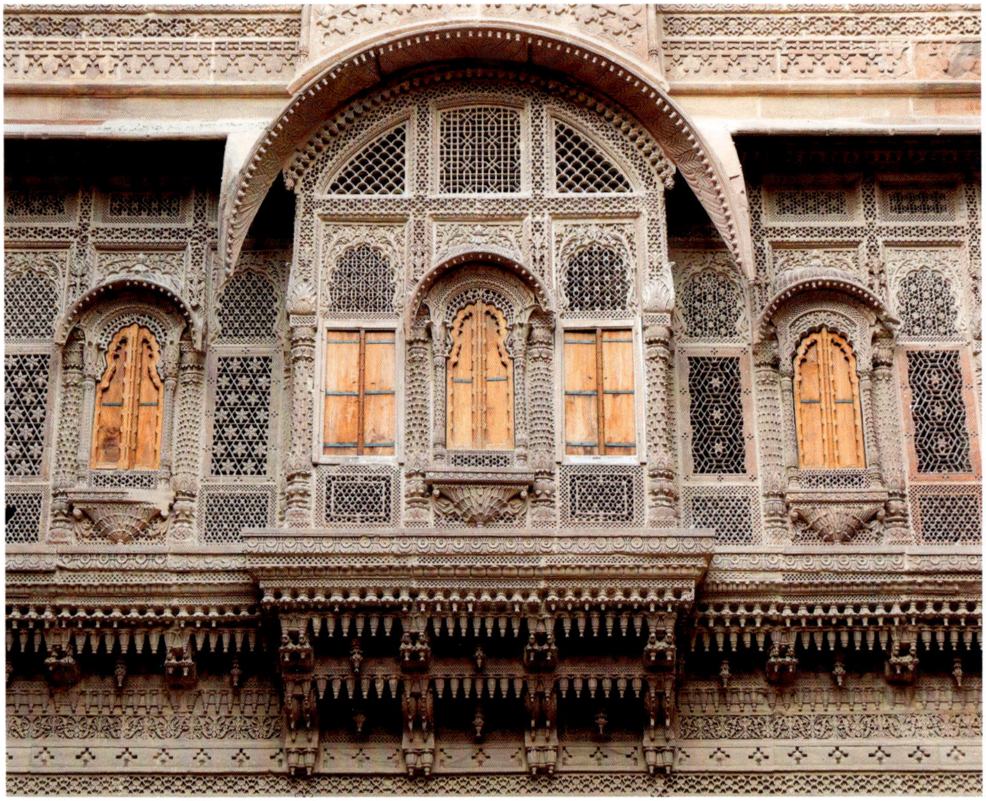

left, fig. 15
Mehrangarh Fort, Jodhpur, Rajasthan, India

opposite, cat. 26
Jali Screen, India (Mughal), 17th century, red sandstone, 143 x 132 x 6 cm
Courtesy of Simon Ray, London

in Rajasthani and other Indo-Islamic architectures, and *mashrabiya* in Arabic residences, were used for sections of the palace dedicated to the king's harem. The harem was the separate part of a Muslim household reserved for wives, concubines, and female servants, and therefore became particularly associated with the domain of women. The clever design of these screens enabled women to see out, often from an upper-floor room, down onto a courtyard where ceremonial functions would take place, while remaining unseen themselves. Although the design began to be used more broadly in different types of buildings and for male and female use, in their original context these carved screens represent a kind of gender role reversal. Indeed, even as they identified a space that both protected and confined women, they also ensured that the male gaze was subordinate to the female and that, notionally at least, the male became the passive recipient of the unseen woman's gaze.

The subject of the woman at the window was especially popular in Indian painting in the late eighteenth century as testified by the number of works that survive from this period. In *Two noblewomen at a window* (c. 1800) [cat. 27], the artist plays on this idea of forbidden views to suggest the beholder has just caught a highly privileged glimpse of two beautiful women through a window explicitly designed to shield them from men's view. Here, two bejewelled ladies appear at a *jharokha* of a palace *zenana* (harem) adorned with beautiful floral textiles. The textile at the top of the window acts like a blind and is rolled up to reveal the women behind, while the second textile, perhaps an ornate rug, has been thrown over the windowsill. One of the women holds a flask and wine cup while the other holds a large lotus flower, perhaps intended as a symbol of Lakshmi, the Hindu goddess of wealth, power and beauty, who traditionally holds the flower.[128]

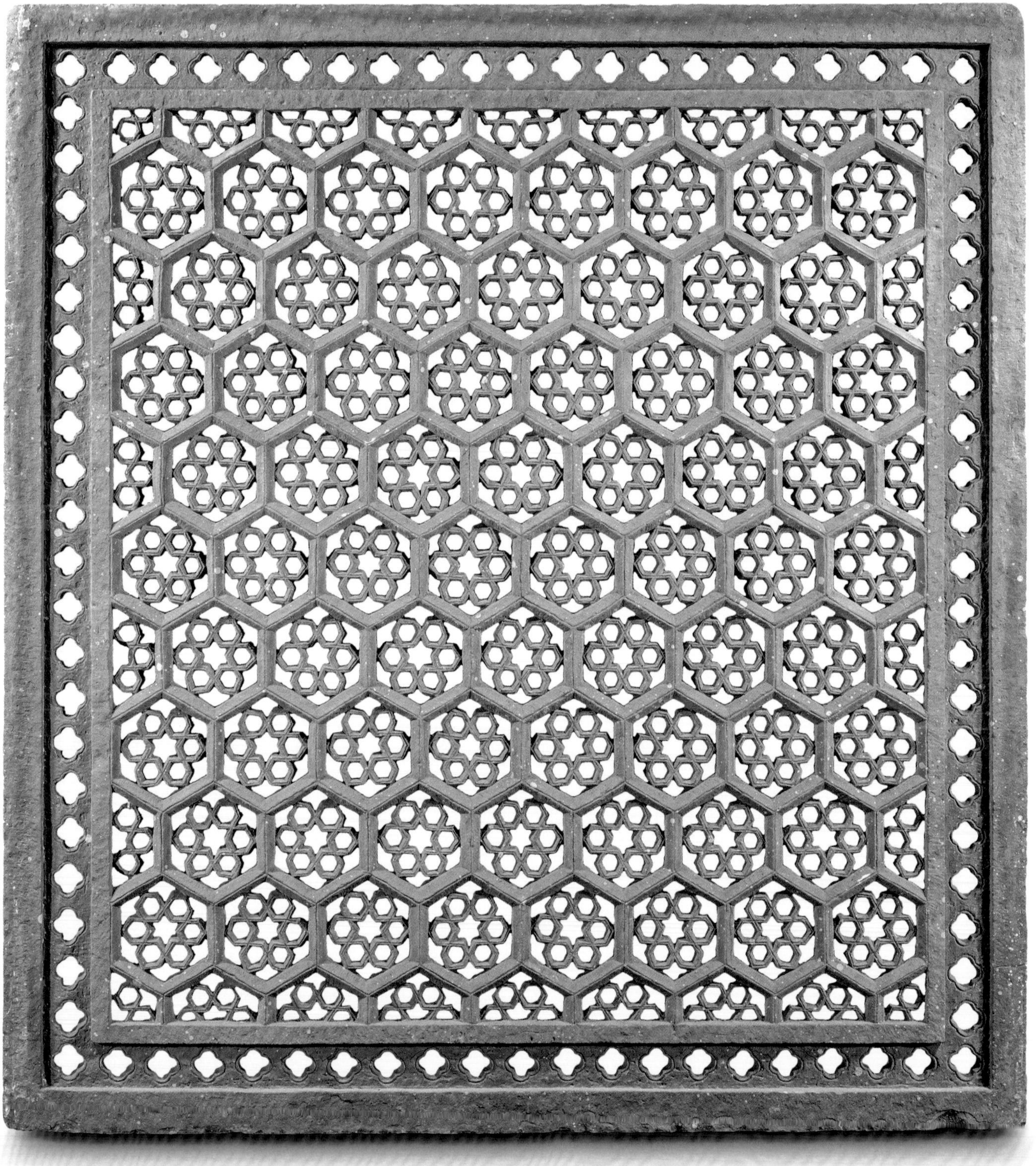

Models and muses at the window

Although artists have portrayed women at windows for millennia, in many of these cases the female figure simply represents a type – a goddess, a saint, a prostitute – or a nameless or idealised woman rather than a distinct person. By the late nineteenth and early twentieth centuries, however, this practice had begun to change and there was a greater interest in representing a specific woman with an identifiable appearance and personality. This may be attributable, in part, to the establishment and increased professionalisation of art academies across Europe and Britain in the late eighteenth and nineteenth centuries which also led to a greater need for models.[129] It is worth noting that the role of the artist's model has changed over time, especially as the meaning and importance of the human figure (and the nude in particular) in art and society has changed.[130] Historically, in periods in which the female nude was especially popular, the models were often of low socio-economic status, poorly paid and associated, correctly or not, with sex work. Some of these models, whether friends, lovers or family members of the artist or paid professionals, sat for an artist for years, establishing a long and intimate relationship that often comes across in the final works. Historically, models have not been credited for much more than their appearance in a given artwork but, more recently, cases have been made for considering models or muses (those who inspire but may not necessarily sit for an artist) as pivotal and active participants if not collaborators in the creation of a work.[131]

Edgar Degas made extensive use of live models, most famously of young ballet dancers but also laundresses, milliners and sex workers.[132] While the precise identity of his *Woman at a Window* (1871–72) [cat. 28] is not known, Degas apparently told his painter friend Walter Sickert that the model was 'une sorte de cocotte' (*cocotte* here used as slang for sex worker) who was starving and whom he paid for her modelling services with a hunk of meat, 'which she fell upon, so hungry was she, and devoured it raw'.[133] To create this work Degas, a master in working with oil on paper, thinned his paint with turpentine to create a more ephemeral effect and, with an economy of line, presents the woman seated in a shadowed *profil perdu* against a bright, light-flooded window looking towards an empty chair, summarily sketched in. This work was painted during the siege of Paris by the Prussian forces (1870–71) which led to a severe food shortage, causing desperate Parisians to slaughter whatever animals were at hand including domestic and later even zoo animals. Degas and his studio must have offered this woman both respite and nourishment while the siege raged outside. The slightly blurred and almost spectral appearance of this unfinished work seems an appropriate reflection of the model's dire situation and the period of devastation in which it was made.

Degas' *Woman at a Window* was eventually acquired by Sickert in 1902, who used it as a means of studying and better understanding the techniques and compositional devices of the French master. Sickert took up the motif of the 'woman in the window' at the beginning of the twentieth century and returned to it throughout his career. Indeed, his particular fondness for the window as an artistic device is apparent from a quote of 1914 in which he likens the way windows frame and limit the light in an indoor landscape to the way the frame of the sonnet form acts on a stream of poetic light.[134] Sickert's *Woman Seated at a Window* (c. 1908–09) [cat. 29] is particularly close to Degas' composition.[135] At the left, a French window illuminates the darker interior and the right side of a young woman's semi-nude body. This is one of several works on this theme painted by the artist in his studio at number 6 Mornington Crescent in London's Camden Town. Here the white translucent lace-edged curtains are drawn aside to reveal a partial view of the greenery of Mornington Crescent Gardens beyond. The woman, presumably a sex worker, is seated on the edge of a daybed

fig. 16
Henri Matisse, *Femme au balcon, fauteuil noir*, 1919, oil on canvas, 66.04 x 50.17 cm

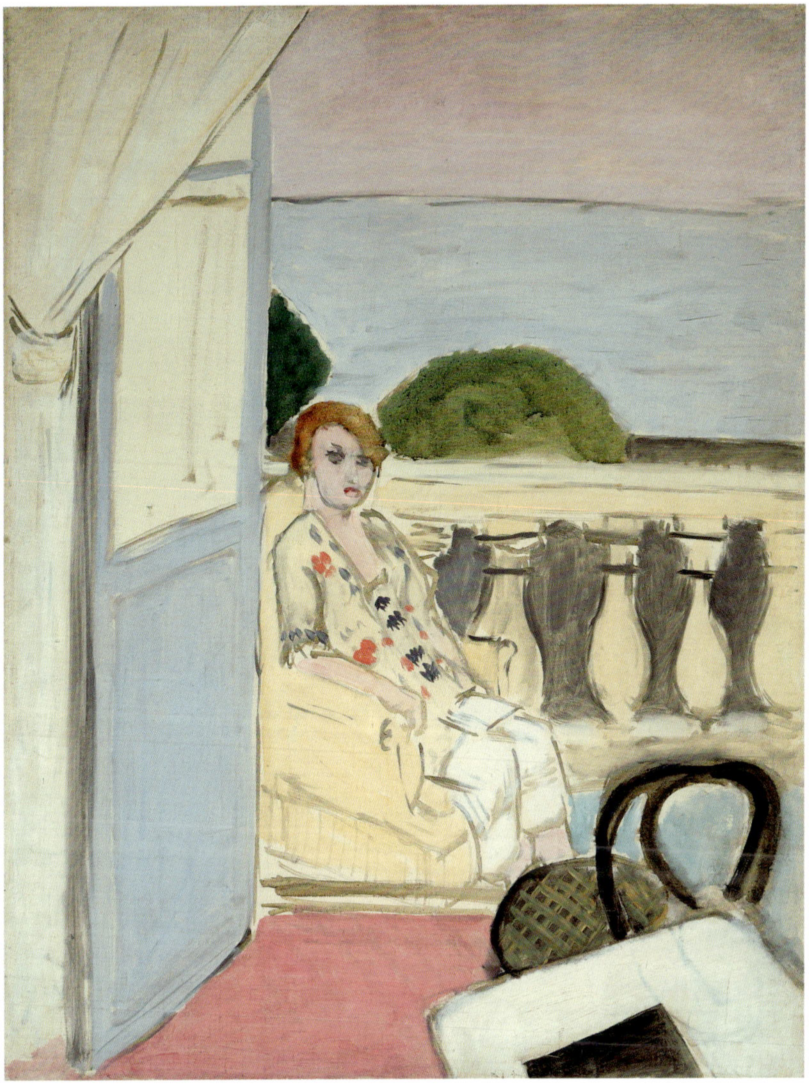

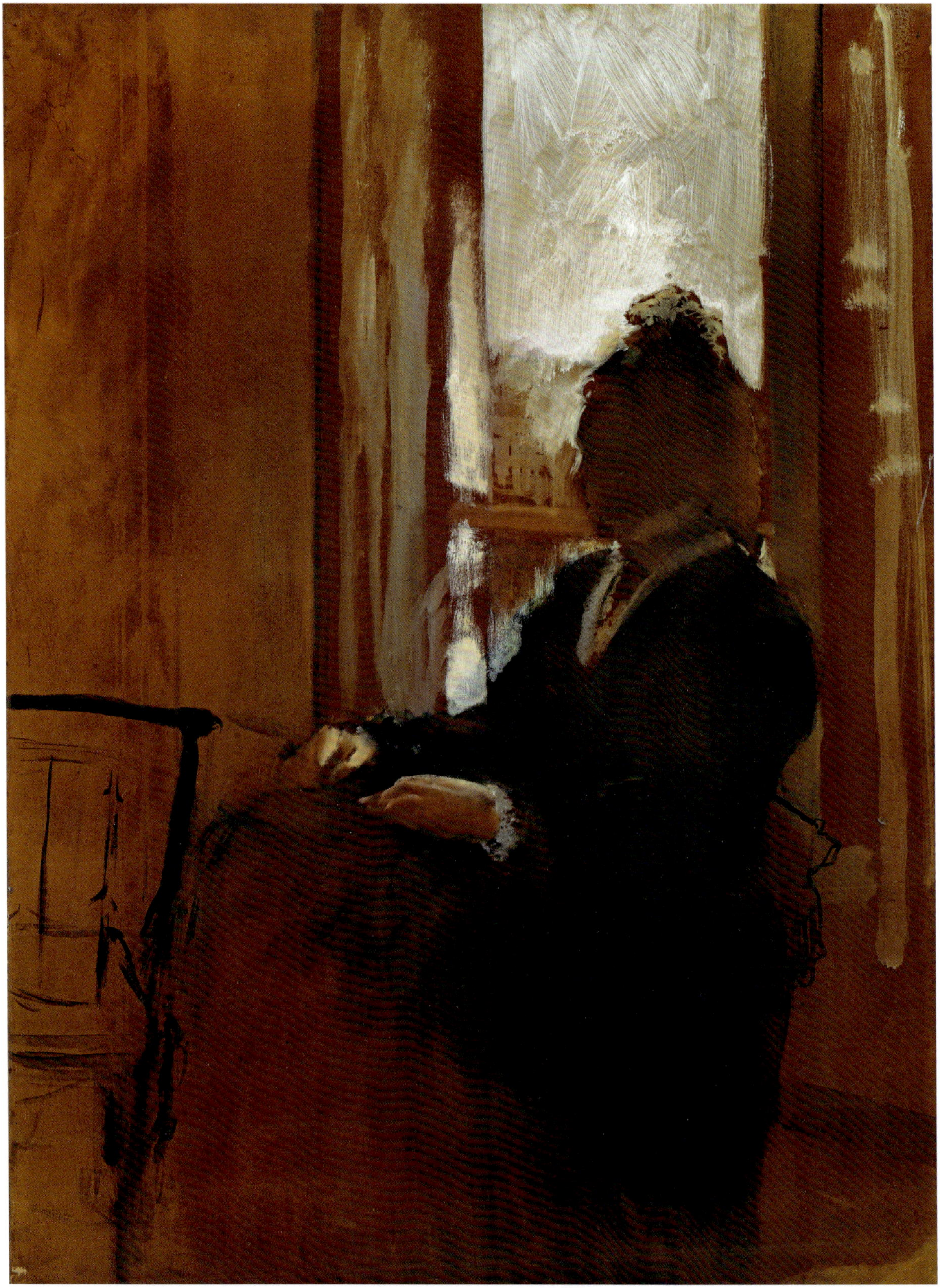

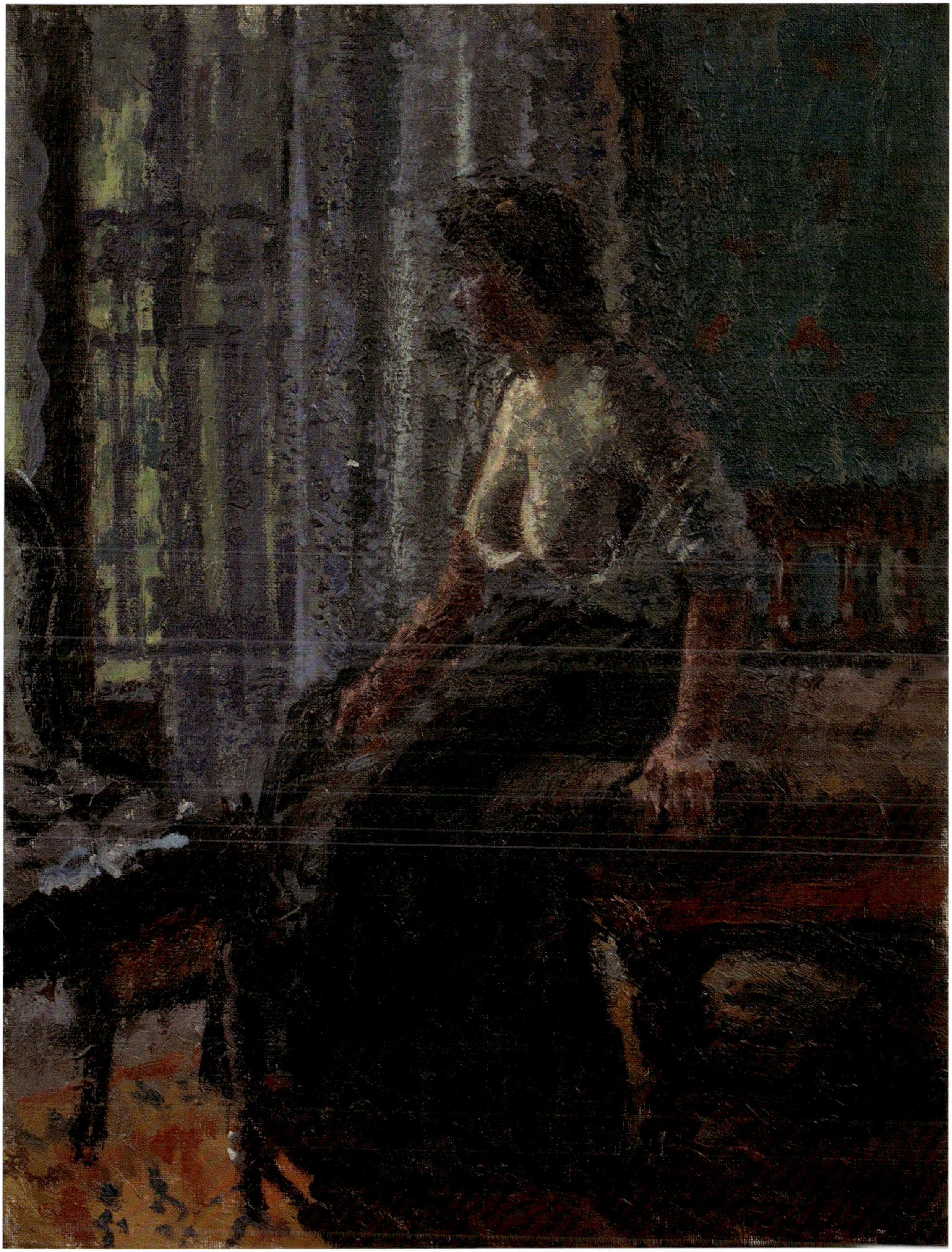

in bright daytime light, her unbuttoned white shirt, still tucked into her skirt at the waist, is parted and lowered to reveal her bust. She turns away from the viewer to look out of the window, as if daydreaming about the world beyond. The oval-backed chair in front of her may be a compositional 'prop' but its inclusion here, as in Degas' work, seems to suggest an absent figure, perhaps the one for whom she undressed. This work, far more sensual than some of Sickert's more frankly sexual compositions, seems to explore the intimacy or perhaps even psychology of the woman's private, solitary, moment.

Of all the twentieth-century artists, however, Henri Matisse was perhaps *the* preeminent painter of the 'woman at the window' composition. 'Windows have always interested me,' Matisse once said, 'because they are a passageway between the exterior and the interior.'[136] Indeed, almost 100 of the artist's works employ a window/door threshold between an intimate, domestic interior and an exterior landscape and many situate a female figure at that threshold.[137] This composition enabled Matisse to experiment with different light effects, contrasting for example a darker interior with the bright light of the Côte d'Azur, and with the spatial relationships between foreground and distance, interior and exterior, as in *Femme au balcon, fauteuil noir* (*Woman on Balcony, Black Armchair*; 1919) [fig. 16]. Painted during Matisse's second sojourn in Nice, this painting shows his room at the Hôtel de la Méditerranée on the Promenade des Anglais. Suffused with light, the room was sparsely but elegantly appointed, with a pink-tiled floor and translucent muslin curtains, here drawn back to reveal French windows with blue shutters which are also opened to reveal a balustraded balcony overlooking the Baie des Anges beyond. The model was to become one of Matisse's favourite muses, appearing in at least 15 of his canvases in this period, both in the nude and in various costumes. The 19-year-old was a local girl, Antoinette Arnoud (or Arnoux) who, rather than becoming Matisse's mistress as some have assumed, was treated by the artist and his wife as an adoptive daughter and considered more of a work partner, collaborator even, than a sexual conquest.[138] Here, framed by the pale blue of the open balcony door-window at the left and of the sky of the horizon behind her, she looks pensive and even a bit annoyed, as if interrupted while reading the book on her lap. Seated outside but facing inwards, with her back to a view of trees and beach beyond, Arnoud is oriented towards an empty chair, table and black book inside the room. The book, which appears in several of Matisse's paintings in this period, is presumably the artist's own note or sketchbook.[139] In this composition, the empty bentwood chair, table and book imply Matisse's presence even though he is not explicitly represented as he is in *The Painting Session* (1919, The National Galleries of Scotland). Matisse's conspicuous absence in *Femme au balcon*, however, effectively invites the viewer to take up his empty seat at the balcony window and to see the model through his eyes.

Matisse's friend and most competitive rival, Pablo Picasso, was similarly partial to the motif of the 'woman in the window' and returned to the subject frequently throughout his career. Picasso and his partner-muse, the artist Françoise Gilot, frequently visited Matisse at his villa in Vence and it was while living in nearby Vallauris that Picasso made his print *La Femme à la fenêtre* (*Woman at the Window*; 1952) [cat. 30] of Gilot at a window.[140] The print is arresting both for its large scale and for how the artist represents Gilot as partially abstracted, with her hands, executed almost entirely in black, pressed up and silhouetted against the white windowpane. The sitter's profile is composed of angular forms in contrasting shades of black and white and illuminated by the window, which creates a dramatic play of light and shadow across her face. Gilot's posture, pressing her hands and body towards the windowpane, suggests anticipation, urgency or even anxiety. This sense is neatly transferred

page 68, cat. 28
Edgar Germain Hilaire Degas, *Woman at a Window*, 1871–72, oil on paper, 61.3 x 45.9 cm
The Courtauld, London (Samuel Courtauld Trust)

page 69, cat. 29
Walter Sickert, *Woman Seated at a Window*, c. 1908–09, oil on canvas, 52 x 40 cm
Private Collection, promised to Petit Palais, Musée Des Beaux-Arts de la Ville de Paris, in memory of Delphine Lévy

cat. 30
Pablo Picasso, *La Femme à la fenêtre* (*Woman at the Window*), 1952, aquatint and drypoint on paper, 90.2 x 63.5 cm
Tate: Presented by Gustav and Elly Kahnweiler 1974, accessioned 1994

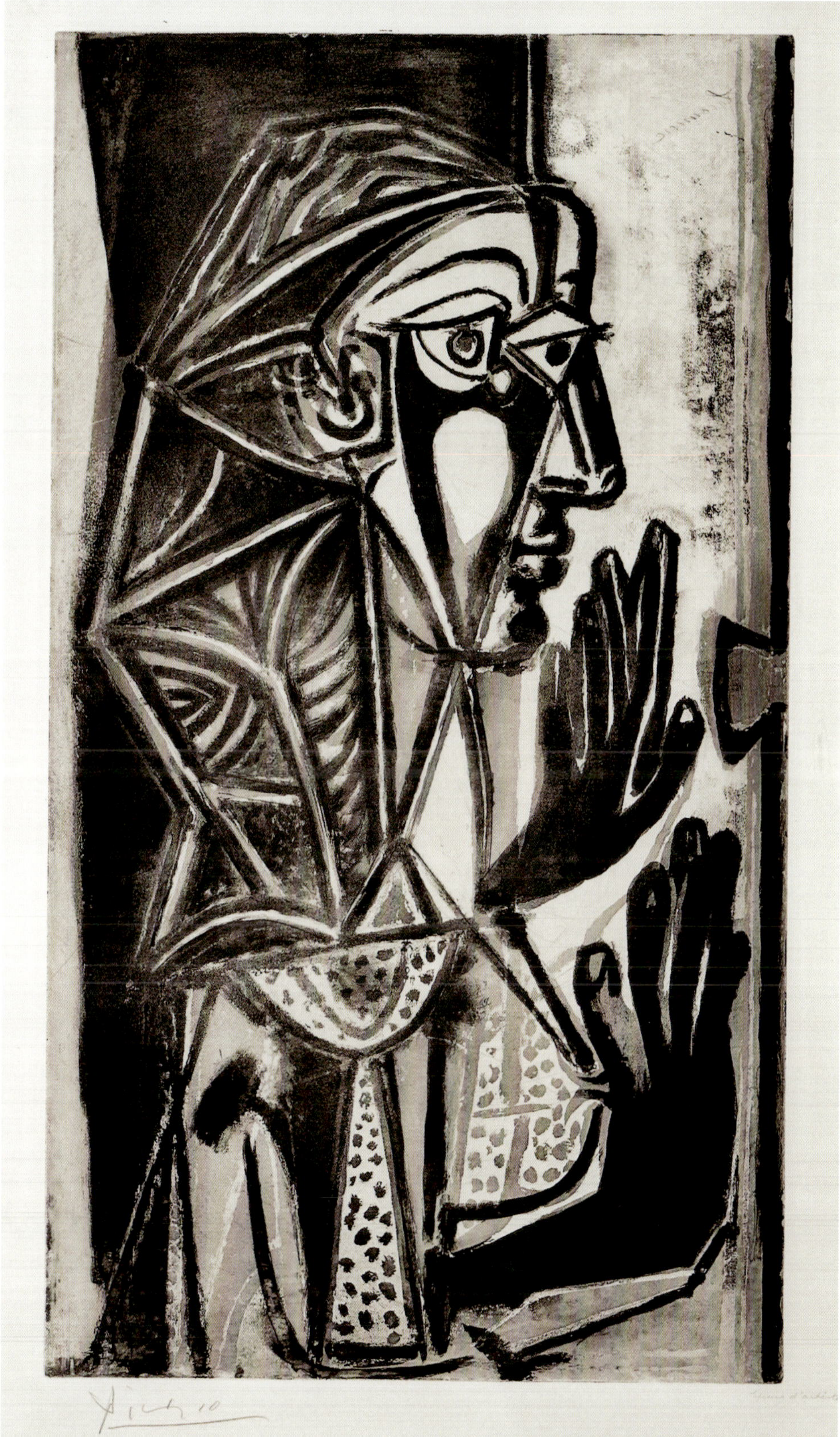

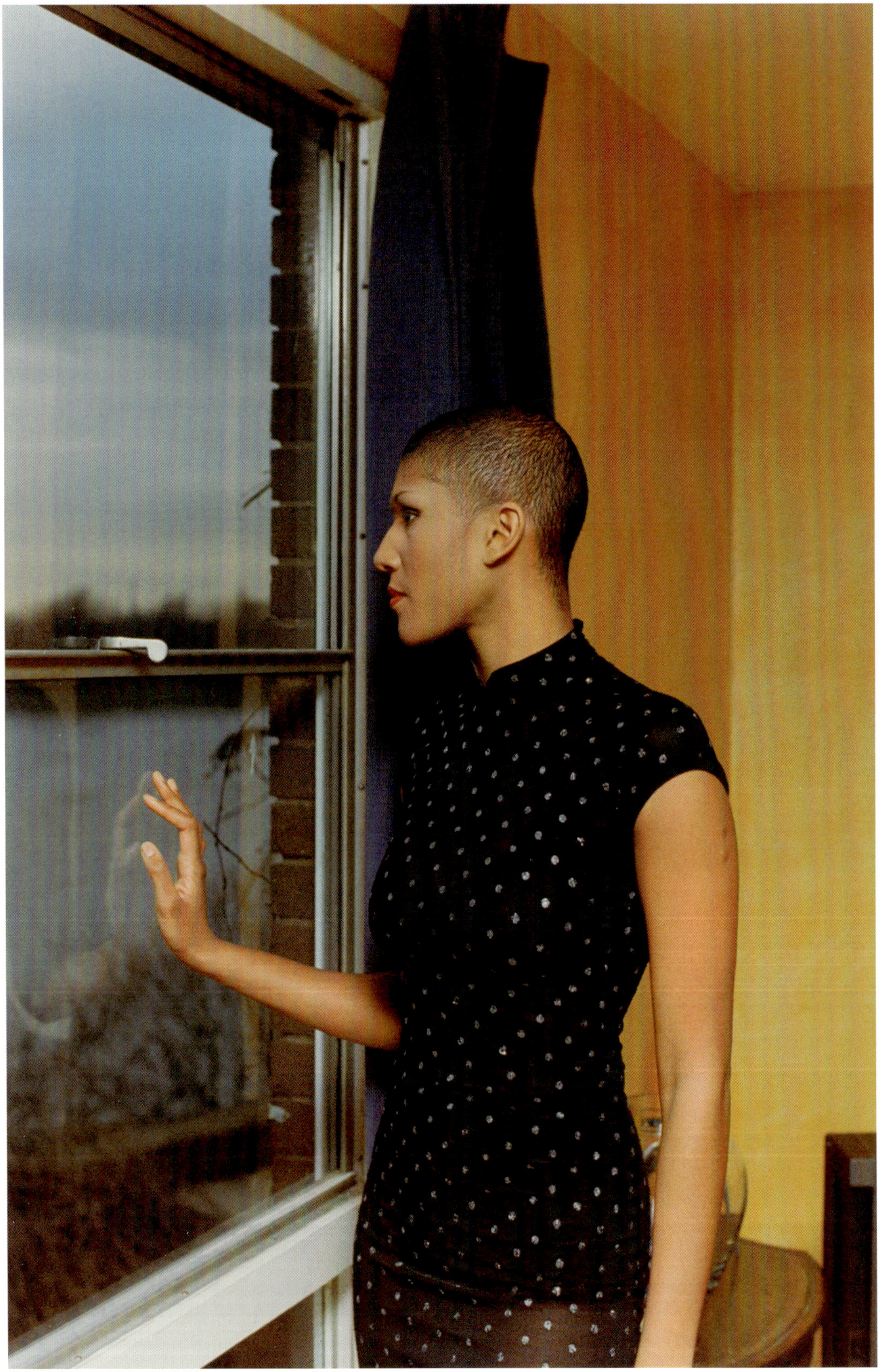

to the beholder whose ability to see what has provoked her rapt attention at the window is frustrated.

The print was made towards the end of Gilot and Picasso's rather tumultuous ten-year relationship (they met when she was 21 and he 61) from 1943 to 1953.[141] During their relationship Gilot had to contend with Dora Maar, Picasso's muse and lover at the time he and Gilot met, Olga Khokhlova, Picasso's wife who apparently often harassed Gilot on the streets of Paris, and Picasso himself who apparently physically abused her and, following their split, discouraged galleries from buying her work. With this in mind, it is hard not to read into the way Gilot presses her hands against the window and seems to gaze wistfully out.

Gilot's gesture of pressing her hands against the windowpane in this type of composition is relatively rare; however, another example is found in the German artist Wolfgang Tillmans' photograph *Smokin' Jo, window* (1995) [cat. 31]. After moving to England to attend art school in the early 1990s, Tillmans then moved to London in 1995, where he began photographing his friends, or 'accomplices' as he describes them, most of whom belonged to the London art, fashion, club and gay scenes.[142] Interested in politics as much as aesthetics, Tillmans explores a wide variety of subjects but especially those associated with homosexuality and gender identity. In *Smokin' Jo, window* he portrays the celebrated Black British house and techno DJ who took her stage name from the heavyweight boxer Smoking Joe Fraser.[143] Jo, born Joanne Joseph, has described her deliberate choice to adopt a gender-ambiguous name as a way of masking her female identity in an attempt to enter what was then an almost entirely male profession. This is one of two photos Tillmans took of Smokin' Jo that year and marks a heady period in her rise to fame just three years after she won the coveted 'number one DJ in the world' award from *DJ Magazine*. Thirty years later, she is still the only woman to have won this prize. While her beauty and talent subsequently led to numerous modelling contracts and endorsement deals, she has described the adoption of this look in the 1990s – 'a number one buzz haircut and baggy tops' – as a means of gaining respect purely for her music rather than for how she looked.[144] Considered in relation to the long history of the 'woman in the window' motif, Tillmans' photograph underscores how women, and perhaps especially women of colour, have sought to manoeuvre within and break away from the confines of societal race and gender constructs. Jo's posture before the window, her right hand gently resting on the glass, captures her on the brink of international fame, and her assured and self-contained demeanour and calm outward gaze convey the sense of a confident woman who is comfortable in her skin but has something to prove. Shown in profile, she does not engage with her surroundings or with the beholder but seems fixed on what lies beyond the window, as if to suggest her focus on navigating beyond the confines not only of this space but of societal norms more broadly.

cat. 31
Wolfgang Tillmans, *Smokin' Jo, window*, 1995, inkjet print on paper, clips, 206.5 x 138 cm
© Wolfgang Tillmans, courtesy Maureen Paley, London

Notes

108. John Farquhar Fraser, John Henry Thomas (eds.), *The Reports of Sir Edward Coke*, 6 vols. (London: Joseph Butterworth and Son, 1826), vol. 5, p. 107.
109. Andrew E. Glantz, 'A Tax on Light and Air: Impact of the Window Duty on Tax Administration and Architecture, 1696–1851', in *Penn History Review*, vol. 15, no. 2 (2008), p. 33.
110. On the window tax see Wallace E. Oates, Robert M. Schwab, 'The Window Tax: A Case Study in Excess Burden', *Journal of Economic Perspectives*, vol. 29, no. 1 (Winter 2015), pp. 163–80.
111. Charles Dickens, *Household Words* (London: Bradbury and Evans, 1850), vol. 1, p. 461.
112. The window tax remained in England until 1851 while a similar tax in France persisted until 1926.
113. Sabine Rewald, *Rooms with a View: The Open Window in the 19th Century*, exh. cat. (New York: Metropolitan Museum of Art, 2011).
114. This type of composition shares some characteristics described as 'absorptive' by Michael Fried in relation to French eighteenth-century pictures. See Michael Fried, *Absorption and Theatricality: Painting and Beholder in the Age of Diderot* (Chicago: University of Chicago Press, 1988).
115. Ibid., pp. 36–39.
116. On this work see Giles Waterfield, *The Artist's Studio*, exh. cat. (Compton Verney, Warwick, 2009; Sainsbury Centre for Visual Arts, Norwich, 2010), p. 95.
117. Grant M. Waters, *Dictionary of British Artists Working 1900–1950* (Eastbourne: Eastbourne Fine Arts Publications, 1975).
118. 'The Art of Isabel Codrington', *The Studio*, vol. 90 (October 1925), p. 217.
119. On Bell, see Frances Spalding, *Vanessa Bell: Portrait of the Bloomsbury Artist* (London: I.B. Tauris, 2016); on the Bloomsbury Group more broadly see Richard Shone, *The Art of Bloomsbury: Roger Fry, Vanessa Bell, and Duncan Grant* (Princeton: Princeton University Press, 1999).
120. This little-known work was exhibited for the first time in 2018 at Piano Nobile Gallery, London and is published in the accompanying catalogue by Richard Shone and Hana Leaper, *From Omega To Charleston: The Art of Vanessa Bell and Duncan Grant 1910–1934* (London: Piano Nobile Publications, 2018).
121. Wendy Baron, *Sickert: Paintings and Drawings* (New Haven: Yale University Press, 2006), pp. 488–89, cat. 571.
122. Amy Boyce Osaki, 'A "Truly Feminine Employment": Sewing and the Early Nineteenth-Century Woman', *Winterthur Portfolio*, vol. 23, no. 4 (1988), pp. 225–41.
123. See discussion of this work and Wall's practice more broadly in Peter Galassi, *Jeff Wall*, exh. cat. (The Museum of Modern Art, New York; The Art Institute of Chicago; San Francisco Museum of Modern Art, 2007); Michael Fried, *Why photography matters as art as never before* (New Haven: Yale University Press, 2008); Sheena Wagstaff, 'Beyond the Threshold', *Tate Etc*, no. 4 (Summer 2005), pp. 40–45.
124. A helpful reference for different kinds of windows and their constructions is Karla J. Nielson, *Window Treatments* (Toronto: John Wiley and Sons, 1990), and for Chinese and Japanese screens in particular see, pp. 280ff.
125. On window screens in Japan, see Gisei Takakuwa, *Shoji: The Screens of Japan* (Kyoto: Mitsumura Suiko Shoin, 1961); Katsuhiko Muramoto, 'In Search of a Relational Body: Reflections on Sustainable Architecture', in Nycole Prowse (ed.), *Intervening Spaces: Respatialisation and the Body* (Leiden: Brill, 2018), pp. 80–100; on Chinese window screens see Daniel Sheets Dye, *Chinese Lattice Designs* (New York: Dower Publications, 1974); and Ma Weidu, *Classical Chinese Doors and Windows* (Beijing: China Architecture & Building Press, 2006).
126. Barbra Teri Okada, *Netsuke: Masterpieces from the Metropolitan Museum of Art*, exh. cat. (New York: The Metropolitan Museum of Art, 1981); Raymond Bushell, *The Inrō Handbook* (Boulder, CO: Weatherhill, 2002).
127. On the traditional placement and use of *jali* and *jharokha*, see Varsha Joshi, *Polygamy and Purdah: Women and Society Among Rajputs* (Jaipur and New Delhi: Rawat Publications, 1995); Molly Emma Aitken, 'Pardah and Portrayal: Rajput Women as Subjects, Patrons, and Collectors', *Artibus Asiae*, vol. 62, no. 2 (2002), pp. 247–80.
128. The lotus is a sacred flower in both Hinduism and Buddhism and has several different meanings but often represents a path to spiritual awakening and enlightenment. On the symbolic associations of the plant in India see James G. Lochtefeld, *The Illustrated Encyclopaedia of Hinduism* (New York: Rosen Publishing Group, 2002), pp. 385–86; Heinrich Robert Zimmer, *Myths and Symbols in Indian Art and Civilization* (Princeton: Princeton University Press, 2015), p. 100.
129. Although academies for painting first arose in Italy in the sixteenth century, they were largely founded across Europe during the eighteenth century. The Royal Academy of Painting and Sculpture in Paris was founded in 1648; the famous Académie des Beaux-Arts (Academy of Fine Arts) was created in 1816 and merged with the older institution. The Royal Academy in London was founded in 1768.
130. On this subject see Kenneth Clark, *The Nude: A Study in Ideal Form* (Princeton: Princeton University Press, 1984), pp. 3–29; Martin Postle, William Vaughn, *The Artist's Model: From Etty to Spencer* (London: Merrell Holberton, 1999).
131. This is also the case in a recent re-assessment of the role of Camille Claudel for Rodin in Nabila Abdel Nabi, Achim Borchardt-Hume, *The Making of Rodin* (London: Tate Publishing, 2021) and several of Matisse's models in Hilary Spurling, *Matisse: The Life* (London: Penguin, 2009); on the subject more broadly see Katie McCabe, *More than a Muse: Creative Partnerships That Sold Talented Women Short* (London: Quadrille, 2020).
132. On this subject see Eunice Lipton, *Looking into Degas: Uneasy Images of Women and Modern Life* (Berkeley: University of California Press, 1986).
133. I'd like to thank Karen Serres for providing me with the source of this anecdote in Sickert's annotated copy of Paul Jamot's 1924 book on Degas which is now in the Collection of the Institut Néerlandais, Fondation Custodia, Paris. There is a second copy of the book, with differing annotations, by Sickert, in the Courtauld Institute of Art Library, London. On the friendship between these two artists see Anna Gruetzner Robins, 'Degas and Sickert: Notes on Their Friendship', *The Burlington Magazine*, vol. 130, no. 1020 (March 1988).
134. Walter Sickert, 'A Stone Ginger' [New Age, 19 March 1914, p. 631] in Anna Gruetzner Robins (ed.), *Walter Sickert: The Complete Writings on Art* (Oxford: Oxford University Press, 2000), p. 344.
135. For a longer discussion of the work see Wendy Baron, *Sickert, Paintings and Drawings* (New Haven: Yale University Press, 2006), p. 371, cat. 352.
136. Jack D. Flam (ed.), *Matisse on Art* (Berkeley: University of California Press, 1994), p. 135; Carla Gottlieb, 'The Role of the Window in the Art of Matisse', *The Journal of Aesthetics and Art Criticism*, vol. 22, no. 4, Summer 1964, pp. 393–423.
137. This was noted in Shirley Neilsen Blum, *Henri Matisse: Rooms with a View* (New York and London: Thames and Hudson, 2010), p. 11.
138. This relationship between Matisse and Antoinette Arnoud, as well as with his other models, has been reconsidered in Hilary Spurling's 2009 biography on the artist; Spurling, p. 318.
139. A similar closed black book appears for example in Matisse's *Interior with a Violin Case*, 1918, The Museum of Modern Art, New York, #86.1934 and *Interior with a Black Book*, 1918, private collection.
140. Brigitte Baer, *Picasso the Printmaker: Graphics from the Marina Picasso Collection*, exh. cat. (Dallas: Dallas Museum of Art, 1983), p. 144; Brigitte Baer, *Picasso peintre-graveur: Catalogue raisonné de l'oeuvre gravé et des monotypes, 1946–1958*, vol. 4 (Bern: Editions Kornfeld, 1988), pp. 160–61.
141. Gilot co-wrote a memoir about her life with the artist which he tried, unsuccessfully to block; see Françoise Gilot, Carlton Lake, *Life with Picasso* (New York: McGraw-Hill, 1964).
142. For Tillmans' discussion of his sitters as 'accomplices' and portraiture as a collaborative process between photographer and 'accomplice', see *Wolfgang Tillmans: Portraits* (New York: Distributed Art Publishers, 2002).
143. Wolfgang Tillmans, *If one thing matters, everything matters* (Berlin: Hatje Cantz, 2003), p. 95.
144. Interview with DJ Paulette in *World Magazine*, 23 May 2015, http://www.dmcworld.net/features/smokin-jo/.

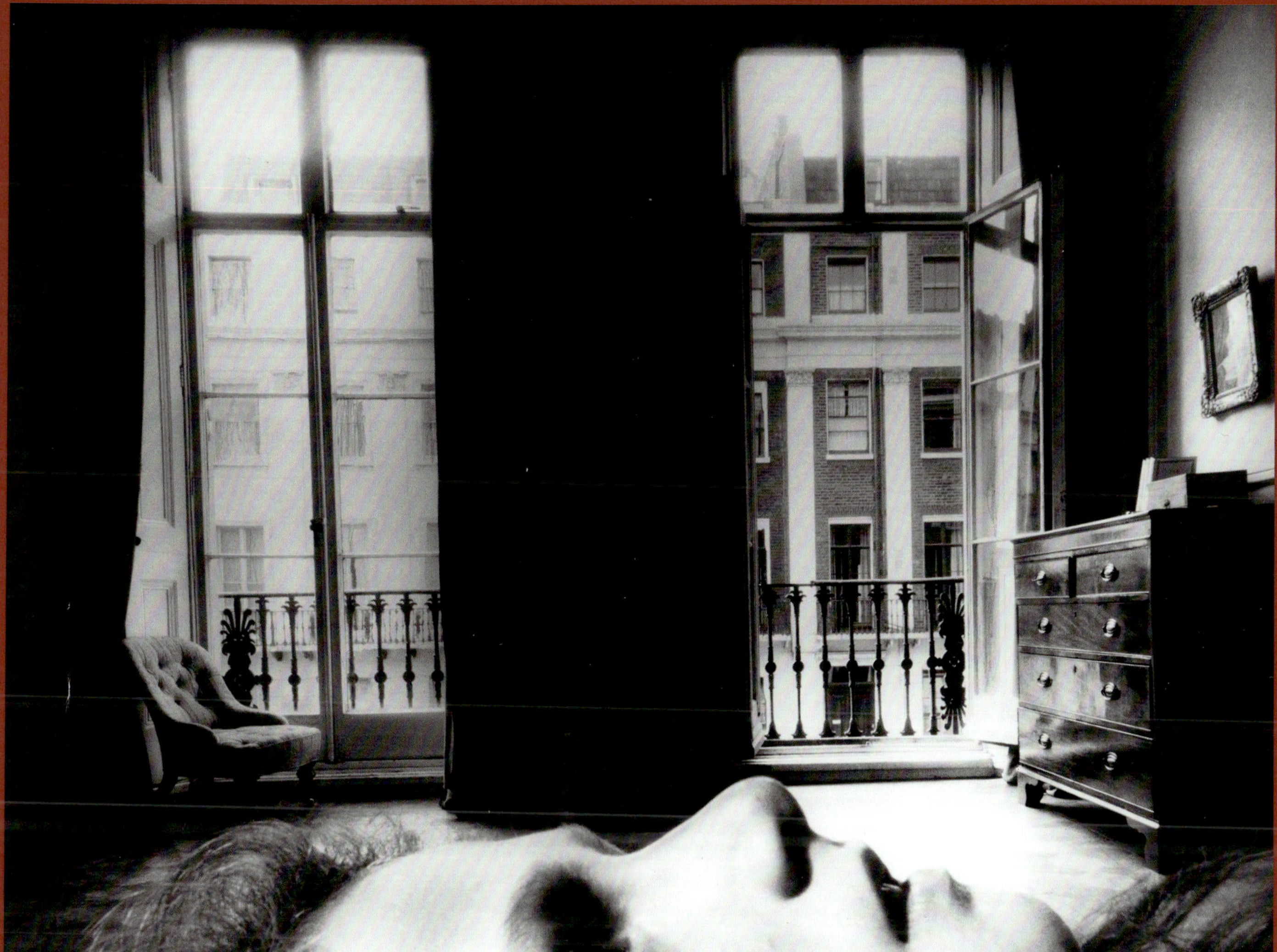

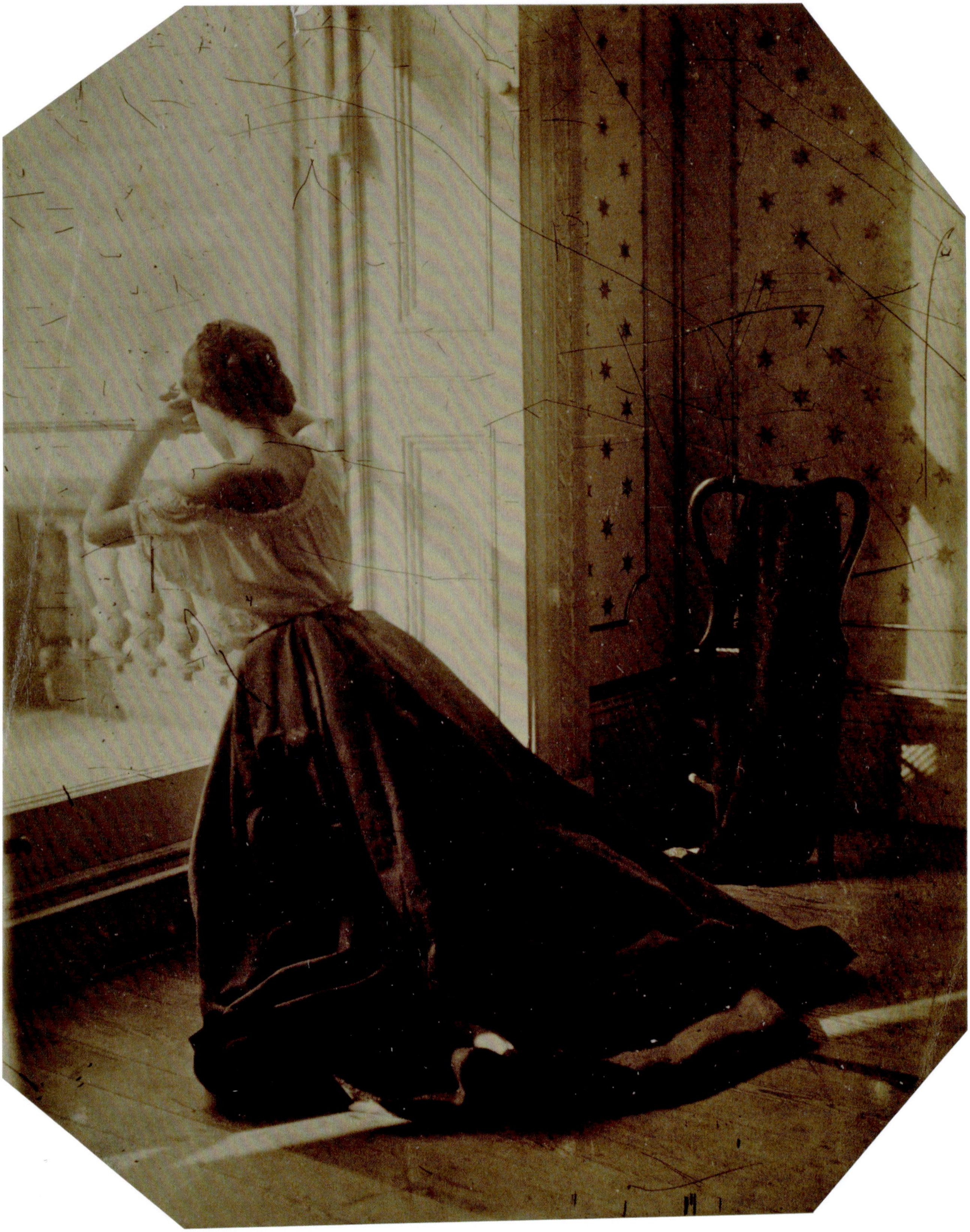

As a consequence of the Industrial Revolution (c.1760–1840), the period towards the end of the nineteenth and beginning of the twentieth century was marked by dramatic change, precipitated in part by several new technological inventions such as electric light. As the need for natural light became less urgent, this aspect of the window's function also shifted and the number of works of art featuring women employing windows as a light source for reading, sewing or playing music also diminished [see cats. 15, 23, fig. 11]. Electric light sources also meant that windows became like display cases for the inhabitants within when illuminated by night [cat. 40].

Developments in glass quality, production and scale led to its adoption as an important building material, especially for commercial and industrial construction.[145] Shop windowpanes also expanded dramatically to become 'show windows' which in turn became a source of inspiration for artists [see cat. 37]. The increased use of glass in industrial construction soon spread to domestic architecture, with the window becoming a display frame or even an entire wall in modernist buildings such as those designed by the German Bauhaus school.

The modernism that marked societal and cultural thinking across the globe also brought new imagery, materials and techniques, such as photography and film, to the 'woman in the window' motif that reflected both the realities and utopian aspirations of modern societies. These works put an increased emphasis on the role of the window as a compositional device rather than a specific reflection of contemporary practice. Indeed, modernist interpretations of the motif often employ windows to play on notions of foreground and background, proximity and distance, or time and space.

Early photography as a 'window'

From the earliest examples of commercial photography onwards, artists working in this medium have used the window as a framing device or conceptual tool.[146] As one of the first photographic subjects, the window is literally and figuratively linked to the process itself. In 1829 William Henry Fox Talbot, a pioneer of photography, even advised that the novice photographer's first subject should always be a window.[147] For practical reasons, windows were used as they provided the light source required for an exposure but they also provided a helpful reference point due to their affinities with the mechanics of photography itself, as an 'opening' or 'viewfinder' through which images are seen and framed. A survey of early nineteenth- and twentieth-century window photographs reveals that the majority feature women looking in or out of them, or that they capture shop windows where the figures peering out are often female mannequins.[148] All of these works seem to play on notions of seeing and being seen, of looking and the right to look, and on framing and display.

Photographers at the window

The advent of photography also marks the earliest instances of female artists taking up the motif of the 'woman in the window'. Indeed women, mostly from Britain and France, took up the medium very early in its development. A prime example is Clementina Maude, the Viscountess Hawarden, a noted Victorian amateur portrait photographer who set up a studio in her elegant home in South Kensington, London in the 1850s.[149] Many of her albumen print portraits are highly autobiographical, featuring her adolescent daughters in dramatic poses, often with their backs to the camera, gazing out of a window in their shared home. In *Clementina Maude, 5 Princes Gardens* (c. 1862) [cat. 32], for example, Lady Hawarden positioned the kneeling figure of her daughter turning away from the viewer at the far left, balancing her form at the far right with the back of the chair oriented towards the corner.

cat. 32
Clementina Viscountess Hawarden, *Clementina Maude, 5 Princes Gardens*, c. 1862, photograph, albumen print from wet collodion negative, 11.8 x 9.5 cm
Victoria and Albert Museum. Given by Lady Clementina Tottenham

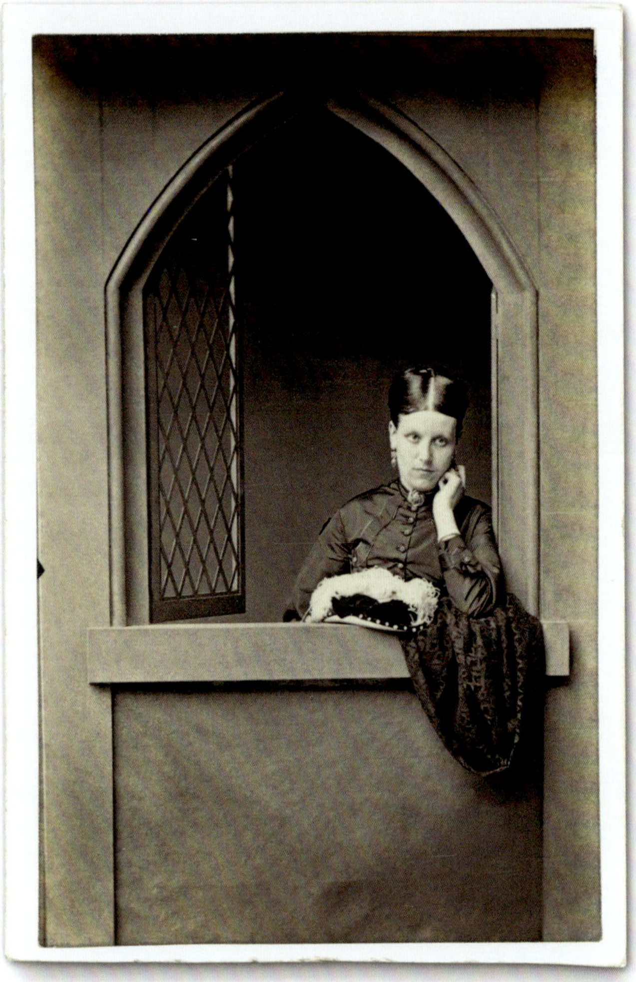

above, cat. 33
James Brennen, *Carte-de-visite, portrait of a woman in an arched window*, 1860s, albumen silver print, 9.5 x 6.4 cm
Wilson Centre for Photography

opposite, cat. 34
***Carte-de-visite, portrait of a woman in an arched window*, late 1880s, albumen silver print, 10.3 x 6.3 cm**
Private Collection, UK

This arrangement sets up a sensual, visual comparison between the curve of the back of the chair, illuminated by the natural light pouring in through the window, and that of the exposed bare shoulder of the young girl. The close cropping of the composition at the model's feet places the viewer in intimate proximity to the young woman, as if enclosed in the small room with her. Lady Hawarden used the room, together with props including clothing, mirrors, the window and balcony, combined with the postures of her sitters to suggest a narrative, albeit an elusive one. It is left to the viewer to interpret the scene but here Clementina Maude's pose, with her forehead leaning against her folded hands at the window, suggests melancholy or longing, while her lack of engagement with the city beyond suggests isolation and perhaps even despair. This work represents a particularly early instance of a female photographer taking up the theme in an especially personal manner, which would inspire female photographers such as Helen Levitt, Vivian Maier and Francesca Woodman over a century later.

Curiously, the theme of the 'woman in the window' was adopted by early photographers to be used as *cartes-de-visite*, a type of small photograph about the size of a modern-day business card that was first patented in Paris and quickly gained popularity in Europe and America.[150] The earliest *cartes-de-visite* were simple, handwritten notecards used by visitors making social calls to the homes of friends, either to present to a doorman or to be left if the hosts were unavailable. These cards became increasingly personalised and were printed with names and addresses and eventually included photographs. In Victorian England in particular, women's *cartes-de-visite* frequently represented them standing at a false 'stage-set' window in the photographer's studio. Two examples of this type show elegant and well-to-do ladies at windows [cats. 33, 34] and can be dated to the late 1800s. They are of particular interest here as they deliberately emulate a type of Dutch seventeenth-century painting showing a woman at a window [see cats. 13–15 and figs. 11–12] popular among British collectors around this date.[151] While this composition must have been intended as a sophisticated manner in which to present oneself to others, it reveals how little was known of the original, rather bawdy, associations of these female figures in Netherlandish pictures.[152] In Augustus W. Wilson's *Carte-de-visite* (late 1800s), for example, he portrays his client at a windowsill surrounded by grapevines, presumably to create a more naturalistic composition. However, in historic works, upon which this photograph draws directly, a woman juxtaposed with bunches of grapes on a vine at a window is understood as an 'easy' woman of loose virtue who is likened to the grape that is easily 'plucked' from the vine, as in

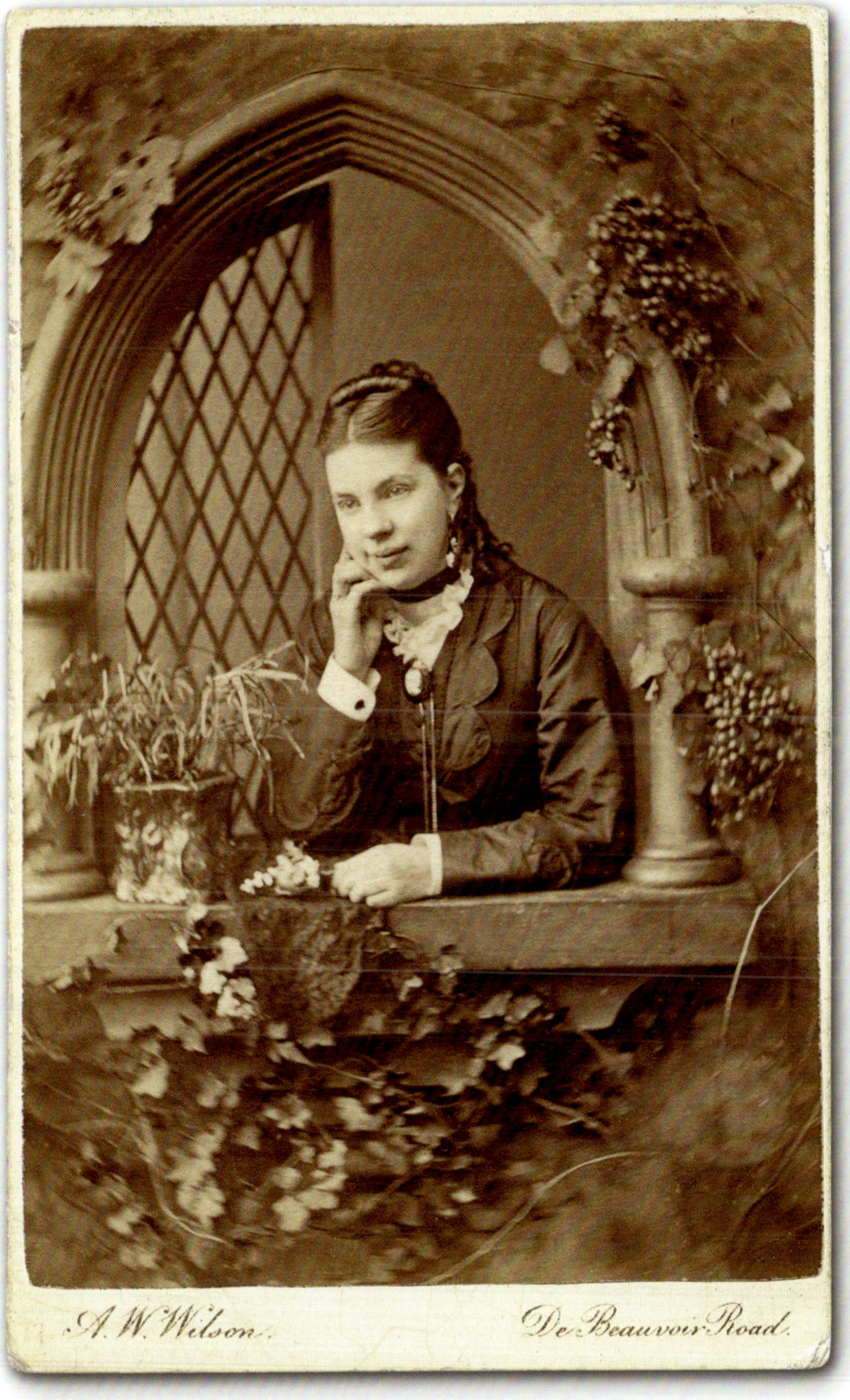
A. W. Wilson.
De Beauvoir Road.

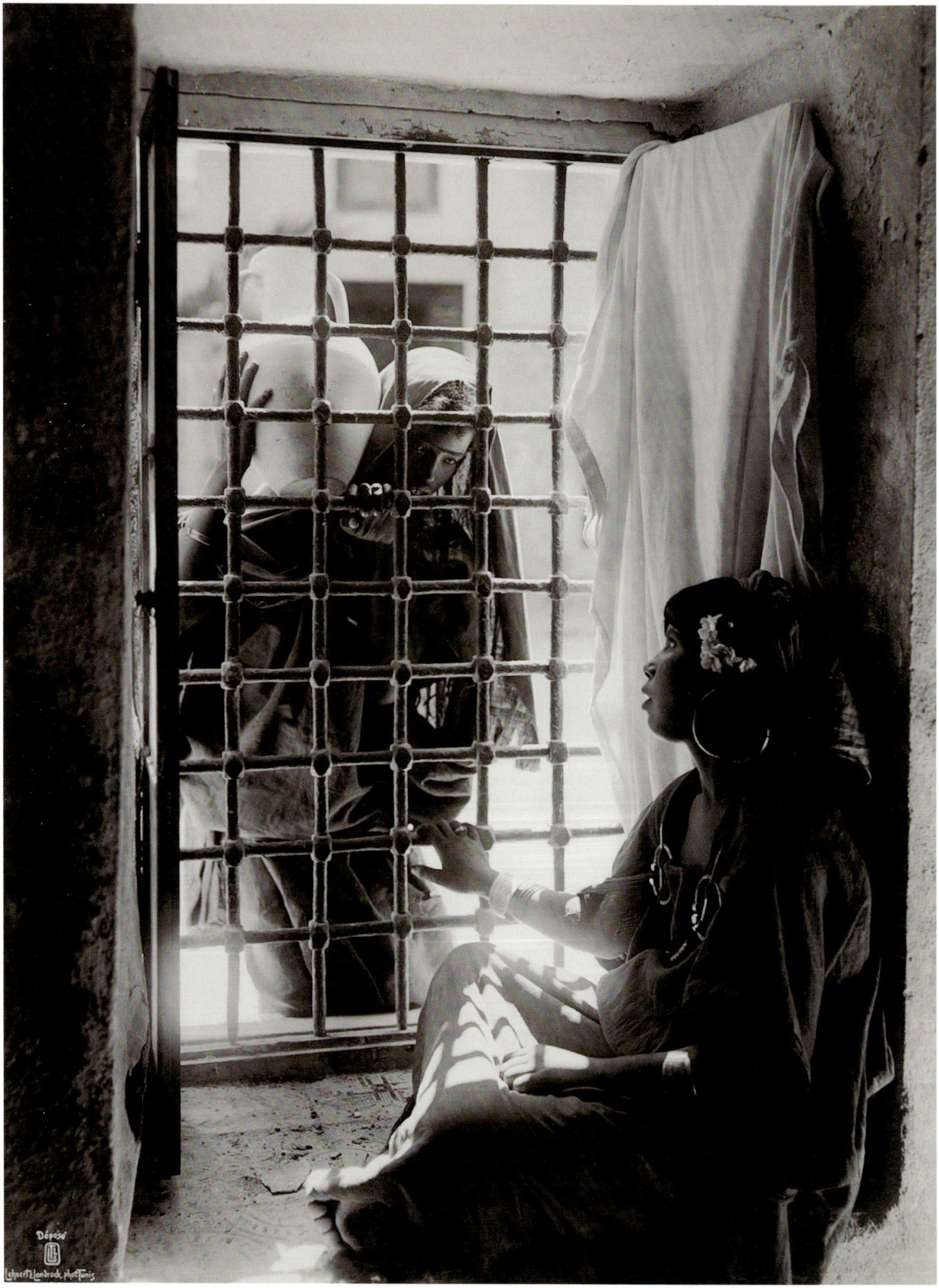
Déposé
Lehnert & Landrock, phot. Tunis

Gerrit Dou's *A Young Woman with a Bunch of Grapes* (1662; Galleria Sabauda, Turin).[153]

Consciously or not, early photographers taking up the motif of the woman at the window were registering complex and evolving ideas about the male gaze but also, increasingly, about the Western gaze. Both are especially evident in the collaborative photographic works of Rudolf Lehnert and Ernest Landrock.[154] Collaborators for over 20 years, Lehnert and Landrock were of Austro-Hungarian and German backgrounds respectively but travelled widely, establishing photographic studios in Tunis and Cairo as well as Leipzig and Munich. Their work is particularly noted for its exploration of 'Orientalist' subjects that concentrate on the romanticised images of the Middle East, which they sold as postcards, souvenir photographs and as reproductions in books. There was a particular Western fascination with Middle Eastern, Asian and North African societies in the nineteenth and twentieth centuries, and artists seeking to evoke these cultures did so through a Western and often condescending and eroticising lens.[155] From the 1860s onwards there was a special interest in and market for photographs of non-Western people in scenes that presented a different sexual morality from that in the West, such as harems.[156] Lehnert and Landrock's *Woman at a window, Tunisia* (c. 1910–15) [cat. 35] is an interesting example as it probably represents a staged tableau, depicting a young, barefoot woman in Egyptian costume, sitting on a floor next to a window that gives on to a street beyond through a metal grille. She appears to converse, through the grille, with another woman carrying a water vase, perhaps an allusion to a society in which centralised water systems were not yet established. The water bearer may also draw on the long history of representation of this figure type in the history of art as painted by artists such as Raphael, Parmigianino and Nicolas Poussin who often associated the shape of a vase with that of the female body and understood both as a kind of 'vessel'.[157] Each figure rests one hand on a crossbar of the metal divider, drawing our attention to it and to the way it imposes a kind of geometric grid over the composition. The grille also sets up a series of contrasts between the two women, between inside and outside, light and dark, action and inaction. The role of the metal bars remains ambiguous: are they for the protection or enclosure of the seated woman? Indeed, Lehnert and Landrock's composition is very much a work of its time which, considered today, might make viewers uncomfortable both for the way it suggests a kind of caged enclosure and for how it seems to stereotype and fetishise ideas about women of colour who were often described as 'exotic' by a predominantly white, male audience.

Film noir

The vulnerability of the lone young, and often beautiful, 'woman in the window' became an important motif in Hollywood thriller and crime dramas known as *film noir* ('dark film') in the 1940s and 1950s. Traditionally focussing on themes of psychological conflict, paranoia, fate and moral ambiguity, these films were shot in black-and-white in a style derived from German expressionist cinematography. One of the greatest proponents of the genre was German director Fritz Lang who immigrated to the US in 1934.[158] In 1944, he directed *The Woman in the Window*, a film believed to have defined the *film noir* genre, which tells the story of a psychology professor who meets and becomes enamoured with a young femme fatale whose painted portrait he observes in a shop window.

The particularly unsettling qualities of the 'woman in the window' motif in *film noir* inspired not only other filmmakers but also a generation of photographers such as Bill Brandt. Brandt's dramatic black-and-white

cat. 35
Rudolf Lehnert and Ernest Landrock, *Woman at a window, Tunisia*, c. 1910–15, gelatin silver print, 23 x 17.6 cm
Wilson Centre for Photography

photograph *Portrait of a Young Girl, Eaton Place* (1955) [cat. 36] evokes a film still and is shot in extreme close-up with a deep-focus profile view of the girl reclining in an elegant apartment punctuated by tall French windows.[159] A departure from the documentary work for which Brandt became known, this more personal, autobiographical work, shows his ten-year-old niece Judith in the sitting room of an apartment that Brandt's wife Eva moved into after their separation. Brandt shot several photographs in this space in Belgravia, London and all three feature the Victorian spoon-backed chair, a piece of furniture that has been described as a surrogate for Eva herself, while Judith, it has been suggested, represents the child that Eva and Bill never had.[160] This low-angled dramatic shot evokes Brandt's favourite film, Orson Welles' *Citizen Kane* (1941), which featured techniques such as deep-focus cinematography, real rooms instead of sets with shots of the ceiling, and chiaroscuro lighting. In *Citizen Kane* style, Brandt here turns his subject into a looming figure shown at an unexpected perspective in a setting made ominous through dramatic lighting effects and an unusual camera angle which places the beholder uncomfortably close to the young girl. Judith's horizontal orientation and the way she seems oblivious to the room around her, and especially of the open window on the right, makes her seem vulnerable. Through lighting effects, Brandt draws the beholder's eye beyond the girl and deeper into the room to take in the windows, one of which is open, the dresser and the painting on the wall as if these might provide clues as to the girl's identity and the reason for her unsettling presence in this room.

Notes

145. There was an extensive use of glass, for example, in the construction of train stations (such as King's Cross Station, London, 1851–52), market halls (Les Halles, Paris, 1835–58) and department stores (Bon Marché, Paris, 1869–87); discussion in Friedberg, pp. 113–15.
146. This was the subject of an exhibition and associated catalogue: Karen Hellman (ed.), *The Window in Photographs* (Los Angeles: Getty Publications, 2013).
147. Letter from Talbot to Lady Mary Lucy Cole, 9 August 1839, from *The Correspondence of William Henry Fox Talbot, Document 10003* cited in Hellman, p. 17, n. 5.
148. See for example Hellman.
149. Graham Ovenden (ed.), *Clementina, Lady Hawarden* (New York: St Martin's Press, 1974); also Carol Mavor, *Becoming: The Photographs of Clementina, Viscountess Hawarden* (Durham, NC: Duke University Press, 1999); and Virginia Dodier, Clementina, *Lady Hawarden: Studies from Life, 1857–1864* (New York: Aperture, 1999).
150. Robin Wichard, Carol Wichard, *Victorian Cartes de Visite* (New York: Bloomsbury, 1999).
151. George IV, for example, may be credited with increasing the taste for such works in England with his collection of Dutch seventeenth-century paintings in the first three decades of the nineteenth century.
152. See discussion of these types of works on pp. 38–42.
153. Eddy de Jongh, 'Grape Symbolism in Paintings of the 16th and 17th Centuries', *Simiolus*, vol. 7, no. 4 (1974).
154. John Hannavy (ed.), *Encyclopedia of Nineteenth-Century Photography* (London: Routledge, 2013), p. 1032.
155. On this subject, see Pascal Baetens, *Nude Photography: The Art and the Craft* (London: Dorling Kindersley, 2007), pp. 14–15.
156. Roger Benjamin, *Orientalist Aesthetics, Art, Colonialism and French North Africa: 1880–1930* (Berkeley: University of California Press, 2003).
157. Elizabeth Cropper, 'On Beautiful Women, Parmigianino, Petrarchismo, and the Vernacular Style', *The Art Bulletin*, vol. 58, no. 3 (1976), pp. 374–94.
158. Tom Gunning, *The Films of Fritz Lang: Allegories of Vision and Modernity* (London: British Film Institute, 2000), see especially Part V 'Framing Desire'.
159. Paul Delany, *Bill Brandt: A Life* (Stanford: Stanford University Press, 2004), p. 244.
160. Ibid.

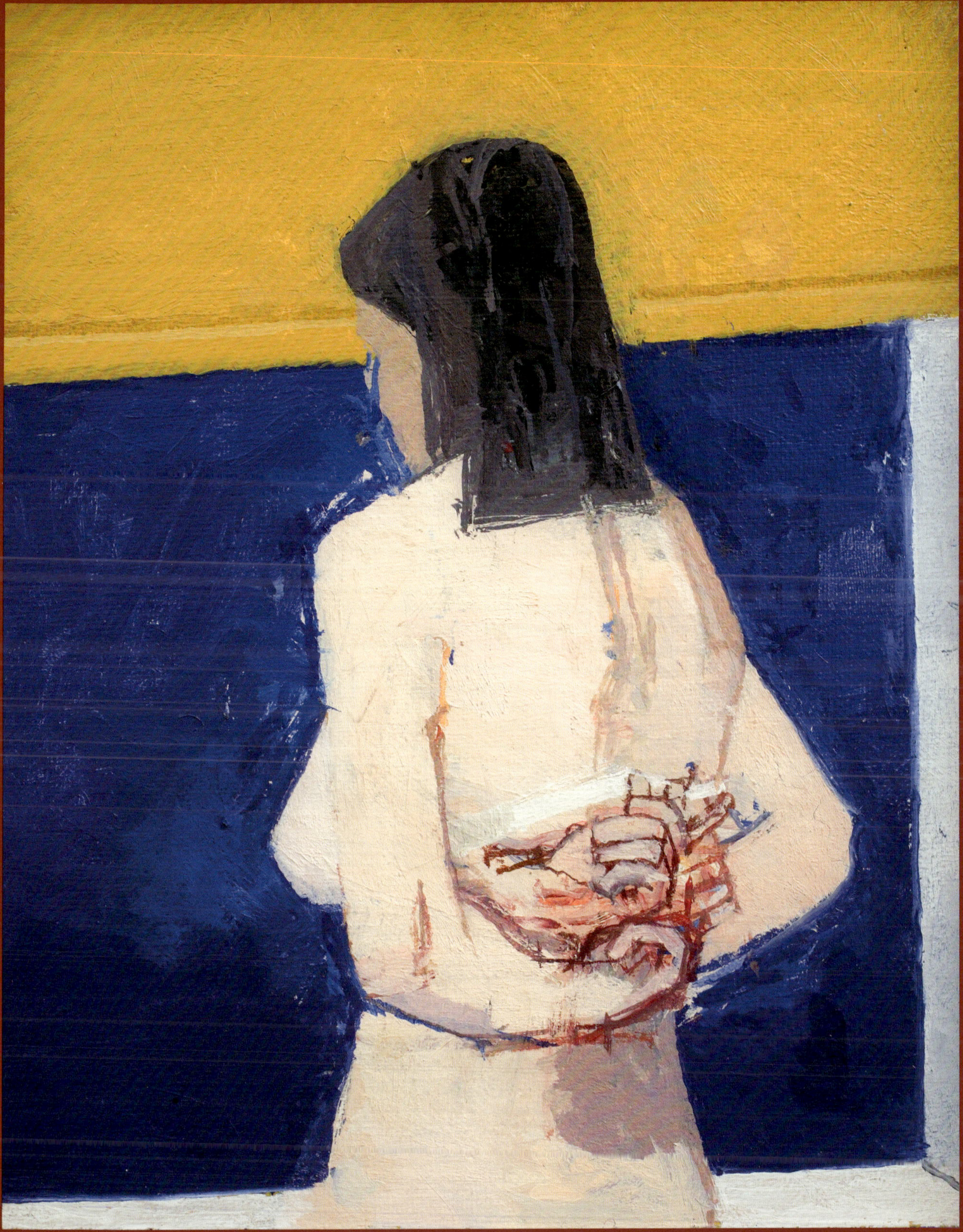

Both during and following the Second World War, the role and presence of women in public life changed. Women who had remained predominantly within the domestic sphere adopted roles formerly taken by the men who were now occupied with the war effort elsewhere. With fewer restrictions on their movements, women were no longer only glimpsed at the window but were on the streets, in the stores and behind the wheels of trucks and aeroplanes. There was also an increase in the number of professional female artists, and their subjects broke away from the genres of still life and portraiture traditionally deemed appropriate for women, to include far more challenging social, political and personal subjects. The women's rights movement of the 1960s and 1970s sought equal rights and opportunities and greater personal freedom for women in every area including politics, work, family and sexuality. This movement challenged long-held notions about the male and female gaze, which had an impact on both actual window gazing and on the representation of women at the window.

Pop art

British pop artist Peter Blake's *Girl in a Window* (1962) [cat. 37] may be seen as a provocative kind of 'commentary' or gloss on the motif of the 'woman in the window'.[161] Here the artist's curious assembly of found objects including a wax head, a photograph, a plastic toy, printed ephemera and a religious token are all framed by an actual repurposed window, illuminated from behind the glass. All the figurative images included are of girls and range from a toy ballerina to an image of the young Queen Elizabeth, all set within a 'domestic' interior as suggested by the addition of curtains, textured wallpaper and a picture rail. The relatively small scale of the objects and the way they are gathered in this vitrine encourage the viewer to approach and peer in, and yet there is something slightly sinister and almost surreal in this assortment of readymade objects. Blake's long and sustained interest in and treatment of windows is evident from his early paintings on the subject from about 1959 onwards. Marrying his interest in windows and vitrines with his love of collecting and of humble found objects and printed ephemera, Blake began creating assemblages such as *Girl in a Window* in the 1960s. In these works, the artist found a successful means of suggesting the sensation of viewing or being viewed through a window in a way that referred to museum methods of enshrining and categorising objects in display cases. *Girl in a Window* seems to encourage the beholder to consider the relationship between viewer and subject as suggested by the way the highly naturalistic wax head seems to reciprocate the gaze in a disconcerting way. The fact that only female figures are shown within the display-case-like window frame brings the issue of gender to the fore. This suggestive arrangement seems to underscore notions of female presentation and performance (the Queen, the mannequin, the ballet dancer) for the viewer and encourages us to think about how we label, categorise and enshrine certain female figures, particularly those in popular culture, as if in a museum or gallery context. In this way, Blake's assemblage blurs the lines between what has traditionally been called 'fine art' and 'popular art' and draws on the long tradition of artists playing on the notion of the window itself as a frame for display.

David Hockney studied alongside Blake at the Royal College of Art in London and both featured in the *Young Contemporaries* exhibition that announced the arrival of British pop art in 1960. Hockney, who works across media including painting, photocollage and, more recently, iPad applications, began experimenting with printmaking in the 1950s and 1960s producing several series of prints he described as 'graphic tales', including

cat. 37
Peter Blake, *Girl in a Window*, 1962, mixed media, 112.4 x 124 x 34 cm
Leeds Museums and Galleries. Purchased with the aid of a grant from the V&A Purchase Grant Fund, 1978

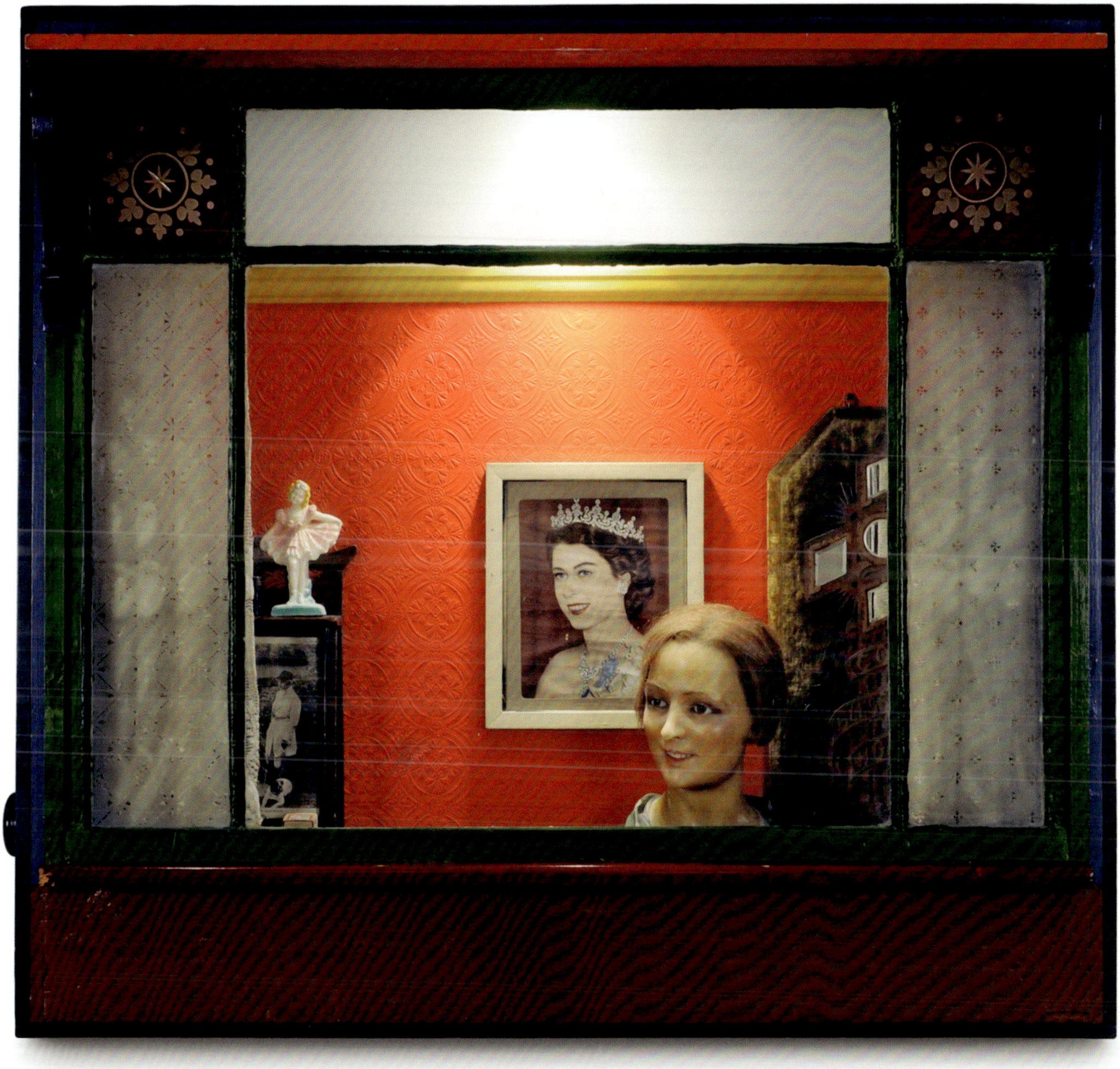

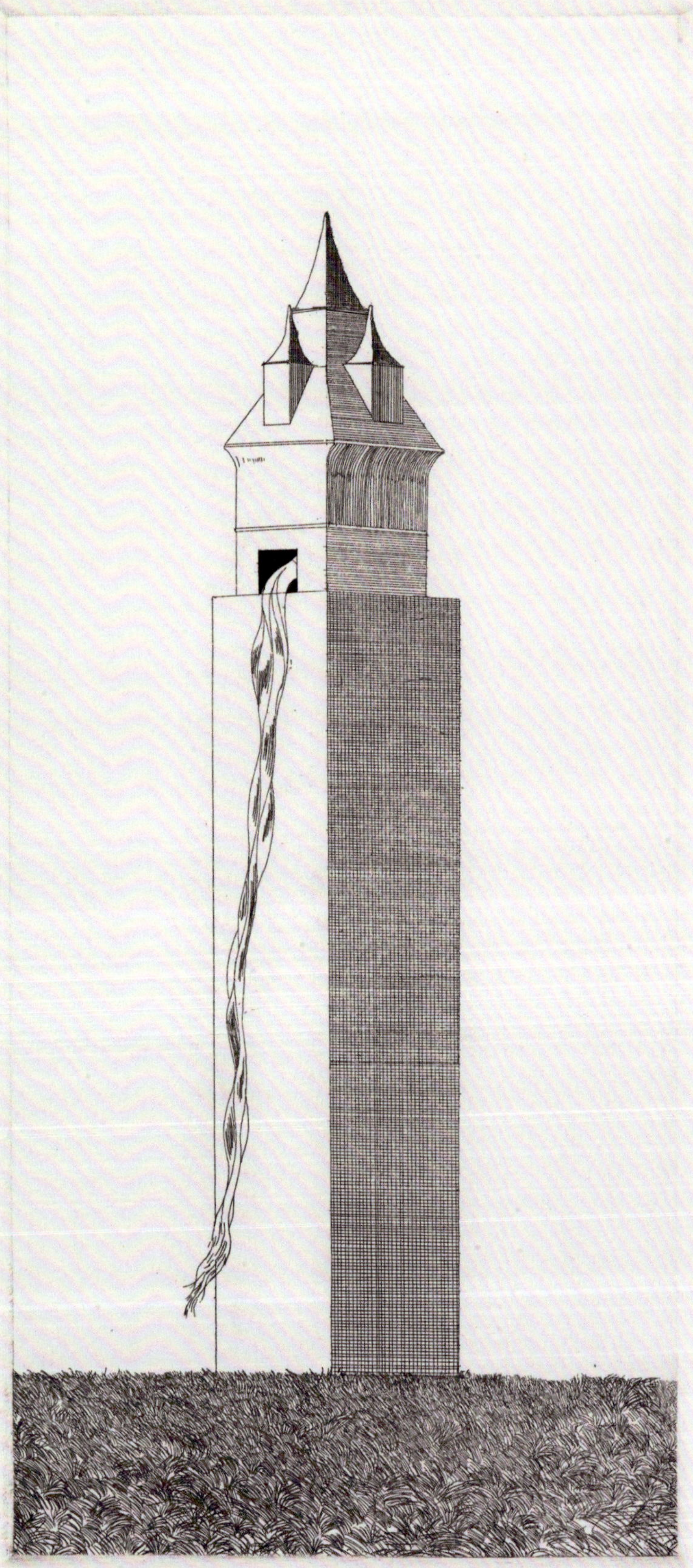

Final State — *David Hockney 1969*

Illustrations for Six Fairy Tales from the Brothers Grimm (1969).[162] In the process of selecting which stories to illustrate, Hockney read over 200 fairy tales compiled by Jacob and Wilhelm Grimm, the nineteenth-century German academics, philologists, cultural researchers and folklorists better known as the Brothers Grimm. Often interpreted as a means of addressing psychological conflicts, these tales were probably intended for the moral edification of both children and adults and seem to reflect the particular social and cultural values of the age.[163] Of these, Hockney was particularly taken with the story of Rapunzel, producing several prints on this theme. According to the Brothers Grimm, when Rapunzel's mother was pregnant, she experienced extreme cravings for the rapunzel (a type of salad leaf also known as rampion) growing in the walled garden belonging to a sorceress who lived next door. Desperate to soothe his wife, Rapunzel's father broke in and stole the rampion only to be caught by the sorceress who requested the baby in exchange.[164] The sorceress took the child, named her after the plant, and eventually locked her in a tower in which the only means of access was through the high window, which could only be reached by climbing up the walls of the tower with the aid of the girl's long hair serving as a rope. When a prince, who happened to be passing by, heard Rapunzel singing and witnessed the way the enchantress gained access to her by climbing up her lowered hair, he too began visiting the young girl and they fell in love. They plotted to escape but were foiled by the enchantress, the prince being thrown from the window and blinded. Scholars have interpreted the tale as a warning about 'precocious sexuality' and that the tower represents a response to 'the threat of female sexuality', the purpose of which was to protect Rapunzel's virginity.[165] The prince's act of entering the tower through Rapunzel's window may also be interpreted as having sexual connotations.[166]

In Hockney's print *The Tower Had One Window* (1969) [cat. 38] Rapunzel is represented only by the locks of her extremely long hair which she lowered, according to the tale, when either the sorceress or the prince called out 'Rapunzel, Rapunzel, lower your hair!' Here, however, neither protagonist is visible, suggesting that perhaps it is the viewer who has summoned her to the window. With only a few economical but well-chosen lines, Hockney evokes the entire story and alludes to the layers of complexity that belie the fairy tale's simple prose.

Between figurativism and abstraction

Another British artist whose oeuvre is marked by its reference to windows – and who would become known for his particular treatment of the picture frame – is Howard Hodgkin. His *Girl by a Window* (1964) [cat. 39] is an early work that straddles the genres of figurativism and abstraction.[167] Although the girl referred to in the title has not been identified, the work may be considered as part of a series of early paintings that refer to Hodgkin's personal experience of London's vibrant 1960s scene through representations of his artist and collector friends such as Robyn Denny, Joe Tilson and his wife, and R.B. Kitaj, among others.[168] All of these 'portraits' however combine recognisable figurative passages with forms and colours that appear entirely abstract and are suggestive while remaining somewhat elusive or 'unresolvable'. Here, with a great economy of line, Hodgkin suggests the form of a reclining woman, perhaps also a member of his artistic circle, before a window. She forms a neat triangle in her reclining pose, with one leg bent and the other extended, propping herself up on one straightened arm. This relaxed posture suggests she has been sitting for an extended time at the window which is painted in the same colourful palette and technique as the figure. Her pose calls to mind that of a reclining Venus or nude female figure as painted by artists ranging from Giorgione in

cat. 38
David Hockney, *The Tower Had One Window*, 1969, etching and aquatint, 45.5 x 31 cm
Mr & Mrs William Iselin

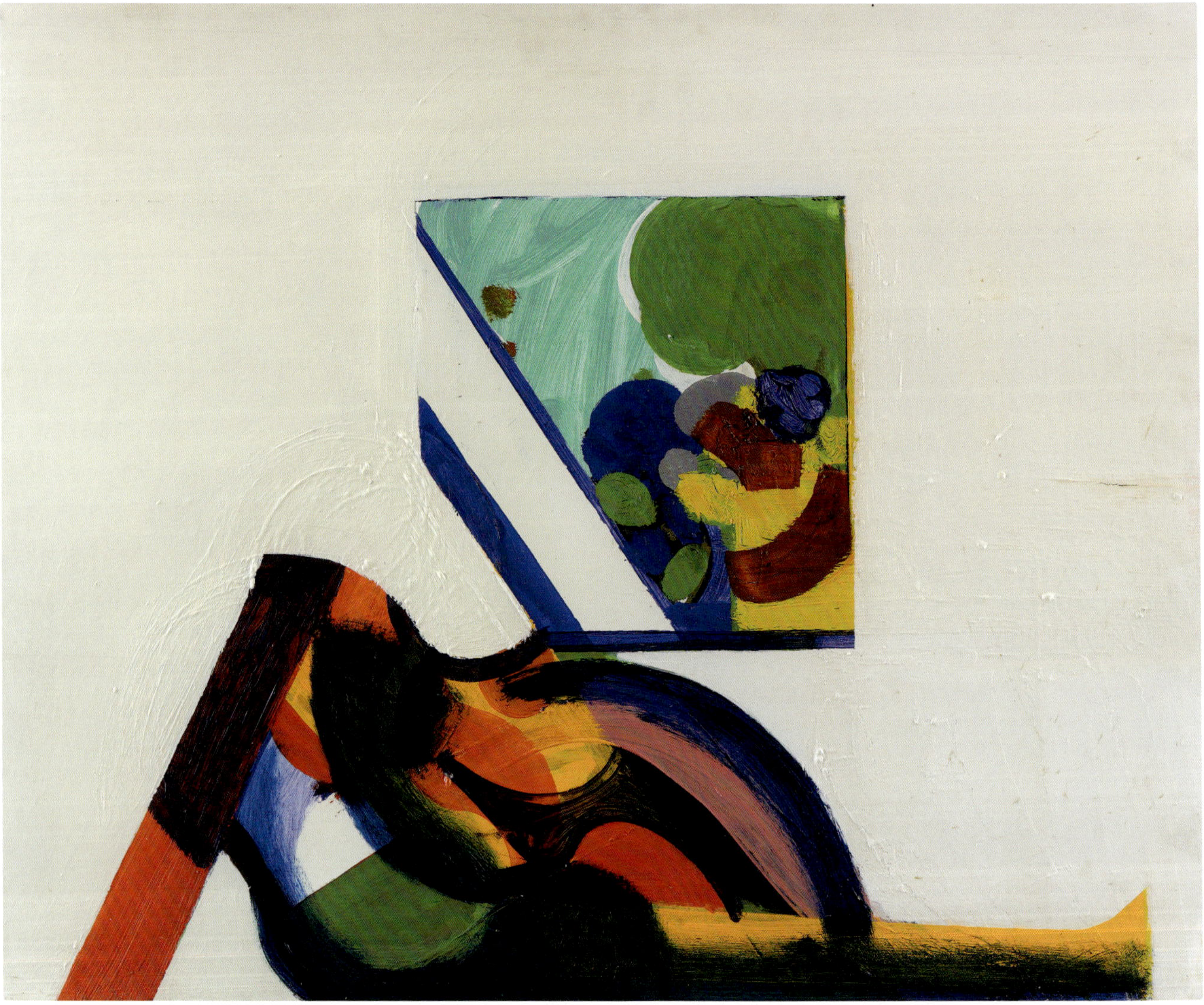

cat. 39
Howard Hodgkin, *Girl by a Window*, 1964, oil on board, 52 x 65 cm
Private Collection, London

the Renaissance to Jean-Auguste-Dominique Ingres, Édouard Manet, Pablo Picasso and Henri Matisse in the nineteenth and twentieth centuries, suggesting that Hodgkin's figure may have more seductive associations.[169] The rectangular form of the painted window echoes that of the canvas, giving the beholder the sense that, in viewing this work, they too are present at a kind of window looking onto the girl and her world. Further, Hodgkin represents his window as if piercing through a white wall in a way that also suggests a coloured painting framed with a white border. This visual effect seems to anticipate Hodgkin's later works which incorporate painted frames as part of the image proper. Indeed, the slippage between notions of framing and of the window recur throughout his oeuvre and would become a distinctive characteristic of his later works.

Euan Uglow, a contemporary of Hodgkin's in London, is known for painting geometric figures based on life drawings and set in interiors, and for his bold use of colour. His *Night Scene* (1995–97) [cat. 40], however, is painted not from life but from memory.[170] Here the artist represents a naked woman at a window whose motions he had clearly witnessed and perhaps half-remembered, as suggested by the slight ambiguity in the woman's gesture which is not immediately identifiable. She is in the process of unhooking her bra, the fiddly nature of which is indicated by the way her hands are repainted several times in slightly different positions, appearing like *pentimenti*, the visible traces of earlier painting beneath layers of paint, that are sometimes visible in historic paintings. The composition is amusing for the way it captures the awkwardness of the gesture and the way a man might watch a woman perform such a familiar yet unfamiliar act. The composition is blocked out in panels of colour in blue, yellow and grey and almost geometrically arranged with the artist's signature measuring marks deliberately left visible. The semi-lowered yellow shade meets the blue of the night sky visible through the window while the grey strip at the right marks the depth of the window frame. In this carefully considered composition, the horizontals converge with the figure at key points so that anyone passing by this window and looking into the lit interior would be obscured from the woman's view by the blind which falls exactly at her eye level, while her modesty is preserved below the waist by the window ledge. The artist locates the viewer inside the room, providing us with a privileged view into the woman's bedroom and the simultaneously intimate and mundane parts of her nightly ritual.

Fragmented and partially concealed bodies

As we have seen, artworks that take up the 'woman looking out of a window' composition often reduce the female figure to a head or a torso by default. In many cases we are given little information about the rest of her body, the space she occupies or any other defining physical or intellectual characteristics. This section, however, explores another category of artworks in this vein – those in which the woman at the window is partially obscured [cats. 28, 42] or reduced to a mere body part, such as a head [cat. 36], a knee [cat. 41], or hair [cat. 38]. Such representations might be deliberately unsettling or intended to protect the identity of the woman portrayed. In many cases, however, these works suggest that the rest of the female figure is irrelevant or even that her (often sexualized) body and body parts are interchangeable with those of another. This type of representation in the history of art has been understood and adopted by the advertising world, where images of 'headless' models are often used to advertise everything from clothes to films and other consumer products.[171] Indeed, by 'decapitating' the woman or fragmenting her body into decontextualized parts, she becomes a passive object

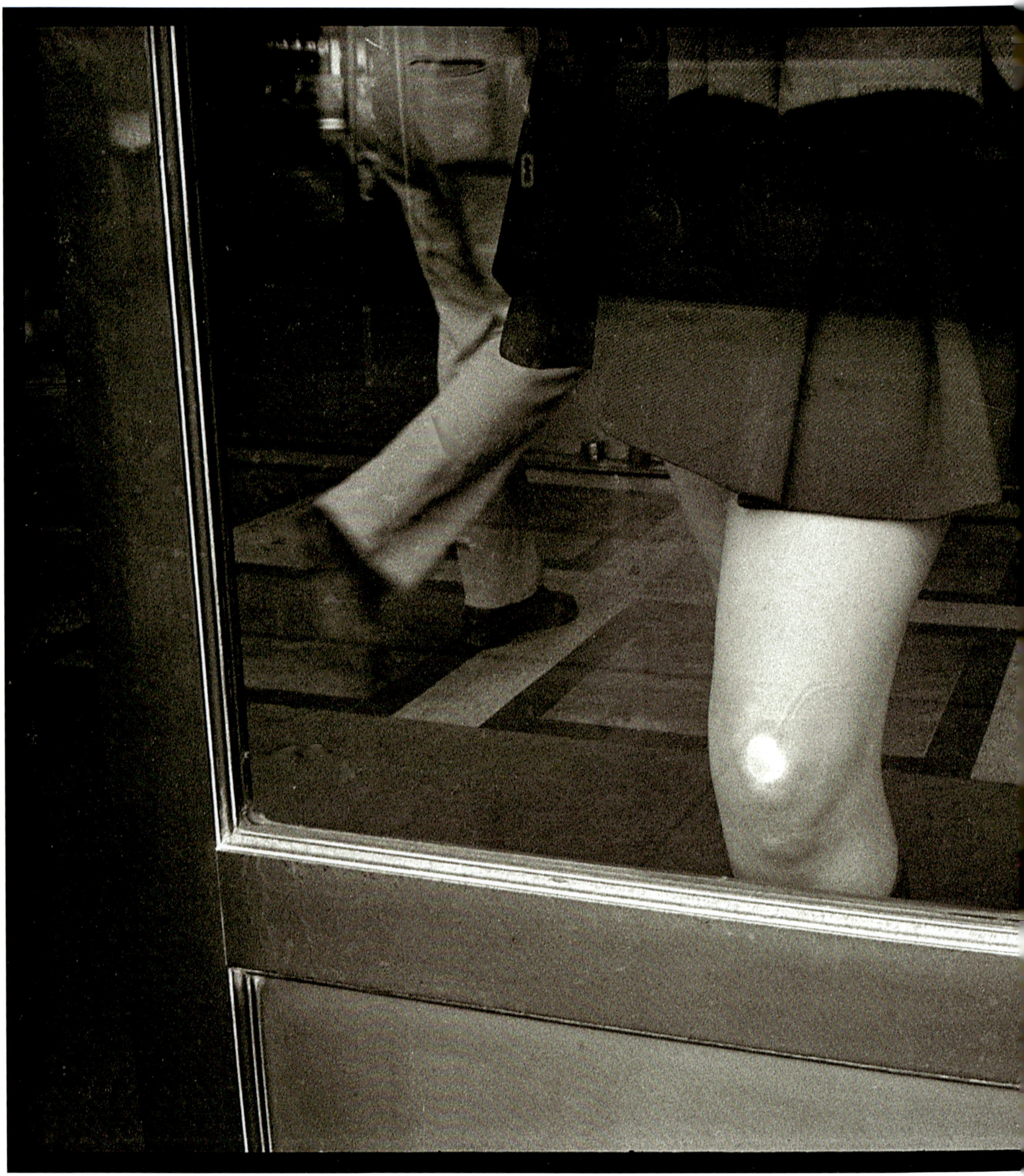

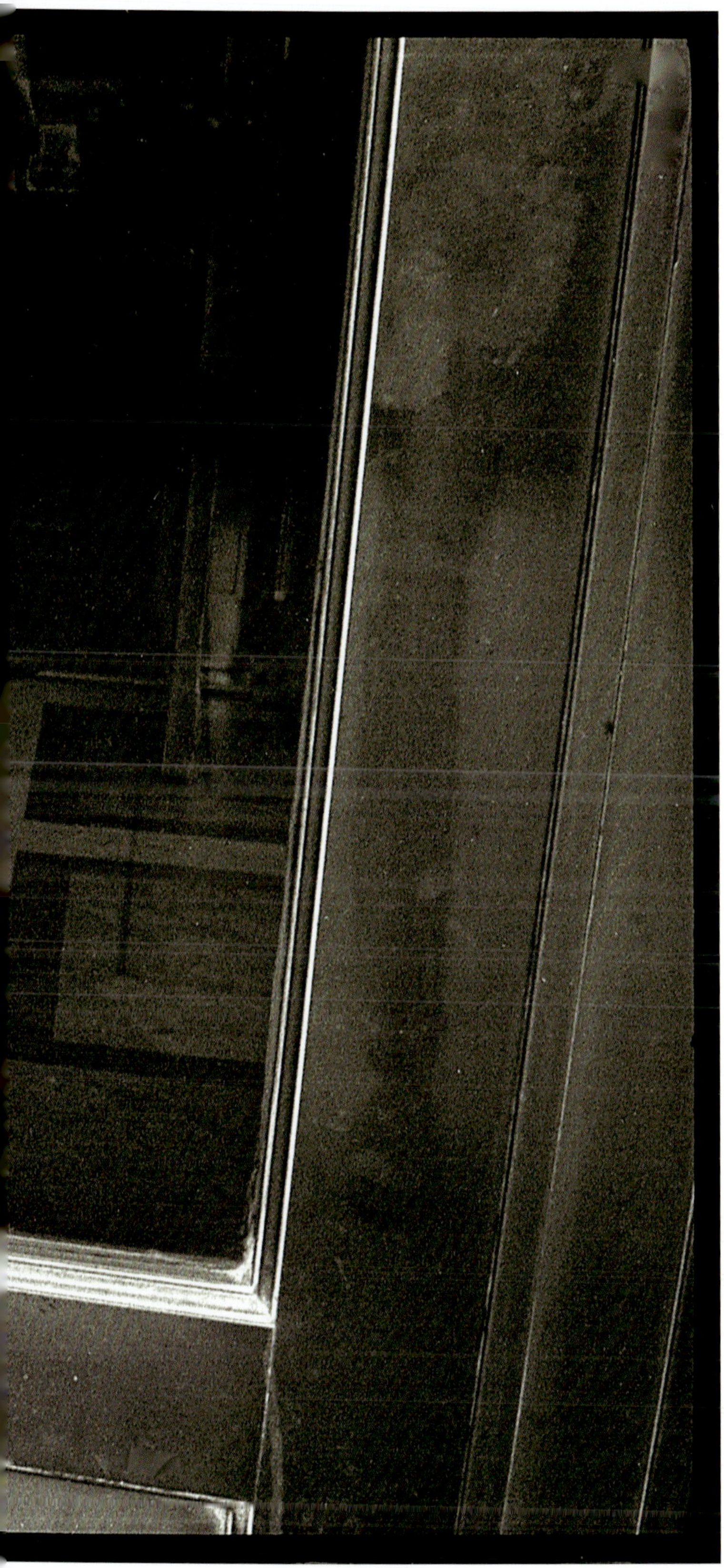

cat. 41
Mark Cohen, *Knee Against Glass*, 1976, printed 2015, gelatin silver print, 30 x 44.8 cm
Victoria and Albert Museum. Purchase funded by the Photographs Acquisition Group

upon which any number of fantasies might be projected. This kind of 'headless' presentation both encourages objectification of the body and, in a technique that might be described as 'aspirational', encourages the viewer to imagine their own face on the body presented. In these kinds of adverts, the issue is not only the potential objectification of the body, and of women in particular, but also implicit racism, as most of these 'headless' female bodies are White, implying their desirability over others. It is not difficult to see how the psychology used by advertisers in fragmenting or partially concealing their models' bodies also applies to images of the 'woman in the window' that do the same.

The American street photographer Mark Cohen creates an unexpected and somewhat fragmented vision of a 'woman at a window' in his *Knee Against Glass* (1976) [cat. 41]. Shot in his native town of Wilkes-Barre, Pennsylvania using a wide-angle lens and a low viewpoint, the photograph showcases both Cohen's 'shoot from the hip' technique and his surrealist sensibility in treating this subject. The woman portrayed is effectively disembodied, represented only by a knee, revealed below a short skirt, pressed against the glass. The framing of the knee and its contact against the glass suggest both containment and pressure against the picture surface, as if it is about to push out into the viewer's space. The severe cropping of the image invites the beholder to imagine the rest of the figure and perhaps even fantasise about her appearance and location. Indeed, by deliberately withholding information, this work draws the viewer in, inviting curiosity about the woman's identity. The composition is simultaneously unsettling, humorous and absurd as it captures and frames a knee as if it was a kind of portrait while the spontaneity of the shot and implied movement of the figure evokes photojournalism or documentary photography. As Cohen shoots from hip height, without looking through the viewfinder, he is often within very close range of his subjects without their knowledge, an aspect that further underscores the voyeurism in this composition.

More recently, British photographer Andrew Jackson has taken up the 'woman in the window' motif to explore issues of gender, race, identity and migration. In *Hand #1, Kingston, Jamaica* (2017) [cat. 42] the woman is seen through, and framed by, a car window. This photograph effectively places the beholder in the place of the driver, here reduced to a blurred male silhouette and extended, beckoning right arm. In this way, Jackson cleverly implicates the viewer within an ambiguous yet clearly uncomfortable narrative. Not only is the driver's face unintelligible but the woman's face is also concealed by her dramatic gesture as she extends her arm with the palm out in a gesture that appears intended to stop his entreaty but which simultaneously obscures her face. The woman's strong 'blocking' move is echoed in the grille, boarded-up window and locked door all visible behind her. Her emphatic rejection of the man's appeal suggests he has made an inappropriate or highly unwelcome proposition. Recent correspondence with the photographer reveals however a more specific, and equally unsettling, reason for the woman's gesture and the concealment of her identity. Jackson indicates that while travelling in Jamaica he asked to take this woman's photograph, to which she agreed but only on the proviso that her face was not revealed. She explained that she was concerned about the work appearing online because Jamaica's recent first female Prime Minister had been embroiled in a national scandal when her face had been Photoshopped onto the naked body of a sex worker and splashed across social media and newspapers. The woman in Jackson's photograph was worried that this could happen to her and that her social standing in her community would be threatened. Accordingly, while this image depicts the

cat. 42
Andrew Jackson, *Hand #1, Kingston, Jamaica*, 2017, photograph, digital C-print, 64.5 x 79.8 cm
Government Art Collection

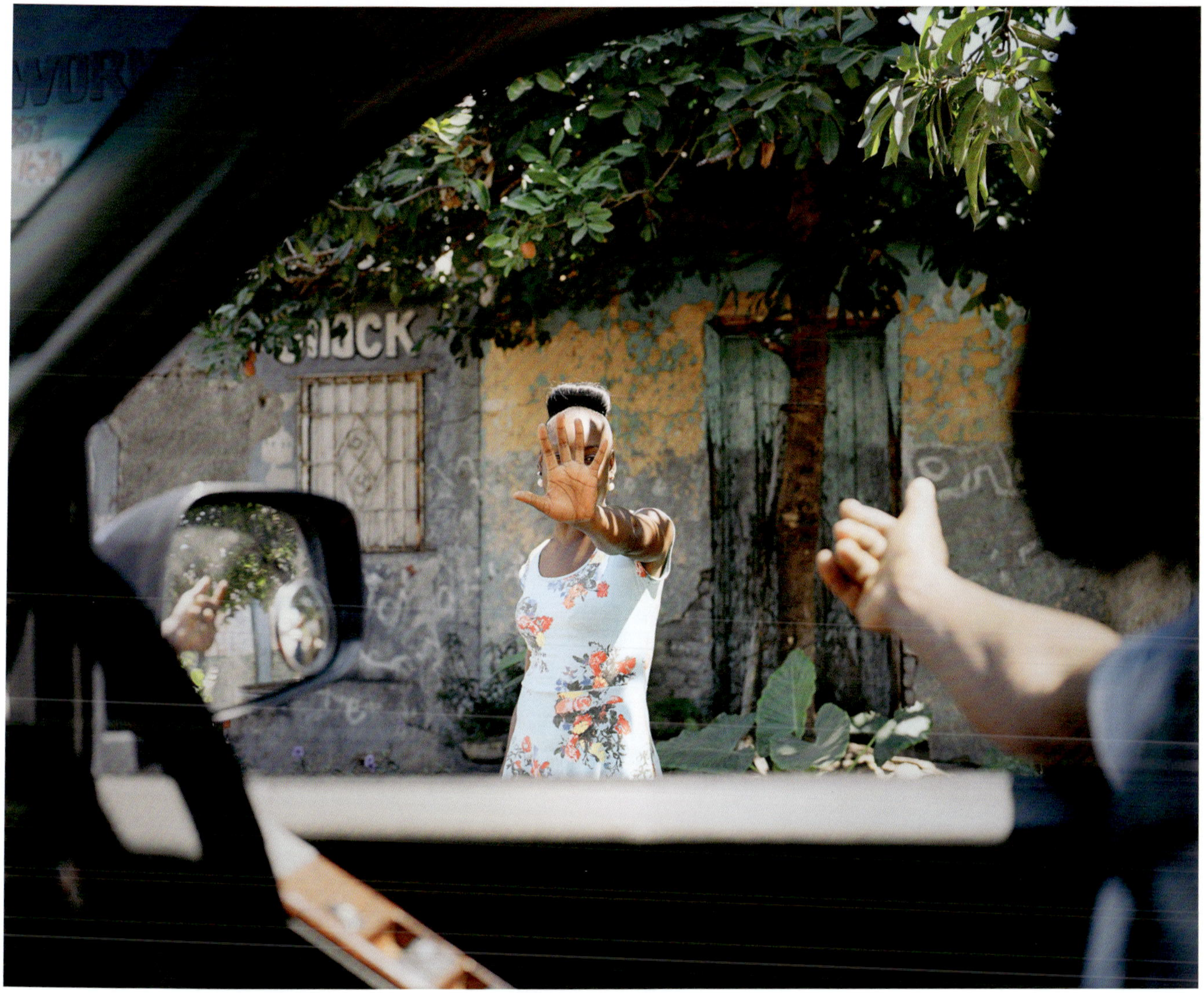

prevention of a portrait being made, as Jackson points out, it actually represents the woman's choice in how she wanted to be represented. Jackson adds that 'in this light, this work explores the issue of consent but also the interchange which occurs within the making of portraits – that interchange between what is revealed by the photographer and what remains hidden of the sitter in the frame.'[172]

The electronic screen as window

Sociological surveys indicate that the popularity of window gazing declined from the 1960s onward, a shift largely attributed to the rise and accessibility of new technologies such as television, which gradually superseded all previous favourite leisure activities.[173] With the invention of the computer, the internet and social media, people – Europeans and North Americans in particular – spend less time looking out of their actual windows and more at the small windows of their computer screens and smartphones.[174] Indeed while screens may be likened to windows for the way they offer the beholder a 'view', it is worth noting how the term 'window', when applied to computer software, refers not to the full expanse of a computer screen but an inset or nested screen within the screen.[175] It was the potential of running multiple programs or displaying different data on different 'windows' on a single screen at the same time that led Microsoft to name their graphical computing product 'Windows' in 1985.[176] The impact of this shift in the way virtual or metaphorical windows were conceived, discussed and used should not be underestimated. It is worth considering therefore how works engaging with the theme of the 'woman in the window' changed after 1960 and after 1985 as the earlier aesthetic and social functions of the window were diminished. Indeed, artists taking up the motif of the woman in the window after these dates do so on

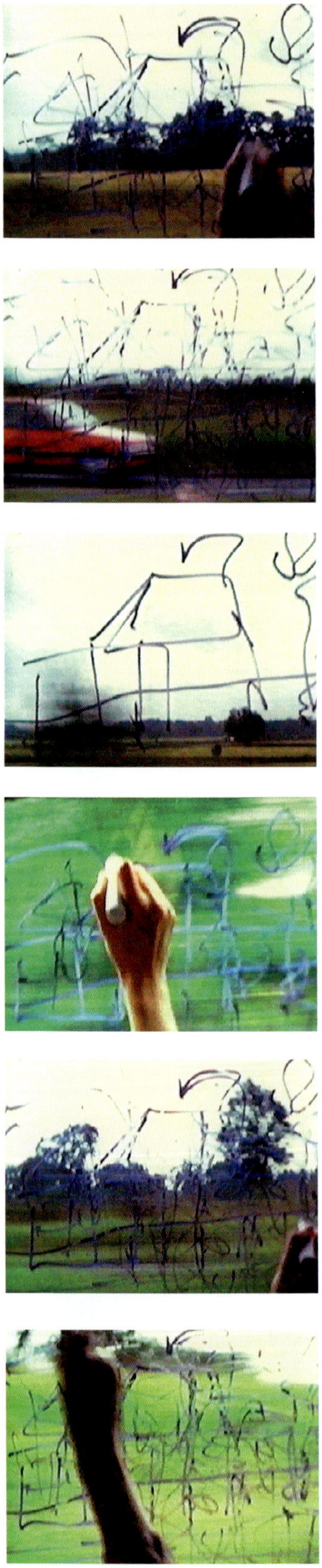

cat. 43
Rachel Lowe, *A Letter to an Unknown Person No.3*, 1998, Betacam SP videotape
Government Art Collection

increasingly symbolic, metaphorical and even abstract terms. In many of these works, the presence of the woman at the window takes on a greater psychological or personal interpretation on the one hand or a broad societal implication on the other.

One artist who plays on the notion of the video screen as window, and combines this with a representation of an actual window, is British artist Rachel Lowe whose work engages with ideas of viewership, space, images and time.[177] Created in 1998, Lowe's *A Letter to an Unknown Person No.3* [cat. 43] offers an unexpected and poignant interpretation of 'the woman in the window' theme. Her short film, recorded in a single take through the window of a car travelling through English landscapes, may be seen as a meditation on the human and ultimately futile desire to capture and hold on to the present. In the film, we see only Lowe's hand, the car window and what she glimpses at speed through the window. The artist's swift, animated hand scribbles with a black marker pen onto the inside of the car window, attempting to record what she sees on the glass. Her lines are looping and enigmatic, like an indecipherable script, as she attempts to trace and capture the fleeting landscape before it disappears. The result is an extraordinary sequence of images in which the views become obscured as Lowe's drawings accrete and become illegible. Representing a kind of nostalgia for the 'now', Lowe's video was made in an era before the smartphone transformed our ability to film and record every moment of our lives. Indeed, in many ways the work dramatises what has become an even greater collective and constant desire to document, capture and relate our own experience as we live it. At the same time, Lowe's work underscores the gap between lived experience and representation. The film is of particular interest in this context as it developed out of Lowe's practice of sketching the view from her studio window on the window itself. This process was initially an attempt to replicate a view but ultimately became more interesting to the artist than the subject itself. In *A Letter to an Unknown Person*, the perspective offered to the viewer is that of the artist; in representing only her hand, the film effectively situates the beholder in her place. Unlike the many works depicting a woman in the window already discussed, this video focuses not on the image of the woman but on her view and her attempts to share her personal experience of it. In some ways, the work is about the inexorable passing of time, about a desire to hold on to experience and about the resultant sense of loss. However, as the title suggests, this experience or performance of looking out of the window and recording its views should be understood as a kind of 'letter'. Accordingly, the viewer of this film is invited to take up two positions: both that of the artist herself and that of the 'unknown person' to whom her missive is addressed.

Notes

161. Christoph Grunenberg, Laurance Sillars (eds.), *Peter Blake: A Retrospective* (London: Tate Publishing, 2007), pp. 58–59, 171.
162. David Hockney, *Six Fairy Tales from the Brothers Grimm: With Illustrations by David Hockney* (London: Royal Academy of Arts, 2018).
163. Scholars have demonstrated, for example, how the brothers added religious and spiritual motifs to these traditional tales and also edited them in light of unfavourable reviews. Their first account of Rapunzel in 1812, for example, describes a sexual relationship between the prince and the girl in the tower, an aspect that was edited out in subsequent editions. On the interpretation of fairy tales, see Bruno Bettelheim, *The Uses of Enchantment: The Meaning and Importance of Fairy Tales* (New York: Knopf, 1976); Sheldon Cashdan, *The Witch Must Die: How Fairy Tales Shape Our Lives* (New York: Basic, 1999); Maria Tatar, *The Annotated Brothers Grimm* (New York: W.W. Norton, 2004), pp. 6–13.
164. Jacob Grimm, Wilhelm Grimm, 'Rapunzel', in Maria Tatar (ed. and trans.), *The Grimm Reader: The Classic Tales of the Brothers Grimm* (New York: W.W. Norton, 2010), pp. 33–38.
165. Ibid, pp. 36–38.
166. Cashdan, p. 157; Kay Stone, 'Things Walt Disney Never Told Us', *The Journal of American Folklore*, vol. 88, no. 347: Women and Folklore (January/March 1975), pp. 46–47.
167. Marla Price, *Howard Hodgkin, The Complete Paintings: Catalogue Raisonné* (London: Thames and Hudson, 2006), cat. 50.
168. Paul Moorhouse, *Howard Hodgkin: Absent Friends*, exh. cat. (London: National Portrait Gallery, 2017).
169. A similar 'odalisque-type' figure appears in Hodgkin's *Mrs Acton in Delhi*, 1967–71. See Price, cat. 94.
170. Richard Kendall, Catherine Lampert (eds.), *Euan Uglow: The Complete Paintings* (New Haven: Yale University Press, 2007), cat. 382, p. 189.
171. Hanna Berg, 'Headless: The role of gender and self-referencing in consumer response to cropped pictures of decorative models', *Psychology & Marketing*, vol. 32, no. 10 (2015), pp. 1002–16.
172. I am grateful to Andrew Jackson for sharing this information and for allowing me to paraphrase and share our correspondence.
173. Jütte, p. 612.
174. The notion of the screens of movies, televisions, computers and handheld devices as 'windows' is discussed extensively by Friedberg.
175. Ibid., pp. 1–2.
176. On Microsoft Windows, see ibid., pp. 228–35.
177. Paul Tebbs, 'Giving and Withholding: The Projection Art of Rachel Lowe', *Afterimage*, vol. 29, no. 2 (September/October, 2001), pp. 5–7.

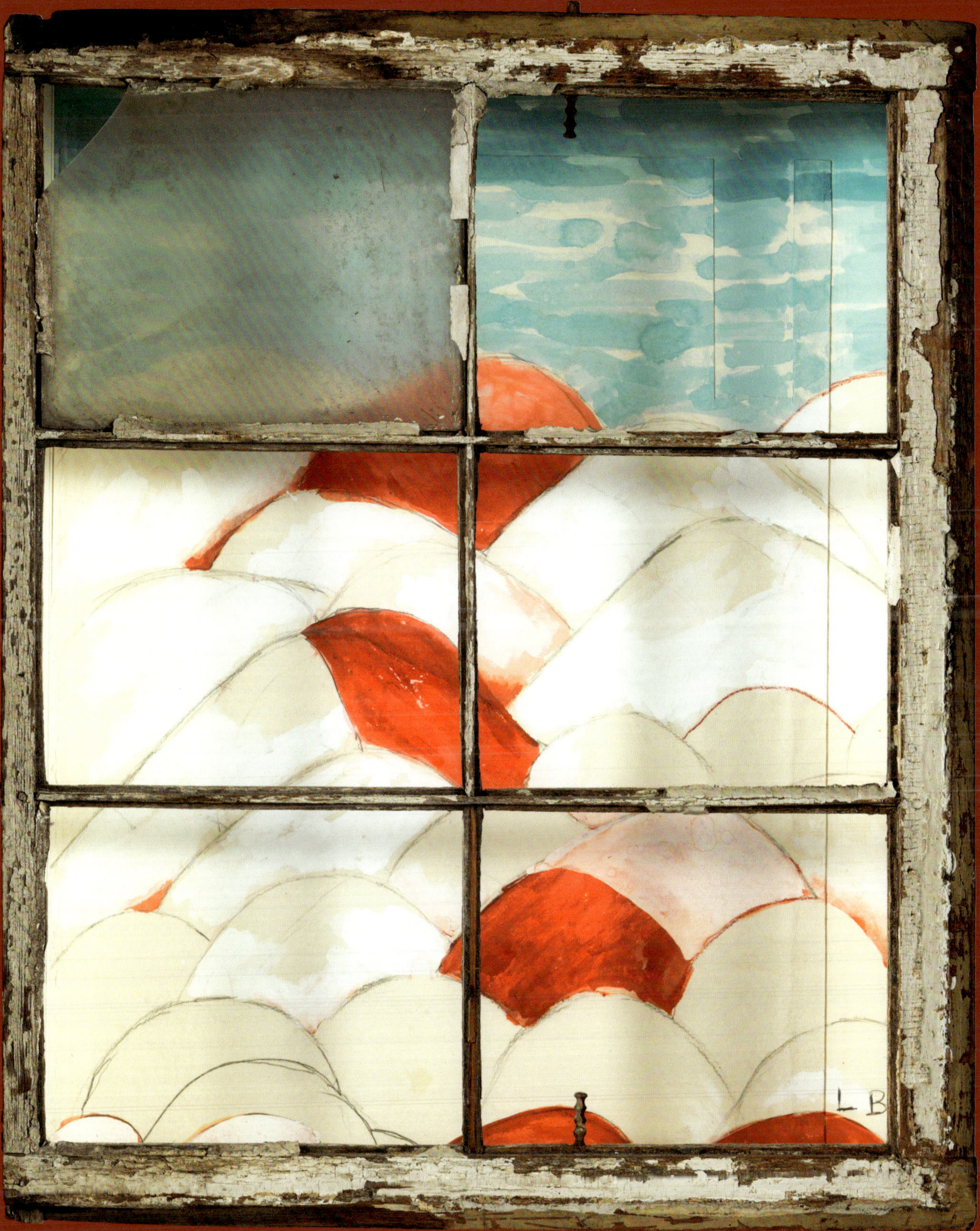
LB

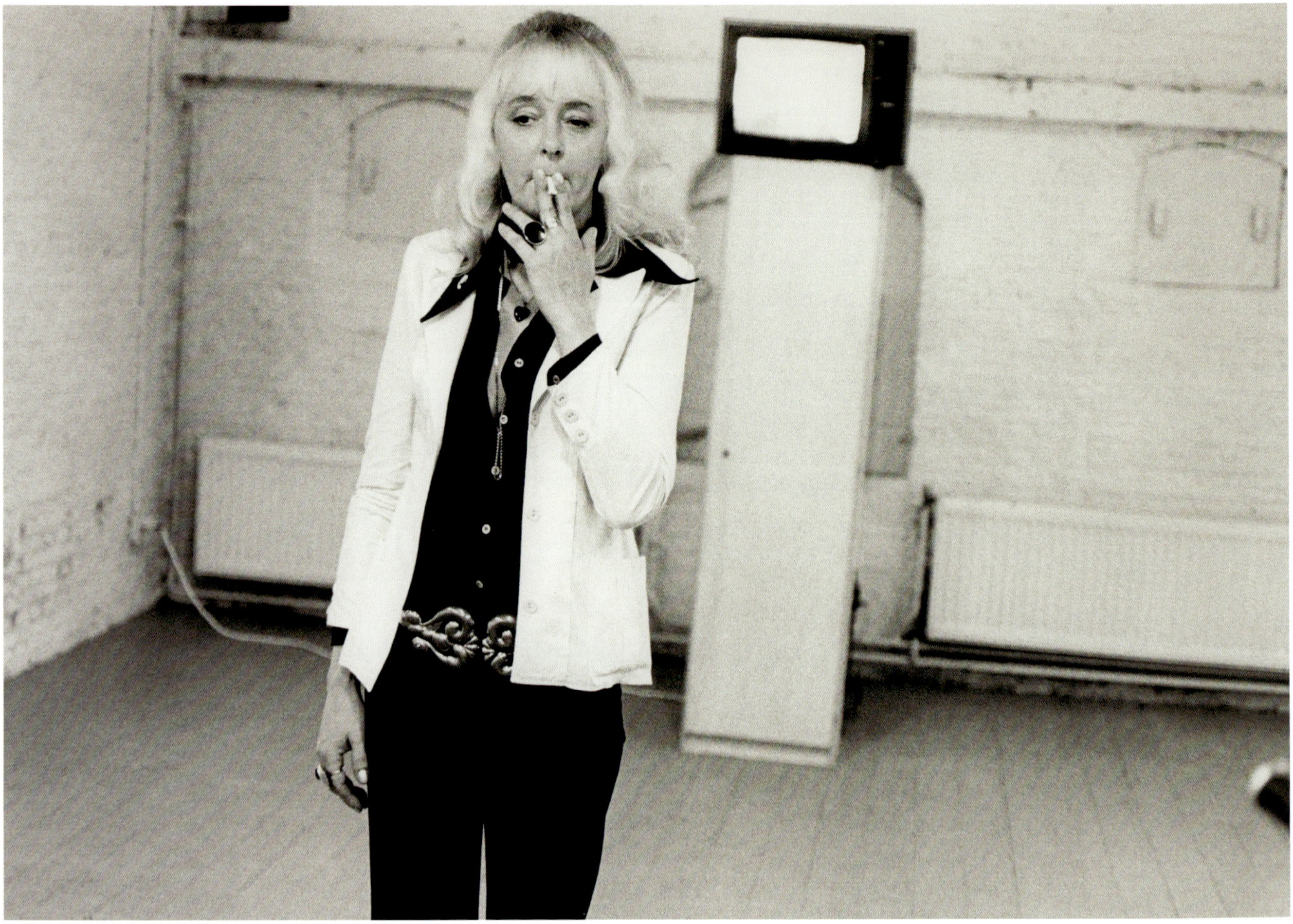

cat. 44
Marina Abramović, *Role Exchange*, 1975, framed black-and-white photographs (diptych), 56 x 80 cm (each)
Collection Irish Museum of Modern Art. Purchased 1995

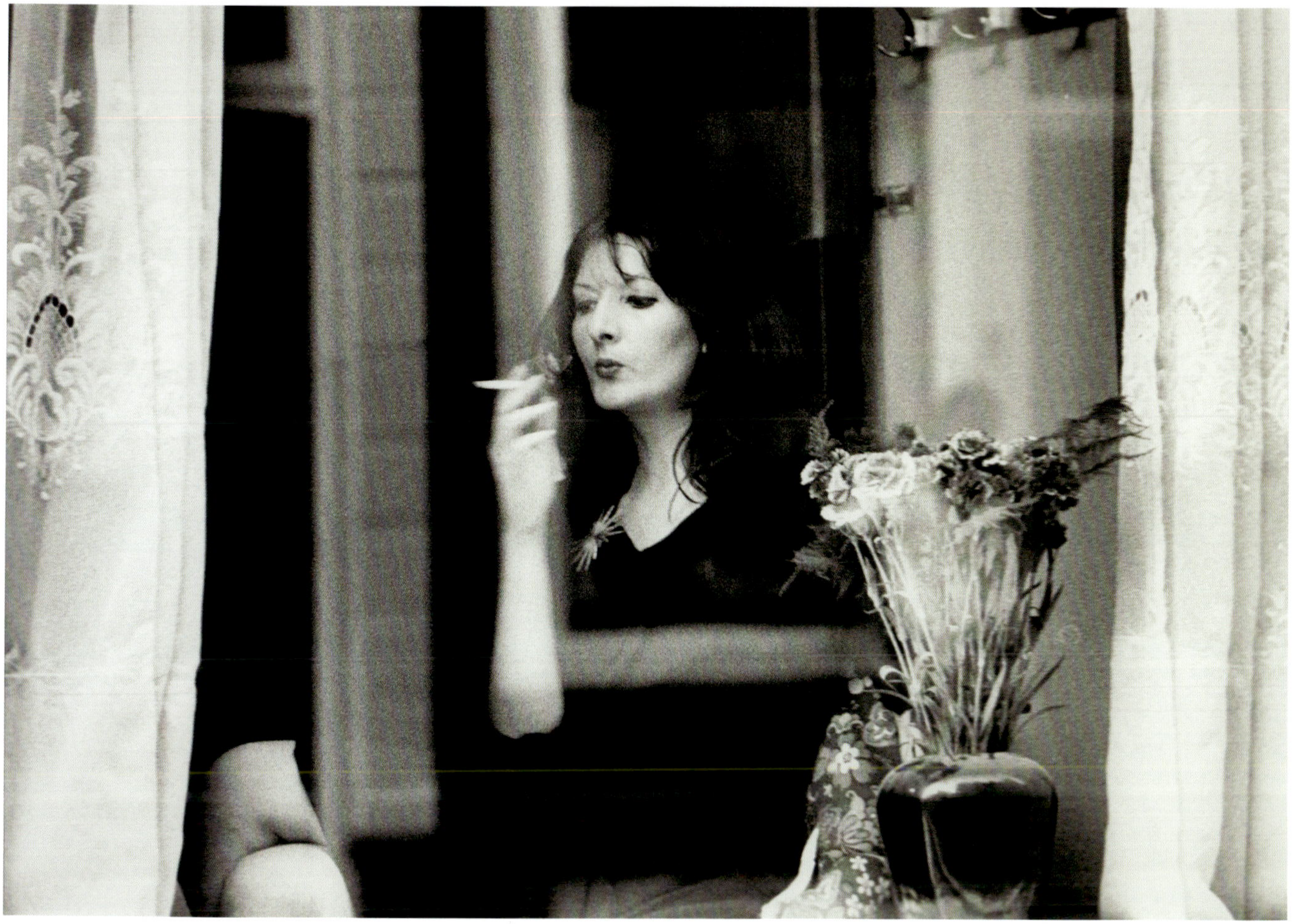

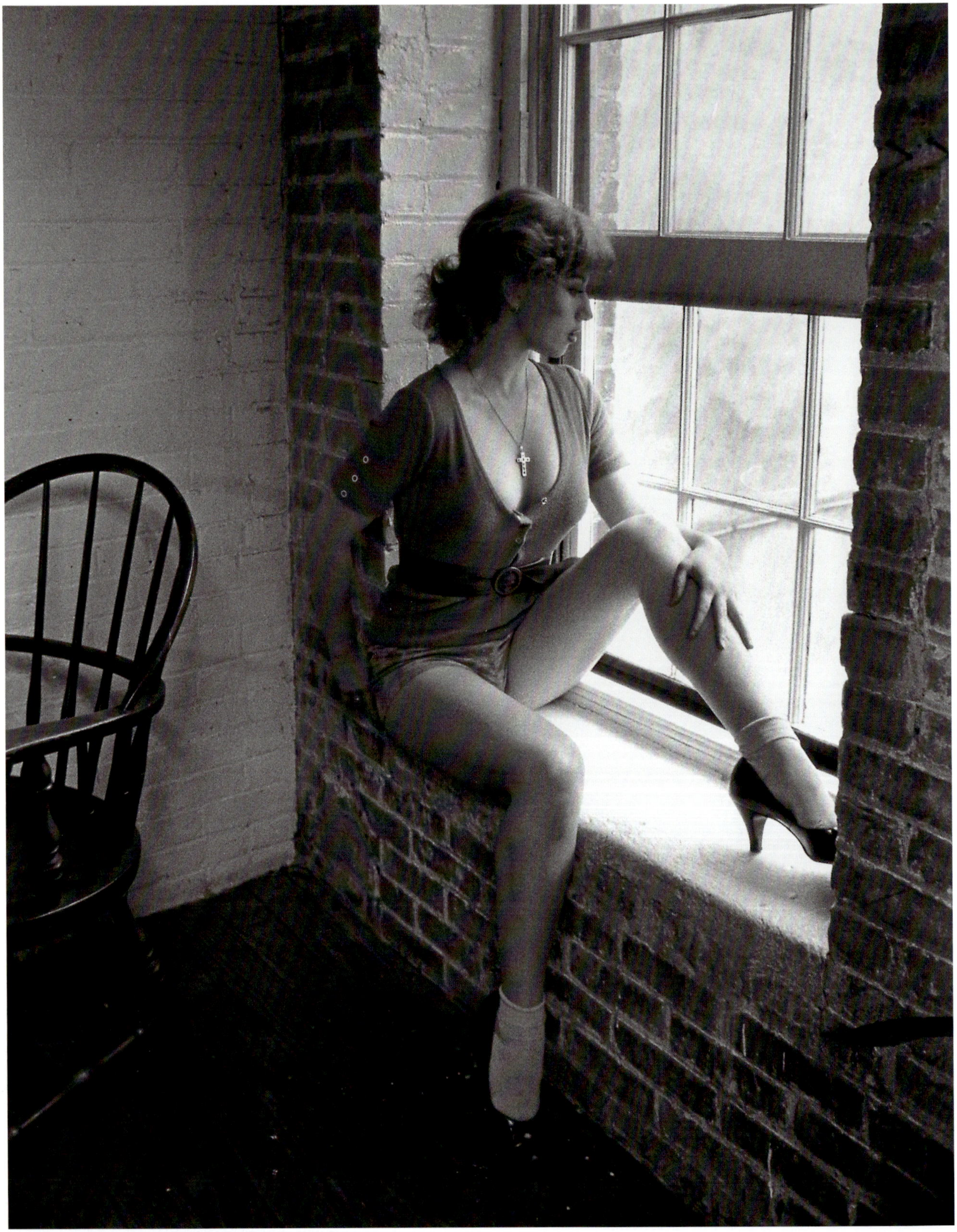

This section explores the work of five contemporary female artists working across different media: Marina Abramović, Cindy Sherman, Louise Bourgeois, Rachel Whiteread and Isa Genzken. The first two artists explore the construction of identity and the nature of representation by using their bodies as both the medium and subject of their work while the following three artists have created works in which the female figure is implied or evoked without being explicitly represented. In drawing attention to the ways in which female artists have adopted and adapted the theme of the 'woman in the window' here, the intention is to underscore how many of these compositions in the history of art were made by men for men and as such largely embody what has long been described by feminist theorists as the 'male gaze'.[178]

Identity and the body

During the late 1960s and early 1970s, feminist performance art grew in importance, particularly amid the civil rights movement and the so-called 'second wave' feminism-fuelled protests in the US. This type of artistic expression soon spread, first to Europe and then further still, with one of its most celebrated pioneers being the Serbian artist Marina Abramović. In 1975 Abramović travelled to Amsterdam for the performance of *Role Exchange* (1975) [cat. 44] which took up one of the most common art historical interpretations of a representation of a woman in a window – that of a sex worker.[179] Indeed, the subject of sexual commerce has preoccupied artists from antiquity onwards and was especially taken up by the male modernist painters focussed on creating images of sex workers, street walkers or '*les filles publiques*'. In the second half of the twentieth century, when female artists took up this theme, their works often challenged contemporary notions of spectatorship, desire and display. Abramović's *Role Exchange* is a prime example, particularly as she took up the role of the 'woman in the window' herself in a performance that deliberately blurred the boundaries between action and representation and between public and private spheres. The performance was documented both through film and photography and this photographic 'diptych' records how Abramović exchanged places with Suze, a female sex worker from the red-light district in Amsterdam.

The artist sat in the sex worker's window while Suze posed as the artist during the opening of an exhibition of Abramović's work at De Appel gallery. The performance was deliberately staged so that each woman was located in an enclosed space that was open and visible to the street through a large, framed picture window and each performed her assigned duties during these public spectacles, acting as each other's alter ego. Of particular interest here is the way that Abramović explored the use of the window as a metaphor for the permeable boundary between the public realm – that is the world of the street which she associates particularly with men – and the private – that is the brothel and the semiprivate world of women. Abramović's performance also drew attention to the window as a site of exchange between commerce and sexuality and between the voyeur and the spectacle. She has said of the performance: 'I was interested in the idea of the windows and the brothel spaces themselves as well as the moral aspects of the architectural space. I was sitting there with everyone looking at me, violently crushing my ego down to zero.'[180] Crucially, Abramović's performance as recorded in these photographs encourages the beholder to consider the power of the viewer over the subject of their gaze and, conversely, what it must be like to be on the receiving end of this scrutiny.

Like Abramović, the American photographer Cindy Sherman explores the construction of identity and the nature of representation by using her own body and transforms herself through a range of disguises to create

cat. 45
Cindy Sherman, *Untitled Film Still*, 1978, gelatin silver print, 25.4 x 20.3 cm

personae that are alternately amusing and disturbing, distasteful and affecting.[181] Her *Untitled Film Still* (1978) [cat. 45] is one in a series of photographs begun in 1977 in which she posed in various guises to evoke the stereotypical feminine characters presented in publicity stills for films from the 1940s and 1950s with a special nod to the work of the film director Alfred Hitchcock. In taking up the motif of the 'woman in the window' Sherman also casts herself as the chief protagonist. Seated at a windowsill wearing a sexually provocative outfit and a prominent cross around her neck, Sherman dangles one bare leg over the window ledge and bends the other as she turns to look down and out of the window in a composition that recalls Hitchcock's *Rear Window* (1954).[182] The woman's ambiguous pose suggests both brazenness and a kind of anxiousness in expression, as she seems to scan the street below. In exploring the stereotypes of femininity and female representation found in popular culture, Sherman draws attention to how they condition our perception and presumptions about the role of women more broadly. In deliberately rendering her photographs ambiguous, yet with the suggestion of narrative, the artist encourages the viewer to examine the work for details that might reveal more of the story. The pendant with a cross, the empty chair, the exposed brick wall and the gaze out of the window all seem to provide clues and suggest meaning yet simply point to the complex ways in which meaning can be visually constructed and manipulated.

Implied presence

Throughout her long career, the French-American artist Louise Bourgeois was deeply engaged with notions of sexuality, architecture, memory, and the body. Her wall sculpture *My Blue Sky* (1989–2003) encapsulates many of these themes in an especially personal and powerful way and demonstrates how personal and powerful the motif can become in the hands of a female artist [cat. 46].[183] Here the female form is echoed in the curves of a mountainous landscape, which seem to undulate, rising and descending like waves, breasts, or cumulus clouds below a loosely rendered blue sky. The white revealed beneath and in between the traces of blue suggests light and air, while the blue recalls Bourgeois's assertion that, for her, the colour represented peace, meditation and escape. The colour red, also evident, signified intense emotion. Such associations are particularly powerful when read against the enclosure of the window which here also serves as a kind of picture frame. The 'window' in this work is an actual window frame, one salvaged from the basement of Bourgeois's own New York home. *My Blue Sky* was created late in the artist's life, when Bourgeois rarely left her house. Accordingly, the wall sculpture has been described as her personal 'lifeline' to the outside world. Like many of Bourgeois's works, this sculpture defies any single interpretation. Rather than reading it as a strictly surrealist, feminist, abstract or highly autobiographical work, it should perhaps be acknowledged as offering all of these possibilities for the beholder.

British artist Rachel Whiteread's sensitivity to space and architecture, together with the sociological and anthropological aspects of her works, which have been described as repositories for memory and meaning, make her an ideal interpreter of the 'woman in the window' theme.[185] As an artist who works primarily in sculpture, typically making casts of everyday objects, furniture and architectural spaces such as chairs, staircases, doors and windows, Whiteread draws attention to the form and use of an object with reference to the texture of its surface, the void within it or space around it. Since the 1990s, Whiteread has made casts of windows in various materials ranging from a translucent resin, to concrete to papier-mâché. Installed at the height

cat. 47
Rachel Whiteread, *Untitled (For WHP)*, 2015, mixed media, two panels (resin and concrete compound), 98 x 49 x 8 cm
Courtesy Rachel Whiteread

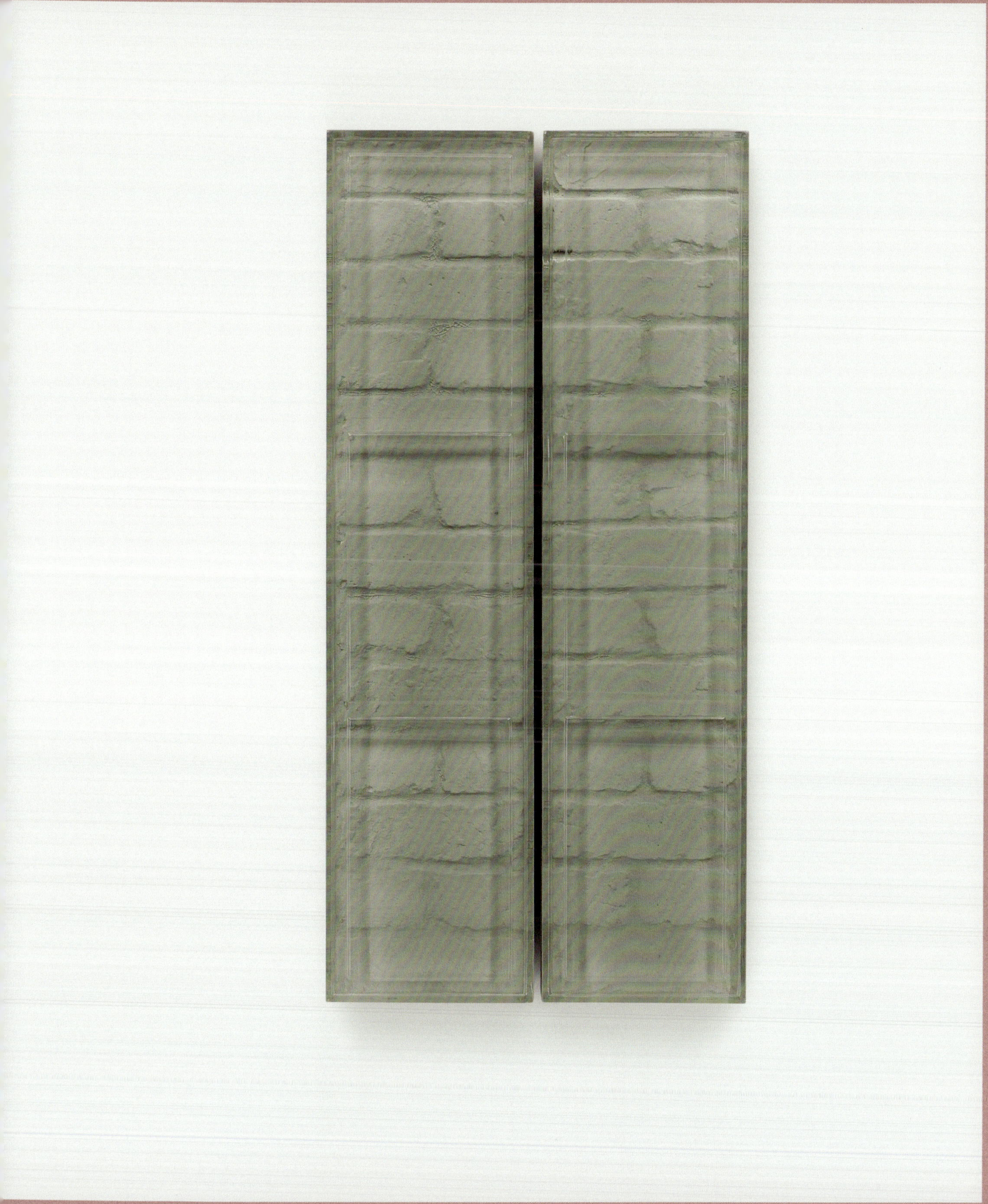

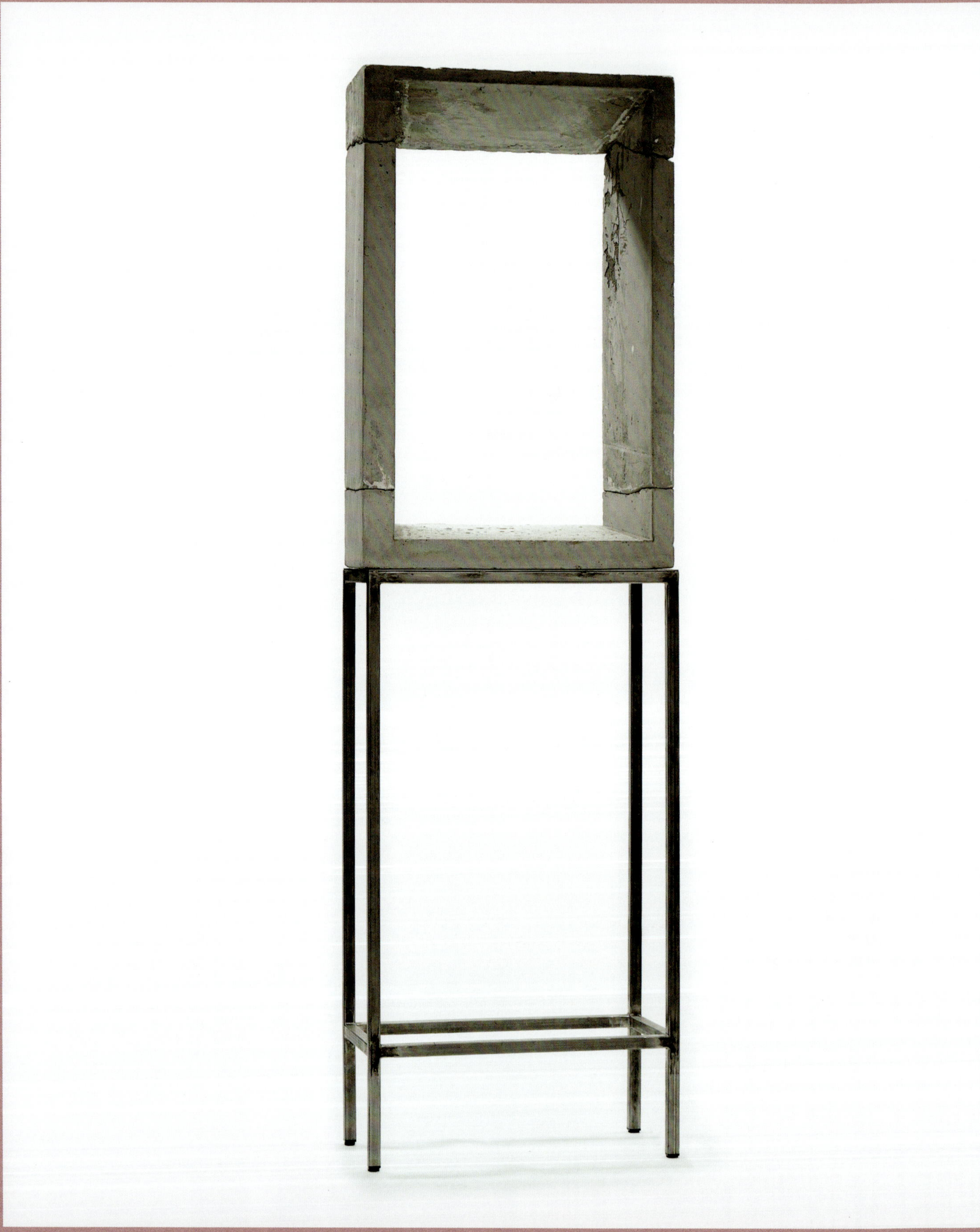

of a domestic window, these casts often initially confuse viewers who feel they are looking at an actual window rather than a negative impression of the original. As casts, these sculptures may be interpreted as a kind of 'ghost' or 'memory' of the absent window. In some ways, they may also be considered records not only of the surfaces of the architectural structures or objects cast but also palpable traces of the marks, the 'wear and tear' that humans leave on their surroundings. Of these window sculptures, *Untitled (for WHP)* (2015) [cat. 47] is perhaps the most personal, as the title refers to the London street where Whiteread lives, the window is modelled on one of her own and the work was intended to hang in her own house. Cast in a translucent grey-blue resin, the window suggests a pale London light pouring through a tall window. However, through this 'window' we see a cast of grey concrete bricks as if to suggest a view out to a neighbouring wall, an experience particularly familiar to those living in dense cities. *Untitled (for WHP)* offers a new interpretation of the 'woman in the window' motif, one in which the woman (the artist) makes the beholder conscious of the space and architecture around them and of the ways these can hinder, condition or facilitate social interaction or 'frame' a particular view onto the world.

Working across a variety of media including photography, film, video, painting and collage, the German artist Isa Genzken's primary focus is sculpture and installation. She uses a variety of materials, including concrete, plaster, wood and textile, and her diverse practice often engages with modernist architecture and the legacies of constructivism and minimalism. The window has been a key motif in Genzken's sculptural practice since the late 1980s when she and her then-husband, the artist Gerhard Richter, designed the König-Heinrich-Platz underground station in Duisburg, filling it with sculptures consisting of poured and stacked slabs of concrete featuring rough openings, windows and interiors. The importance of the motif for Genzken is reinforced by the title of her mid-career survey in 1992, *Everybody Needs At Least One Window*.[186] In the early 1990s, Genzken began a series of 'Fenster' (window) sculptures: raw concrete shapes mounted on delicate steel frames or plinths. *Fenster* (1990) [cat. 48] belongs to this series and is, in fact, a kind of hybrid object as it is at once a sculpture, a frame, a concrete cast of an abstract form and a functional window that is activated by the presence of a viewer looking through it.[187] The steel plinth supporting the 'window' seems to refer to the display of sculptures in museums, signalling their status as 'works of art', while at the same time forming an inextricable part of the sculpture itself. The combination of heavy, exposed concrete atop a delicate plinth feels precarious, and indeed part of the fascination of this object is how it negotiates the delicate balance between weight, structure and gravity. Placed in the centre of a room rather than on a wall, the 'Fenster' also subverts the notion of interior and exterior. Deliberately ambiguous, Genzken's 'Fensters' have been described as 'window-like objects', objects mounted to evoke 'windowness' or windows framing 'emptiness'. Considered in the context of this study, the artist herself may be understood as the implied 'woman in the window'. Alternatively, the three-dimensional nature of this work, which encourages viewers to move around or peer through it, invites visitors to experience what it feels like to be both the subject and object of a window gaze. Genzken's *Fenster* is at once abstract and real; an object that acquires meaning through context and the act of looking.

Conclusion

The action of looking out of windows was one of the favourite leisure pursuits of pre-modern Europeans but, as we have seen, it is also one that can be traced back to the female viewers of spectacles in ancient Minoan-

cat. 48
Isa Genzken, *Fenster*, 1990,
concrete, steel, 257.5 x 38 x 77 cm
Private Collection, London

Mycenaean civilisations. Although men and women have long participated in the pleasurable and social practice of window gazing, it was predominantly the presence of a woman at a window that was represented, debated, controlled and desired. Catholics, Protestants and Muslims seem to have diverged in their moral evaluations of this practice, and governments and legislation-making bodies were regularly enlisted to defend either one's right to see out or not to be seen depending on the particular culture, period and location of the debate. Indeed, this debate is ongoing as evidenced by the recent case of the inhabitants of a block of luxury flats with floor-to-ceiling windows who tried to sue Tate Modern in London when the gallery built a new viewing platform that effectively allows visitors to look into the windows of the adjacent building. Attempting to sue for their loss of privacy – and what the Romans would have termed 'good *prospectus*' – the homeowners lost the case but are currently appealing this decision. The London press however, has largely supported the initial ruling, stating, for example, that 'cities bring out the voyeur in us all'.[188] The case represents a reversal of sorts, one in which visitors left the carefully curated spaces and labelled artworks of the gallery and climbed to the top of the building to look outwards instead, onto the city and its inhabitants. In some ways, the gallery's new viewing platform may be seen to promote a return to window gazing. What the 'local inhabitants versus Tate' case also reminds us is that, throughout the history of the 'woman in the window' composition just examined, we find attempts to distinguish between legitimate and illegitimate gazes, between public and private and between female gazes and male ones. Indeed, in tracing the history of this motif and in identifying the key cultures and periods in which it became prevalent and why, this study offers a new perspective onto the social, cultural and gendered history of vision.

Notes

178. See note 7.
179. Anna Novakov (ed.), 'Role Exchange: Desire, Beauty and the Public', in *Veiled Histories: The Body, Place and Public Art* (New York: Critical Press, 1997); Anna Novakov, 'Point of Access: Marina Abramović's 1975 Performance Role Exchange', *Woman's Art Journal*, vol. 24, no. 2 (Autumn 2003–Winter 2004), pp. 31–35.
180. Quoted in Novakov, 'Role Exchange: Desire, Beauty and the Public', p. 27.
181. See Peter Galassi, *Cindy Sherman: The Complete Untitled Film Stills* (New York: Museum of Modern Art, 2003); Erika Balsom, 'In the Company of Images: Untitled Film Stills', in Paul Moorhouse (ed.), *Cindy Sherman* (London: National Portrait Gallery, 2019).
182. In the film, a photographer with a broken leg is confined to a wheelchair and spends his time watching his neighbours through the rear window of his Greenwich Village apartment, speculating on their behaviour and lives, becoming convinced that one of them has committed murder.
183. Frances Morris (ed.), *Louise Bourgeois* (London: Tate Publishing, 2007), p. 133.
184. Louise Bourgeois interview with Cecilia Bloomberg, 16 October 1998 in ibid., p. 83.
185. Ann Gallagher, Molly Donovan (eds.), *Rachel Whiteread* (London: Tate Publishing, 2017).
186. The exhibition was held at the Renaissance Society at the University of Chicago, 14 May –28 June 1992.
187. These sculptures were shown and discussed more recently in a monographic show at Whitechapel Gallery in 2009; see the accompanying catalogue by Iwona Blazwick, Yve-Alain Bois, Penelope Curtis, *Isa Genzken: Open Sesame!* (Cologne: Walther König Verlag, 2009).
188. Fiona Sturges, 'Tate Modern's Neighbours Missed the Point: Cities Make Voyeurs of Us All', *The Guardian* (16 February 2019).

EPILOGUE
THE PANDEMIC WINDOW

The first version of this exhibition and its associated catalogue were prepared for autumn 2020 but were postponed due to the global COVID-19 pandemic. During this period, the subject of the 'woman in the window' took on a new resonance and meaning as, around the world, everyone became familiar with lockdowns intended to limit the highly transmissible virus and the challenges associated with staying at home. For a lot of people, the role and importance of the window came to the fore in ways they had probably rarely, if ever, considered previously. Many of those lucky enough to have windows allowing access to light, air and an outside view, came to treasure them while those with limited access to windows felt particularly trapped and disconnected from the outside world.[189] In many respects, windows began to serve the roles they had performed centuries ago but which had become obsolete or unnecessary in contemporary society. Windows again became primary sites of communication where conversations were had, letters were passed, drawings and messages were posted, food and other key supplies were deposited, and gifts were offered. Windows at once provided visual access to and physical protection from the outside world. So, for example, we experienced first-hand or read stories about grandparents meeting their new grandchildren 'through the window' or neighbours entertaining each other by singing or playing music from their open windows.

While medical communities around the world played a critical role in researching the virus, treating patients and advocating for our physical wellbeing, cultural institutions sought to support mental, intellectual and creative wellbeing in other ways.[190] A particularly successful and moving community project spearheaded by the Duchess of Cambridge and the National Portrait Gallery was inaugurated in the early summer of 2020. Called 'Hold Still', the project sought to create a

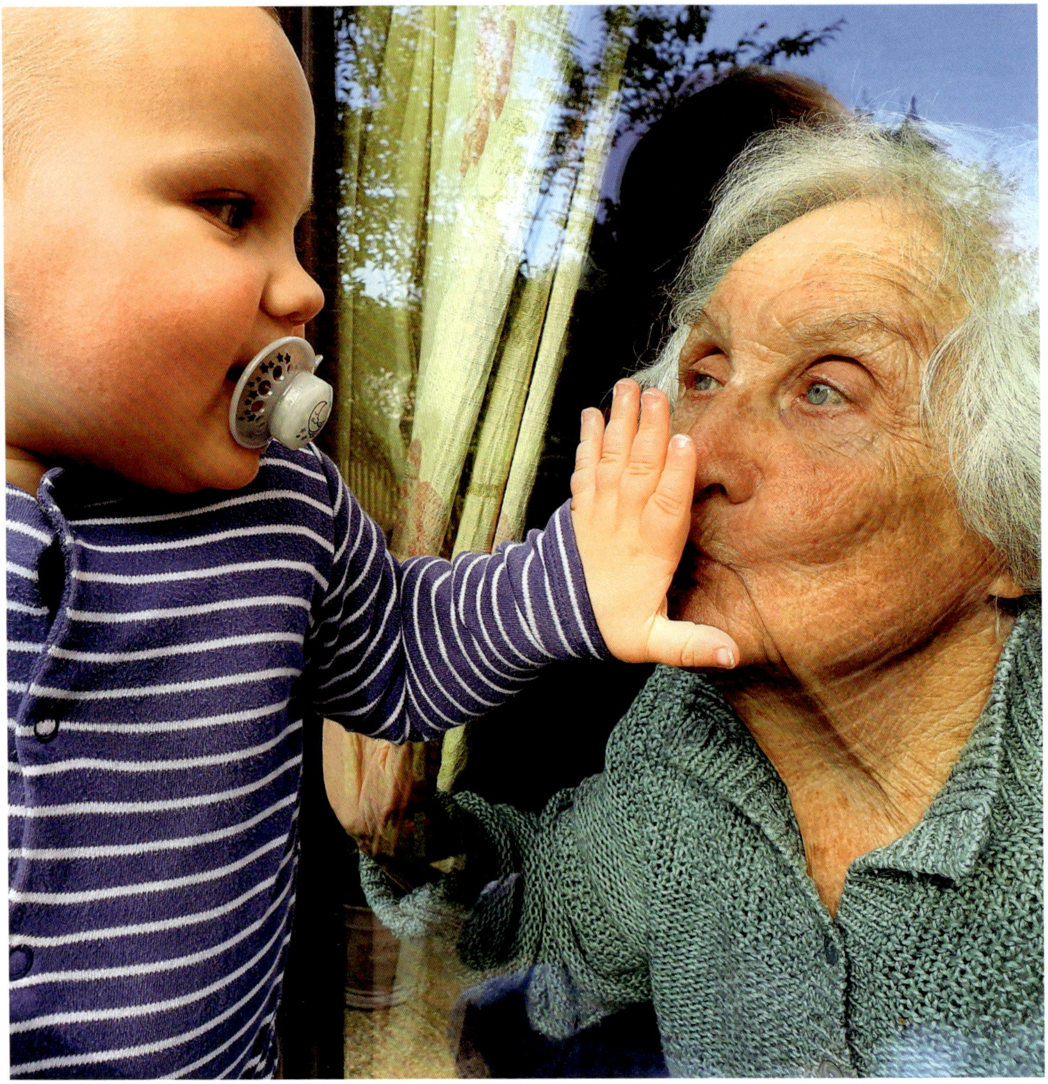

collective portrait of the UK during lockdown and people of all ages from across the country were invited to submit a photographic portrait. A large number of submissions showcased a window, testifying the degree to which it became a 'lifeline' for so many in this period. Interestingly, many of these photos highlighted the experience of women in particular and while everyone, regardless of age or gender, experienced challenges during the pandemic, several studies indicate that women were disproportionately negatively impacted. [191] During lockdown, women, on average, shouldered more of the domestic responsibilities as well as looking after vulnerable parents or neighbours, suffered more domestic abuse, continued to be paid less than their male counterparts and especially struggled to balance family and work obligations. Two of the photographs selected for 'Hold Still' stand out in this context. The first *Glass Kisses* [cat. 49] by Steph James was taken in Cowfold, West Sussex in 2020. Of the work, James says: 'This is a photograph of my one-year-old little boy and his 88-year-old Great Grandma, who miss each other so much at the moment. I captured this beautiful moment between them whilst dropping off groceries. Kisses through glass.' The second, *Dadi's Love* [cat. 50] by Simran Janjua, taken in London on 20 June 2020, shows Janjua's sister-in-law with her grandmother ('*Dadi*' in Punjabi) meeting through a window after months of being apart. Reflecting on this event, Janjua said: 'In this moment I felt the depth of love they feel for each other, capturing both the joy and longing in their eyes; separated by a window, but connected by love.' Both photographs, taken by women of women, capture such intimate, affectionate and personal moments and yet are part of a familiar, collective experience. Every one of us may now feel a new empathy or understanding of what it means to be the 'woman at the window'.

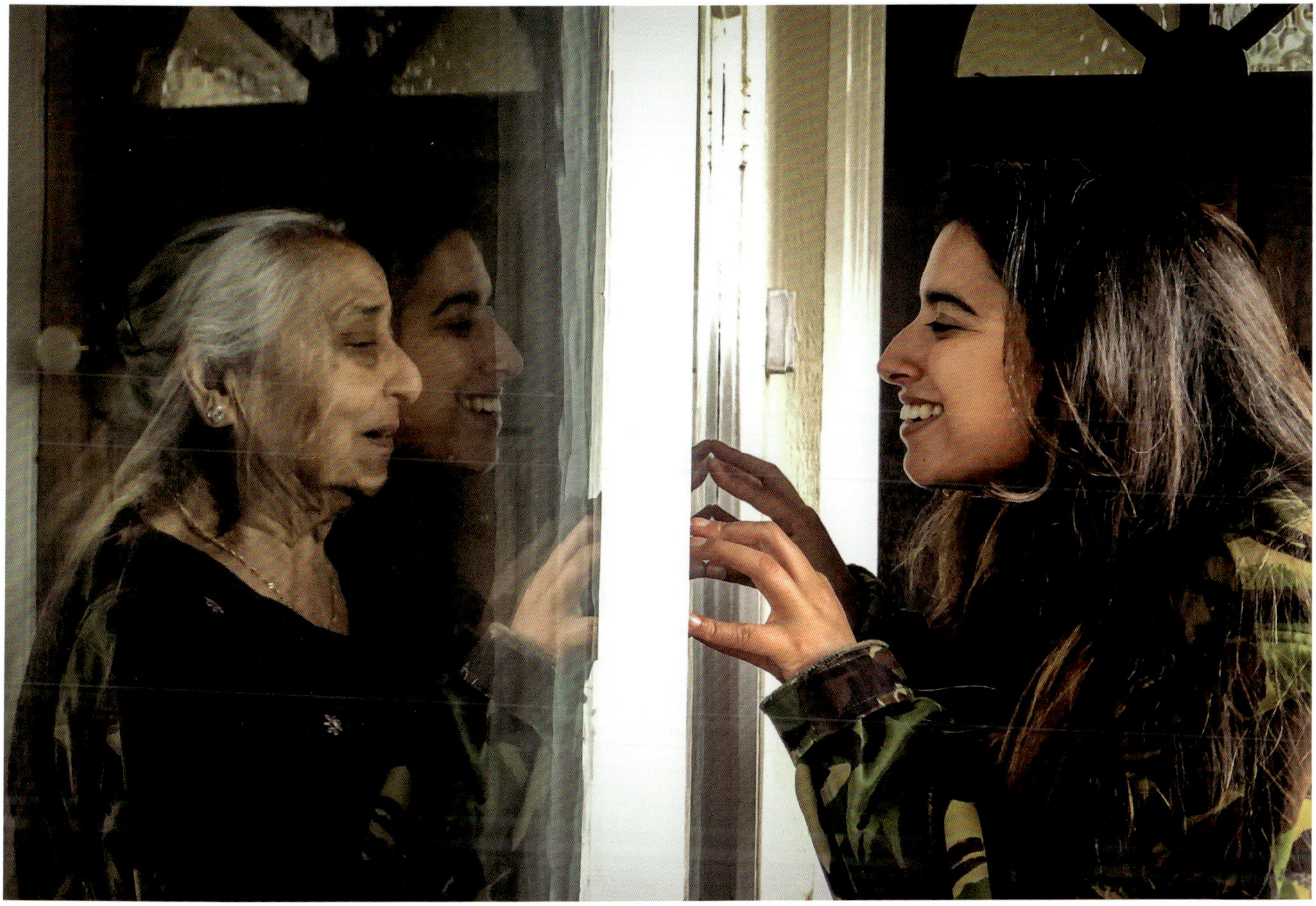

left, cat. 49
Steph James, *Glass Kisses*, 2020
From the National Portrait Gallery's HOLD STILL project

right, cat. 50
Simran Janjua, *Dadi's Love*, 2020
From the National Portrait Gallery's HOLD STILL project

Notes

189. See, for example, Becky Kleanthous, 'An Ode to Windows', *Architectural Digest* (21 April 2020).

190. Numerous online conferences were organised to assess the role of cultural institutions in the pandemic and programmes were set out to provide access to stimulating and uplifting online events, images and information. The International Committee for Museums and Collections of Modern Art, for example, hosted an online conference on precisely this theme, titled 'Reframing Museums Symposium: What Role do Cultural Institutions Play in the Pandemic?' (17 November 2020).

191. A study by the United Nations, for example, demonstrated how the pandemic underscored society's reliance on women both on the front line and at home, while simultaneously exposing structural inequalities across every sphere, from health to the economy, security to social protection. There was a marked rise in violence against women and in domestic violence in particular. See, for example, a study by Anu Madgavkar, Olivia White, Mekala Krishnan, Deepa Mahajan, Xavier Azcue published by the McKinsey Global Institute, 'COVID-19 and Gender Equality: Countering the Regressive Effects' (15 July 2020), https://www.mckinsey.com/featured-insights/future-of-work/covid-19-and-gender-equality-countering-the-regressive-effects; this was also reported by a number of studies by the UN in a dedicated webpage on 'How COVID-19 impacts women and girls'.

BIOGRAPHY

Jennifer Sliwka is an art historian, curator and lecturer based at King's College London where she convenes a collaborative MA with the National Gallery and oversees the Visual Commentary on Scripture project (thevcs.org). She specialises in Italian Renaissance and Baroque art and is particularly interested in transhistorical studies, tracing artistic themes and techniques across centuries and collaborating with contemporary artists. She received her PhD from the Johns Hopkins University, MA from the Courtauld Institute of Art and BA from the University of Toronto. Her research has been supported by the Getty Research Institute, the Kress Foundation, the Metropolitan Museum of Art and the Villa I Tatti, The Harvard Center for Italian Renaissance Studies.

Before joining King's, she worked, from 2007 to 2017, as a curator at the National Gallery, curating exhibitions including: *Devotion by Design: Italian Altarpieces before 1500* (2011), *Visions of Paradise: Botticini's Palmieri Altarpiece* (2015–16) and *Monochrome: Painting in Black and White* (2017–18).

BIBLIOGRAPHY

– Abdel Nabi, Nabila and Achim Borchardt-Hume. *The Making of Rodin*. London: Tate Publishing, 2021.
– Aitken, Molly Emma. 'Pardah and Portrayal: Rajput Women as Subjects, Patrons, and Collectors.' *Artibus Asiae*, vol. 62, no. 2 (2002), pp. 247–80.
– Alberti, Leon Battista. *On Painting and On Sculpture: The Latin Texts of De Pictura and De Statua*. Translated by Cecil Grayson. London: Phaidon, 1972.
– Alberti, Leon Battista. *On the Art of Building in Ten Books*. Translated by Joseph Rykwert, Neil Leach, Robert Tavernor. Cambridge, MA: The MIT Press, 1991.
– Alberti, Leon Battista. *I libri della famiglia*. Turin: G. Einaudi, 1994.
– Alberti, Leon Battista. *The Family in Renaissance Florence*. Translated by Renée Neu Watkins. Long Grove, IL: Waveland Press, 2004.
– Albertus Magnus. *De Laudibus Beatae Mariae Virginis*. Strasbourg: Johann Mentelin, [c. 1474].
– Albright, W.F. 'Further Light on the History of Israel from Lachish and Megiddo.' *Bulletin of the American Schools of Oriental Research, vol.* 68 (1937), pp. 22–26.
– Alighieri, Dante. *Vita nuova*. Translated by Mark Musa. Bloomington: Indiana University Press, 1973.
– Aschkenasy, Nehama. *Woman at the Window: Biblical Tales of Oppression and Escape*. Detroit: Wayne State University Press, 1998.
– Athenaeus. *The Deipnosophists*. Translated by Charles Burton Gulick. London: William Heinemann; New York: G. P. Putnam's Sons, 1927–41.
– Baer, Brigitte. *Picasso the Printmaker: Graphics from the Marina Picasso Collection*. Exh. cat. Dallas: Dallas Museum of Art, 1983.
– Baer, Brigitte. *Picasso peintre-graveur: Catalogue raisonné de l'oeuvre gravé et des monotypes, 1946–1958*. Bern: Editions Kornfeld, 1988.
– Baer, Ronni with contributions by Arthur K. Wheelock, Jr., Annetje Boersma, *Gerrit Dou 1613–1675: Master Painter in the Age of Rembrandt*. Exh. cat. Washington, London, The Hague, 2000.
– Baetens, Pascal. *Nude Photography: The Art and the Craft*. London: Dorling Kindersley, 2007.
– Bahrani, Zainab. *Women of Babylon: Gender and representation in Mesopotamia*. London and New York: Routledge, 2001.
– Balsom, Erika. 'In the Company of Images: Untitled Film Stills.' In *Cindy Sherman*, edited by Paul Moorhouse. London: National Portrait Gallery, 2019.
– Baring-Gould, Sabine and John Fisher. *The Lives of the British Saints: The Saints of Wales and Cornwall and Such Irish Saints as Have Dedications in Britain*. 4 vols. London: C.J. Clark, 1911.
– Barnett, Richard David. *A Catalogue of the Nimrud Ivories: With Other Examples of Ancient Near Eastern Ivories in the British Museum*. London: British Museum Press, 1957.
– Baron, Wendy. *Sickert: Paintings and Drawings*. New Haven: Yale University Press, 2006.
– Bartrum, Giulia. *German Renaissance Prints 1490–1550*. Exh. cat. London: British Museum Press, 1995.
– Bartrum, Giulia. *Albrecht Dürer and his Legacy*. Exh. cat. London: British Museum Press, 2002.
– Baudelaire, Charles. 'Windows', 1869. In *Paris Spleen*. Translated by Louise Varèse. New York: New Directions, 1970.
– Beauchamp Walters, Henry and Edgar John Forsdyke, Cecil Harcourt Smith. *Catalogue of the Greek and Etruscan vases in the British Museum I–IV*. London: British Museum Press, 1893.
– Benjamin, Roger. *Orientalist Aesthetics, Art, Colonialism and French North Africa: 1880–1930*. Berkeley: University of California Press, 2003.
– Bernhard, Thomas. *Old Masters*. Translated by Ewald Osers. London: Quartet, 1989.
– Berg, Hanna. 'Headless: The role of gender and self-referencing in consumer response to cropped pictures of decorative models.' *Psychology & Marketing*, vol. 32, no. 10 (2015), pp. 1002–16.
– Bettelheim, Bruno. *The Uses of Enchantment: The Meaning and Importance of Fairy Tales*. New York: Knopf, 1976.
– Birch, Samuel and Sir Charles Thomas Newton. *A Catalogue of the Greek and Etruscan Vases in the British Museum*. London: William Nichol, 1851.
– Blazwick, Iwona and Yve-Alain Bois, Penelope Curtis. *Isa Genzken: Open Sesame!* Exh. cat. Cologne: Walther König Verlag, 2009.
– Blum, Gerd. 'Epikureische Aufmerksamkeit und euklidische Abstraktion: Alberti, Lukrez und das Fenster als Bild gebendes Dispositiv.' In *Imagination und Repräsentation: Zwei Bildsphären der frühen Neuzeit*, edited by Horst Bredekamp, Christiane Kruse, Pablo Schneider. Leiden: Brill, 2010, pp. 79–118.
– Bomfor, Kate, Ann Sumner and Giles Waterfield, eds. *Rembrandt's Girl at a Window*. London: Dulwich Picture Gallery, 1993.
– Boyce Osaki, Amy. 'A "Truly Feminine Employment": Sewing and the Early Nineteenth-Century Woman.' *Winterthur Portfolio*, vol. 23, no. 4 (1988), pp. 225–41.
– Boyd Brown, Christopher and Jaroslav Pelikan, Helmut T. Lehmann, eds, trans., *Luther's Works*. 55 vols. St. Louis, MO: Concordia Press, 1957–86.
– Bredius, A. (revised by H. Gerson). *Rembrandt: The Complete Edition of the Paintings*. London: Phaidon, 1971.
– Broedel, Hans Peter. *The 'Malleus Maleficarum' and the Construction of Witchcraft: Theology and Popular Belief*. Manchester: Manchester University Press, 2003.
– Brooten, B.J. *Love between Women: Early Christian Responses to female Homoroticism*. Chicago: University of Chicago Press, 1998.
– Brucker, Gene. *Renaissance Florence*. New York: Wiley, 1969.
– Bushell, Raymond. *The Inrō Handbook*. Boulder, CO: Weatherhill, 2002.
– Cashdan, Sheldon. *The Witch Must Die: How Fairy Tales Shape Our Lives*. New York: Basic, 1999.
– Cherix, Christophe and Esther Adler. *Saar: Black Girl's Window*. Exh. cat. New York: Museum of Modern Art, 2019.

– Chevalier, Tracey and Colin Wiggins. *Tom Hunter: Living in Hell and Other Stories*. Exh. cat. London: National Gallery Publications, 2005.
– Chu, John. 'Windows of Opportunity: The Fantasy Figure and the Spirit of Enterprise in the Early Eighteenth Century.' In *Fancy in Eighteenth-Century Visual Culture, Oxford University Studies in the Enlightenment*, edited by Melissa Percival and Muriel Adrien. Liverpool: Voltaire Foundation, 2020, pp. 49–67.
– Clark, Kenneth. *The Nude: A Study in Ideal Form*. Princeton: Princeton University Press, 1984).
– Cowen Orlin, Lena. 'Boundary Disputes in Early Modern London.' In *Material London, c. 1600*, edited by Lena Cowen Orlin. Philadelphia: University of Pennsylvania Press, 2000, pp. 344–76.
– Crane, Mary Thomas. 'Illicit Privacy and Outdoor Spaces in Early Modern England.' *Journal of Early Modern Cultural Studies*, vol. 9, no. 1 (Spring–Summer 2009), pp. 4–22.
– Cropper, Elizabeth. 'On Beautiful Women, Parmigianino, Petrarchismo, and the Vernacular Style.' *The Art Bulletin*, vol. 58, no. 3 (1976), pp. 374–94.
– D'Angelo, M.R. 'Women Partners in the New Testament.' *Journal of Feminist Studies in Religion*, vol. 6, no. 1 (Spring 1990), pp. 65–86.
– Davies, Glenys. 'The Significance of the Handshake Motif in Classical Funerary Art.' *American Journal of Archaeology*, vol. 89, no. 4 (October 1985), pp. 627–40.
– De Jongh, Eddy. 'Grape Symbolism in Paintings of the 16th and 17th Centuries.' *Simiolus*, vol. 7, no. 4 (1974), pp. 166–191.
– De Jongh, Eddy, ed. *Tot Lering en Vermaak: Betekenissen van Hollandse genrevoorstellingen uit de zeventiende eeuw*. Exh. cat. Amsterdam: Rijksmuseum, 1976.
– De Jongh, Eddy. 'A Bird's-Eye View of Erotica: Double Entendre in a Series of Seventeenth-Century Genre Scenes.' In *Questions of Meaning: Theme and Motif in Dutch Seventeenth-Century Painting*, edited by Eddy de Jongh. Translated by Michael Hoyle. Leiden: Primavera, 2000, pp. 22–46.
– Delany, Paul. *Bill Brandt: A Life*. Stanford: Stanford University Press, 2004.
– De Marchi, Andrea and Francesco Caglioti, eds. *Verrocchio, il Maestro di Leonardo*. Exh. cat. Florence: Mandragora, 2019.
– Dickens, Charles. *Household Words*. London: Bradbury and Evans, 1850.
– Dodier, Virginia. *Clementina, Lady Hawarden: Studies from Life, 1857–1864*. New York: Aperture, 1999.
– Ducos, Blaise and Lara Yeager-Crasselt, eds. *Rembrandt, Vermeer and the Dutch Golden Age: Masterpieces from The Leiden Collection and the Musée du Louvre*. Exh. cat. Abu Dhabi: Saqi Books, 2019.
– Drerup, Heinrich. 'Bildraum und Realraum in der römischen Architektur.' *Mitteilungen des Deutschen Archäologischen Instituts, Römische Abteilung*, no. 66 (1959), pp. 147–74.
– Eggenter, Marco. *L'amor 'Scortese' – Morale e sessualità nel Medioevo Cristiano*. Iseo: Universitas Ysei, 2018.
– Evans, Mark and Stefan Weppelmann. *Botticelli Reimagined*. Exh. cat. London: Abrams and Chronicle, 2016.
– Farquhar, Fraser, and John Henry Thomas, eds. *The Reports of Sir Edward Coke*, 6 vols. London: Joseph Butterworth and Son, 1826.
– Fauth, Wolfgang. *Aphrodite Parakyptus: Untersuchungen zum Erscheinungsbild der vorderasiatischen Dea Prospiciens*. Wiesbaden: Franz Steiner, 1967.
– Ferretti, Emanuela. 'Palazzo Farnese.' In *Michelangelo, architetto a Roma*, edited by Mauro Mussolin. Cinisello Balsamo: Silvana Editoriale, 2009, pp. 158–69.
– Flam, Jack D., ed. *Matisse on Art*. Berkeley: University of California Press, 1994.
– Foley, Michael P., ed. *Augustine: Confessions*. Translated by F.J. Sheed. Indianapolis: Hackett, 2006.
– Freud, Sigmund. *The complete introductory lectures on psychoanalysis*. Translated and edited by James Strachey. London: Allen and Unwin, [1971].
– Franits, Wayne E. *Paragons of Virtue: Women and Domesticity in Seventeenth-Century Dutch Art*. Cambridge: Cambridge University Press, 1993.
– Fried, Michael. *Absorption and Theatricality: Painting and Beholder in the Age of Diderot*. Chicago: University of Chicago Press, 1988.
– Fried, Michael. *Why Photography Matters as Art as Never Before*. New Haven: Yale University Press, 2008.
– Friedberg, Anne. *The Virtual Window: From Alberti to Microsoft*. Cambridge, MA: MIT Press, 2006.
– Funnell, Peter and Charlotte Gere, Jan Marsh, Pamela Nunn. *Pre-Raphaelite Sisters*. Exh. cat. London: National Portrait Gallery, 2019.
– Gallagher, Ann and Molly Donovan, eds. *Rachel Whiteread*. London: Tate Publishing, 2017.
– Galassi, Peter, ed. *Jeff Wall*. Exh. cat. New York: The Museum of Modern Art, 2007.
– Galassi, Peter. *Cindy Sherman: The Complete Untitled Film Stills*. Exh. cat. New York: Museum of Modern Art, 2003.
– Giambullari, Bernardo. *Canzone per andare in maschera carnesciale facte da piu persone*. Florence: Bartolomeo dei Libri, c. 1515.
– Gillow, John. *African Textiles: Colour and Creativity across a Continent*. London: Thames and Hudson, 2003.
– Gilot, Françoise and Carlton Lake. *Life with Picasso*. New York: McGraw-Hill, 1964.
– Glantz, Andrew E. 'A Tax on Light and Air: Impact of the Window Duty on Tax Administration and Architecture, 1696–1851.' *Penn History Review*, vol. 15, no. 2 (2008), pp. 1–23.
– Gruetzner Robins, Anna. 'Degas and Sickert: Notes on Their Friendship.' *The Burlington Magazine*, vol. 130, no. 1020 (March 1988), pp. 198, 210–11, 225–29.
– Gruetzner Robins, Anna, ed. *Walter Sickert: The Complete Writings on Art*. Oxford: Oxford University Press, 2000.
– Godfrey, Sima. 'Baudelaire's Windows.'

L'Esprit Créateur, vol. 22, no. 4: The Poet as Art Critic (Winter 1982), pp. 83–100.
– Gottlieb, Carla. 'The Role of the Window in the Art of Matisse.' *The Journal of Aesthetics and Art Criticism*, vol. 22, no. 4, Summer (1964), pp. 393–423.
– Gottlieb, Carla. *The Window in Art: From the Window of God to the Vanity of Man: A Survey of Window Symbolism in Western Painting*. New York: Abaris, 1981.
– Greenstein, Jack. 'The Vision of Peace; Meaning and Representation in Ambrogio Lorenzetti's Sala Della Pace Cityscapes.' *Art History*, vol. 4, no. 11 (1988), pp. 492–510.
– Grosfilley, Anne. *African Wax Print Textiles*. London: Prestel, 2018.
– Grunenberg, Christoph and Laurance Sillars, eds. *Peter Blake: A Retrospective*. London: Tate Publishing, 2007.
– Gunning, Tom. *The Films of Fritz Lang: Allegories of Vision and Modernity*. London: British Film Institute, 2000.
– Hannavy, John, ed. *Encyclopedia of Nineteenth-Century Photography*. London: Routledge, 2013.
– Hellman, Karen, ed. *The Window in Photographs*. Exh. cat. Los Angeles: Getty Publications, 2013.
– Herodotus, *Herodotus the Histories*. Translated by Aubrey De Sélincourt and John Marincola. London: Penguin Books, 2003.
– Herbig, Reinhard. 'Fensterstudien an antiken Wohnbauten in Italien.' *Mitteilungen des Deutschen Archäologischen Instituts, Römische Abteilung*, no. 44 (1929), pp. 260–321.
– Hlavackova, Hana and Hana Seifertova. 'La Madone de Most: Imitation et symbole.' *Revue de l'Art*, vol. 67 (1985), pp. 59–65.
– Hoak, Dale. 'Art, Culture, and Mentality in Renaissance Society: The Meaning of Hans Baldung Grien's Bewitched Groom (1544).' *Renaissance Quarterly*, vol. 38, no. 3 (1985), pp. 488–510.
– Hockney, David. *Six Fairy Tales from the Brothers Grimm: With Illustrations by David Hockney*. Exh. cat. London: Royal Academy of Arts, 2018.
– Hofstede de Groote, C. *A Catalogue Raisonné of the Works of the Most Eminent Dutch Painters of the Seventeenth Century*, 10 vols. London, Stuttgart and Paris, 1907–26.
– Homer, *The Iliad*. Translated by Robert Fitzgerald and Gregory Nagy. London: David Campbell, 1992.
– Hondius, Dienke. 'Black Africans in Seventeenth-Century Amsterdam.' *Renaissance and Reformation/Renaissance et Réforme*, vol. 31, no. 2 (Spring 2008), pp. 87–105.
– Horn, Hans-Jürgen. 'Respiciens per fenestras, prospiciens per cancellos: Zur Typologie des Fensters in der Antike.' *Jahrbuch für Antike und Christentum*, vol. 10 (1967), pp. 30–60.
– Horn, Hans-Jürgen. 'Fenster.' *Reallexikon für Antike und Christentum: Sachwörterbuch zur Auseinandersetzung des Christentums mit der Antiken Welt*, vol. 7 (1969), pp. 732–47.
– Inglis, Erik. *The Hours of Mary of Burgundy: Codex Vindobonensis 1857, Vienna, Osterreichische Nationalbibliothek*. London: H. Miller, 1995.
– Jerome. *Select Letters of St. Jerome*. Translated by F.A. Wright. Cambridge, MA: Harvard University Press, 1933.
– Jacob-Friesen, Holger and Julia Carrasco, Johanna Scherer, eds. *Hans Baldung Grien: heilig/unheilig*. Exh. cat. Berlin and Munich: Deutscher Kunstverlag, 2019.
– Joshi, Varsha. *Polygamy and Purdah: Women and Society Among Rajputs*. Jaipur and New Delhi: Rawat Publications, 1995.
– Jütte, Daniel. 'Das Fenster als Ort sozialer Interaktion: Zu einer Alltagsgeschichte des Hauses im vormodernen Europa.' In *Das Haus in der Geschichte Europa: Sozialer Raum, Identitätsort, Ordnungskonzepts*, edited by Inken Schmidt-Voges and Joachim Eibach. Berlin: De Gruyter Oldenbourg, 2015, pp. 467–83.
– Jütte, Daniel. 'Window Gazes and World Views: A Chapter in the Cultural History of Vision.' *Critical Inquiry*, vol. 42, no. 3 (Spring 2016), pp. 611–46.
– Keegan, P. 'Plato, Feminist Philosophy, and the Representation of Culture: Butler, Irigaray, and the Embodied Subjectivity of Ancient Women.' *Journal of Interdisciplinary Gender Studies*, vol. 7, no. 1–2 (Nov 2003), pp. 90–105.
– Keel, Othmar and Christoph Uehlinger. *Gods, Goddesses, and Images of God in Ancient Israel*. Translated by Thomas H. Trapp. Minneapolis: Fortress Press, 1998.
– Kendall, Richard and Catherine Lampert, eds. *Euan Uglow: The Complete Paintings*. New Haven: Yale University Press, 2007.
– Kent, Dale. 'Women in Renaissance Florence.' In *Virtue and Beauty: Leonardo's Ginevra de' Benci and Renaissance Portraits of Women*, edited by David Alan Brown. Exh. cat. Washington D.C.: National Gallery of Art, 2001, pp. 25–47.
– Kent, F.W. *Household and Lineage in Renaissance Florence: The Family Life of the Capponi, Ginori and Rucellai*. Princeton: Princeton University Press, 1977.
– Kent, F.W. 'La famiglia patrizia florentina nel quattrocento. Nuovi orientamenti nella storiografia recente.' In *Palazzo Strozzi: Meta Millenio 1480–1080*, edited by Daniela Lamberini. Rome: Istituto Della Enciclopedia Italiana, 1991, pp. 70–91.
– Klapisch-Zuber, Christiane. *Women, Family and Ritual in Renaissance Italy: Collected Essays*. Translated by Lydia G. Cochrane. Chicago: University of Chicago Press, 1985.
– Klapisch-Zuber, Christiane. 'Images without Memory: Women's Identity and Family Consciousness in Renaissance Florence.' In *Fenway Court: Imaging the Self in Renaissance Italy*, edited by Hilliard T. Goldfarb. Boston: Isabella Stewart Gardner Museum, 1992, pp. 37–44.
– Kleanthous, Becky. 'An Ode to Windows.' *Architectural Digest*. https://www.architecturaldigest.com/story/ode-to-windows-during-coronavirus-social-distancing (published 21 April 2020).
– Koja, Stephan and Uta Neidhardt, Arthur K. Wheelock Jr. *Johannes Vermeer: Vom Innehalten*. Exh. cat. Dresden: Staatliche Kunstsammlungen, 2021.
– Kuehn, Thomas. *Law, Family and Women: Towards a Legal Anthropology in Renaissance Italy*. Chicago: University of Chicago Press, 1993.
– Kyle, Donald G. *Sport and Spectacle in the Ancient World*. Hoboken: Wiley-Blackwell, 2014.
– LGRH. 'The Art of Isabel Codrington.' *The Studio*, vol. 90 (October 1925), p. 217.
– Liedtke, Walter A. *Vermeer and the Delft School*. Exh. cat. New York: Metropolitan Museum of Art, 2001.
– Lipton, Eunice. *Looking into Degas: Uneasy Images of Women and Modern Life*. Berkeley: University of California Press, 1986.
– Lochtefeld, James G. *The Illustrated Encyclopaedia of Hinduism*. New York: Rosen Publishing Group, 2002.
– Lucian of Samosata, *Lucian's Dialogues of the Gods*. Edited by Nicholas Jeeves. Translated by H. & F. Fowler and William Tooke. Cambridge: The PDR Press, 2016.
– Luther, Martin. *D. Martin Luthers Werke: Kritische Gesamtausgabe*. Edited by J.K.F. Knaake, 73 vols. Weimar: H. Böhlaus, 1883–2009.
– Luther, Martin. *Luther's Works*. Translated by H. T. Lehmann, 55 vols. St. Louis: Concordia Publishing House, 1957–86.
– Macey, Patrick Paul. *Bonfire Songs: Savonarola's Musical Legacy*. Oxford: Clarendon Press, 1998.
– Mancoff, Debra N. *Jane Morris: The Pre-Raphaelite Model of Beauty*. San Francisco: Pomegranate, 2000.
– Markham Schulz, Anne. *Antonio Rizzo Sculptor and Architect*. Princeton: Princeton University Press, 1983.
– Marsh, Jan. *Black Victorians: Black People in British Art, 1800–1900*. Exh. cat. London: Lund Humphries, 2005.
– Matter, Anne. *The Voice of My Beloved: The Song of Songs in Western Medieval Christianity* Philadelphia: University of Pennsylvania Press, 2011.
– Mavor, Carol. *Becoming: The Photographs of Clementina, Viscountess Hawarden*. Durham, NC: Duke University Press, 1999.
– Mayes, A.D. 'The Historical Context of the Battle against Sisera.' *Vetus Testamentum*, vol. 19, no. 3 (1969), pp. 353–60.
– McCabe, Katie. *More Than a Muse: Creative Partnerships That Sold Talented Women Short*. London: Quadrille, 2020.
– McClure, Laura. *Courtesans at Table: Gender and Greek Literary Culture in Athenaeus*. London: Routledge, 2003.
– Moorhouse, Paul. *Howard Hodgkin: Absent Friends*. Exh. cat. London: National Portrait Gallery, 2017.
– Morris, Frances, ed. *Louise Bourgeois*. Exh. cat. London: Tate Publishing, 2007.
– von Müller, Achatz. 'Der Politiker am Fenster: Zur historischen Ikonographie eines "lebenden Bildes".' In *Homo Pictor*, edited by Gottfried Boehm. Leipzig: De Gruyter, 2001, pp. 323–38.
– Mulvey, Laura. 'Visual Pleasure and Narrative Cinema.' *Screen*, vol. 16, no. 3 (Autumn 1975), pp. 6–18.

– Muramoto, Katsuhiko. 'In Search of a Relational Body: Reflections on Sustainable Architecture.' In *Intervening Spaces: Respatialisation and the Body*, edited by Nycole Prowse. Leiden: Brill, 2018, pp. 80–100.
– Neilsen Blum, Shirley. *Henri Matisse: Rooms with a View*. New York and London: Thames and Hudson, 2010.
– Nielson, Karla J. *Window Treatments*. Toronto: John Wiley and Sons, 1990.
– Norman, Diana. *Painting in Late Medieval and Renaissance Siena (1260–1555)*. New Haven: Yale University Press, 2003.
– *Notes and Queries*. Oxford: Oxford University Press, 1869.
– Novakov, Anna, ed. 'Role Exchange: Desire, Beauty and the Public.' In *Veiled Histories: The Body, Place and Public Art*. New York: Critical Press, 1997.
– Novakov, Anna. 'Point of Access: Marina Abramović's 1975 Performance Role Exchange.' *Woman's Art Journal*, vol. 24, no. 2 (Autumn 2003–Winter 2004), pp. 31–35.
– Oates, Wallace E. and Robert M. Schwab. 'The Window Tax: A Case Study in Excess Burden.' *Journal of Economic Perspectives*, vol. 29, no. 1 (Winter 2015), pp. 163–80.
– Opaschowski, Horst W. *Pädagogik der freien Lebenszeit*. Opladen: Leske + Budrich, 1996.
– Orlandi, Nazareno, ed. *Bernardine of Siena: Sermons*. Translated by Helen Josephine Robins. Siena: Tipografia Sociale, 1920.
– Orme, Nicholas. *The Saints of Cornwall*. Oxford: Oxford University Press, 2000.
– Ovenden, Graham, ed. *Clementina, Lady Hawarden*. New York: St Martin's Press, 1974.
– Ovid. *Ovid Metamorphoses*. Translated by R J Tarrant. Oxford: Oxford University Press, 2004.
– Ovid. *Ovid: The Love Poems*. Translated by A.D. Melville. Oxford: Oxford University Press, 2008.
– Ovid. *Ovid's Heroides*: A New Translation and Critical Essays. Edited by Paul Murgatroyd, Bridget Reeves and Sarah Parker. Abingdon; New York, NY: Routledge, 2017.
– Online Etymology Dictionary, 'window (n.).' https://www.etymonline.com/word/window.
– Packer, Lelia and Jennifer Sliwka. *Monochrome: Painting in Black and White*. Exh. cat. London: National Gallery Publications, 2017.
– Pancratius Crausius, Petrus. 'Disputatio Juridica, De Jure Fenestrarum = Vom Fenster-Recht.' In *Illustri Academia Jenensi Anno MDCLXIX. Habita*. Halle Magdeburg: Litteris Hendelianis, 1730.
– DJ Paulette. 'Interview with Smokin' Jo.' *DMC World Magazine*, 23 May 2015. http://www.dmcworld.net/features/smokin-jo/.
– Pavlovskis, Zoja. *Man in an Artificial Landscape: The Marvels of Civilization in Imperial Roman Literature*. Leiden: Brill, 1973.
– Paolozzi Strozzi, Beatrice and Marc Bormand, eds. *La Primavera del Rinascimento: La Scultura e le Arti a Firenze 1400–1460*. Exh. cat. Florence: Mandragora, 2013.
– Penny, Nicholas. *The Sixteenth-Century Italian Paintings. National Gallery Catalogues: Volume II: Venice 1540–1600*. London: National Gallery Publications.
– Périer-D'Ieteren, Catheline. *Dieric Bouts: The Complete Works*. Brussels: Mercatorfonds, 2006.
– Petrarch, Francesco. *Canzoniere*. Edited by Piero Cudini. Milan: Grandi Libri Garzanti, 1974.
– Postle, Martin and William Vaughn. *The Artist's Model: From Etty to Spencer*. London: Merrell Holberton, 1999.
– Price, Marla. *Howard Hodgkin, The Complete Paintings: Catalogue Raisonné*. London: Thames and Hudson, 2006.
– Pseudo-Apollodorus and C Julius Hyginus. *Apollodorus' Library and Hyginus' Fabulae: two handbooks of Greek mythology*. Translated and introduced by R. Scott Smith and Stephen Trzaskoma. Indianapolis: Hackett Publishing., 2007.
– Randolph, Adrian. *Engaging Symbols: Gender, Politics, and Public Art in Fifteenth-Century Florence*. New Haven: Yale University Press, 2002.
– Reeves, Eileen. *Painting the Heavens: Art and Science in the Age of Galileo*. Princeton: Princeton University Press, 1997.
– Rewald, Sabine. *Rooms with a View: The Open Window in the 19th Century*. Exh. cat. New York: Metropolitan Museum of Art, 2011.
– Rubin, Patricia L. and Alison Wright, eds. *Renaissance Florence: The Art of the 1470s*. Exh cat. London: National Gallery Publications, 1999.
– Salzer, Anselm. *Sinnbilder und Beiworte Mariens in der deutschen Literatur und lateinischen Hymnenpoesie des Mittelalters*. Darmstadt: Wissenschaftliche Buchgesellschaft, 1967.
– Savage, Anne and Nicholas Watson. *Anchoritic Spirituality: Ancrene Wisse and Associated Works*. New York: Paulist Press, 1991.
– Schama, Simon. 'Wives and Wantons: Versions of Womanhood in 17th Century Dutch Art.' *Oxford Art Journal*, vol. 3, no. 1, Women in Art (April 1980), pp. 5–13.
– Schedensack, Christine. *Nachbarn im Konflikt: Zur Entstehung und Beilegung von Rechtsstreitigkeiten um Haus und Hof im frühneuzeitlichen Münster*. Münster: Aschendorff, 2007.
– Schleusener-Eichholz, Gudrun. *Das Auge im Mittelalter*. Vol. 2. Munich: W. Fink, 1985.
– Schneider, Norbert. *Vermeer, 1632–1675: Veiled Emotions*. Cologne: Taschen, 2016.
– Schroeder, Joy A. 'The Rape of Dinah: Luther's Interpretation of a Biblical Narrative.' *Sixteenth Century Journal*, vol. 28, no. 3 (Autumn 1997), pp. 775–91.
– Seeman, Don. 'The Watcher at the Window: Cultural Poetics of a Biblical Motif.' *Prooftexts*, vol. 24, no. 1 (Winter 2004), pp. 1–50.
– Sennett, Richard. *The Conscience of the Eye: The Design and Social Life of Cities*. New York: Alfred A. Knopf, 1992.
– Servius. *Servianorum in Vergilii carmina commentariorum. Vol. III, Quod in aeneidos libros III-V explanationes continet*. Edited by Arthur Frederick Stocker, Albert Hartman Travis and Richard Treat Bruère. Oxford: E Typographeo universitatis, 1965.

– Shaw, Diane. 'The Construction of the Private in Medieval London.' *Journal of Medieval and Early Modern Studies*, vol. 26 (Autumn 1996), pp. 447–66.
– Shaw, Maria C. 'The Bull-Leaping Fresco from below the Ramp House at Mycenae: A Study in Iconography and Artistic Transmission.' *The Annual of the British School at Athens*, vol. 91 (1996), pp. 167–90.
– Sheets Dye, Daniel. *Chinese Lattice Designs*. New York: Dower Publications, 1974.
– Shefer, Elaine. 'The Bird in the Cage in the History of Sexuality: Sir John Everett Millais and William Holman Hunt.' *Journal of the History of Sexuality*, vol. 1, no. 3 (January 1991), pp. 446–80.
– Shone, Richard. *The Art of Bloomsbury Roger Fry, Vanessa Bell, and Duncan Grant*. Princeton: Princeton University Press, 1999.
– Shone Richard and Hana Leaper. *From Omega To Charleston: The Art of Vanessa Bell and Duncan Grant 1910–1934*. Exh. cat. London: Piano Nobile Publications, 2018.
– Siegfried, Susan L. *The Art of Louis-Léopold Boilly: Modern Life in Napoleonic France*. New Haven: Yale University Press, 1995.
– Simons, Patricia. 'Mantegna's Battle of the Sea Gods: The Material and Thematic Interaction of Print and Sculpture.' In *Prints in Translation, 1450–1750: Image, Materiality, Space*, edited by Suzanne Karr Schmidt and Ed Wouk. London: Routledge, 2017, pp. 89–135.
– Sofer, Barbara. 'The Human Spirit: Sisera's mother.' *The Jerusalem Post*. https://www.jpost.com/magazine/opinion/the-human-spirit-siseras-mother (published 21 October 2011).
– Strabo. *The Geography of Strabo: In Eight Volumes*. Translated by Horace Leonard Jones and John Robert Sitlington Sterrett. London: W. Heinemann, 1954–1970.
– Smith, A.H. and F.N. Pryce. *Corpus Vasorum Antiquorum: Great Britain 2, British Museum 2*. London: British Museum Press, 1926.
– Skinner, Quentin. 'Ambrogio Lorenzetti's Buon Governo Frescoes: Two Old Questions, Two New Answers.' *Journal of the Warburg and Courtauld Institutes*, vol. 62 (1999), pp. 1–28.
– Sluijter, Eric Jan. 'Een stuck waerin een jufr: voor de spiegel van Gerrit Douw.' *Antiek*, vol. 23 (October 1988), pp. 150–61.
– Spalding, Frances. *Vanessa Bell: Portrait of the Bloomsbury Artist*. London: I.B.Tauris, 2016.
– Spurling, Hilary. *Matisse: The Life*. London: Penguin, 2009.
– Stambaugh, John E. *The Ancient Roman City*. Baltimore: The Johns Hopkins University Press, 1998.
– Stone, Kay. 'Things Walt Disney Never Told Us.' *The Journal of American Folklore*, vol. 88, no. 347: Women and Folklore (January/March 1975), pp. 46–47.
– Strobl, Alice and Alfred Weidinger, eds. *Oskar Kokoschka, Works on Paper: The Early Years, 1897–1917*. Exh. cat. New York: Solomon R. Guggenheim Museum, 1994.
– Stupperich, Reinhard. 'Zur dextrarum iunctio auf frühen römischen Grabreliefs.' *Boreas*, vol. 6, (1983), pp. 143–50.
– Sturges, Fiona. 'Tate Modern's Neighbours Missed the Point: Cities Make Voyeurs of Us All.' *The Guardian*. https://www.theguardian.com/commentisfree/2019/feb/16/tate-modern-angry-neighbours-cities-voyeurs (published 16 February 2019).
– Surh, Dominique. 'Old Woman at a Window with a Candle' (2017). In *The Leiden Collection Catalogue*, 2nd edition, edited by Arthur K. Wheelock Jr. New York, 2017–20. https://theleidencollection.com/artwork/an-oldwoman-at-a-niche-by-candlight/ (archived May 2020).
– Takakuwa, Gisei. *Shoji: The Screens of Japan*. Kyoto: Mitsumura Suiko Shoin, 1961.
– Tatar, Maria. *The Annotated Brothers Grimm*. New York: W.W. Norton, 2004.
– Tatar, Maria, ed. and trans. *The Grimm Reader: The Classic Tales of the Brothers Grimm* New York: W.W. Norton, 2010.
– Tebbs, Paul. 'Giving and Withholding: The Projection Art of Rachel Lowe.' *Afterimage*, vol. 29, no. 2 (September/October, 2001), pp. 5–7.
– Teri Okada, Barbra. *Netsuke: Masterpieces from the Metropolitan Museum of Art*. Exh. cat. New York: The Metropolitan Museum of Art, 1981.
– Tillmans, Wolfgang. *Portraits*. New York: Distributed Art Publishers, 2002.
– Tillmans, Wolfgang. *If one thing matters, everything matters*. Berlin: Hatje Cantz, 2003.
– Tomas, Natalie. *A Positive Novelty: Women and Public Life in Renaissance Florence*. Clayton: Monash University Publications in History, 1992.
– Treuherz, Julian and Elizabeth Prettejohn, Edwin Becker, eds. *Dante Gabriel Rossetti*. Exh. cat. London: Thames and Hudson, 2003.
– Turner, Jane, ed. *The Dictionary of Art*. New York and London: Grove / Macmillan, 1996.
– Schweitzer, Eva and Andreas Austilat. *A Tramp in Berlin: New Mark Twain Stories & An Account of Twain's Berlin Adventures*. New York: Berlinica Publishing LLC, 2013.
– Verdi, Richard. *The Parrot in Art: From Dürer to Elizabeth Butterworth*. London: Scala Publishers in association with the Barber Institute of Fine Arts, The University of Birmingham, 2007.
– Virgil. *Virgil's Eclogues*. Translated by Len Krisak. Philadelphia: University of Pennsylvania Press, 2012.
– Wagstaff, Sheena. 'Beyond the Threshold.' *Tate Etc*, no. 4 (Summer 2005), pp. 40–45.
– Walker, Susan and Andrew Burnett. 'A Relief with Portrait of Two Women.' In *Augustus, Handlist of the Exhibition and Supplementary Studies, British Museum Occasional Paper, no. 16*. London: The British Museum, 1981, pp. 43–47.
– Waterfield, Giles. *The Artist's Studio*. Exh. cat. London: Paul Holberton Publishing, 2009.
– Waters, Grant M. *Dictionary of British Artists Working 1900–1950*. Eastbourne: Eastbourne Fine Arts Publications, 1975.
– Washbourne, Rose Mary. 'Aphrodite Parakyptousa "the Woman at the Window": The Cypriot Astarte-Aphrodite's Fertility Role in Sacred Prostitution and Rebirth.' *Report of the Department of Antiquities of Cyprus* (1999), pp. 163–77.
– Washbourne, Rose Mary. *Out of the Mouths of Pots: Towards an Interpretation of the Symbolic Meaning of Cypriot Bronze Age Funerary Artefacts Including Examples in the University of Canterbury's Logie Collection*. Jonsered: Paul Åströms Forlag, 2000.
– Weidu, Ma. *Classical Chinese Doors and Windows*. Beijing: China Architecture & Building Press, 2006.
– Weinberg, Gail S. 'D.G. Rossetti's ownership of Botticelli's "Smeralda Brandini" [sic].' *Burlington Magazine*, vol. 146, no. 1210 (January 2004), pp. 20–26.
– Weller, Dennis P. *Small Treasures: Rembrandt, Vermeer, Hals, and Their Contemporaries*. Exh. cat. Raleigh, NC: North Carolina Museum of Art, 2014.
– van de Wetering, A *Corpus of Rembrandt Paintings: Vol. 4 The self-portraits (1625–1669)*. Dordrecht: Springer, 2005.
– Whitlum Cooper, Francesca, ed. *Boilly: Scenes of Parisian Life*. Exh. cat. London: National Gallery Publications, 2019.
– Wichard, Robin and Carol Wichard. *Victorian Cartes de Visite*. New York: Bloomsbury, 1999.
– Woods-Marsden, Joanna. *Renaissance Self-Portraiture: The Visual Construction of Identity and the Social Status of the Artist*. New Haven: Yale University Press, 1998.
– Zanker, Paul. 'Grabreliefs römischer Freigelassener.' *Jahrbuch des Deutschen Archäologischen Instituts*, vol. 90 (1975), pp. 267–315.
– Zimmer, Heinrich Robert. *Myths and Symbols in Indian Art and Civilization*. Princeton: Princeton University Press, 2015.

PICTURE CREDITS

Catalogue images
Cats. 1, 3: © The Trustees of the British Museum. All rights reserved
Cat. 2: Image © Tullie House Museum, Carlisle
Cat. 4: © Royal Academy of Arts, London; photographer: John Hammond
Cat. 5: Royal Collection Trust / © Her Majesty Queen Elizabeth II 2022
Cat. 6: © The National Gallery, London. Salting Bequest, 1910
Cat. 7: Courtesy of Daniel Katz Gallery, London
Cat. 8: Courtesy of Sam Fogg, London
Cats. 9, 32: © Victoria and Albert Museum, London
Cat. 10: Bradford Art Galleries and Museums, West Yorkshire, UK © Bradford Museums & Galleries / Bridgeman Images
Cat. 11: By permission of the British Library, C.8.g.9
Cats. 12, 15: Dulwich Picture Gallery, London
Cat. 13: Image courtesy of The Leiden Collection, New York
Cat. 14: © National Trust Images
Cat. 16: © Tom Hunter
Cat. 17: © The National Gallery, London. Presented by Emilie Yznaga, 1945
Cat. 18: © Foundation Oskar Kokoschka / DACS 2021. Photo: Victoria and Albert Museum, London
Cat. 19: © Ajarb Bernard Ategwa / Jack Bell Gallery
Cat. 20: © Matthew Hollow
Cat. 21: Photograph reproduced with the kind permission of the Russell-Cotes Art Gallery & Museum, Bournemouth
Cat. 22: © Estate of Vanessa Bell. All rights reserved, DACS 2021. Photo: Private Collection, Courtesy PIANO NOBILE, Robert Travers (Works of Art) Ltd.
Cat. 23: Crown Copyright: UK Government Art Collection
Cat. 24: Courtesy of the artist
Cats. 25, 27: Image © Ashmolean Museum, University of Oxford
Cat. 26: Courtesy of Simon Ray, London
Cat. 28: The Courtauld, London (Samuel Courtauld Trust)
Cat. 29: Private Collection, promised to Petit Palais, Musée des Beaux-Arts de la Ville de Paris, in memory of Delphine Lévy
Cat. 30: © Succession Picasso / DACS, London 2021. Photo: Tate
Cat. 31: © Wolfgang Tillmans, courtesy Maureen Paley, London
Cats. 33, 35: Wilson Centre for Photography
Cat. 34: Private Collection, UK
Cat. 36: © Bill Brandt Archive
Cat. 37: © Peter Blake. All rights reserved, DACS. Photo: Leeds Museums and Galleries
Cat. 38: © David Hockney. Photo: Richard Schmidt
Cat. 39: © The Estate of Howard Hodgkin
Cat. 40: © The Estate of Euan Uglow / Bridgeman Images. Photo: Private Collection, Courtesy PIANO NOBILE, Robert Travers (Works of Art) Ltd.
Cat. 41: © Mark Cohen
Cat. 42: © Andrew Jackson. Photo: Crown Copyright: UK Government Art Collection
Cat. 43: © Rachel Lowe. Photo: Crown Copyright: UK Government Art Collection
Cat. 44: © Marina Abramović. Courtesy of the Marina Abramović Archives / DACS 2021. Photo: Collection Irish Museum of Modern Art, purchased, 1995
Cat. 45: © Cindy Sherman. Courtesy the artist and Hauser & Wirth
Cat. 46: © The Easton Foundation / VAGA at ARS, NY and DACS, London 2021. Photo: Christopher Burke
Cat. 47: © Rachel Whiteread. Photo: Prudence Cuming Associates. Courtesy Gagosian
Cat. 48: © DACS 2021. Photo: Courtesy Galerie Daniel Buchholz, Berlin/Cologne/New York
Cat. 49: © Steph James
Cat. 50: © Simran Janjua

Comparative illustrations
Fig. 1: funkyfood London - Paul Williams / Alamy Stock Photo
Figs. 2, 3: © The Trustees of the British Museum. All rights reserved
Fig. 4: akg-images / Erich Lessing
Fig. 5: ÖNB / Vienna, Cod. 1857 fol. 14 v: Gebetbuch Karls des Kühnen von Burgund
Fig. 6: © The National Gallery, London. Bought 1878
Fig. 7: © bpk / Skulpturensammlung und Museum für Byzantinische Kunst, SMB / Antje Voigt
Fig. 8: Digital image courtesy of the Getty's Open Content Program
Fig. 9: Courtesy of The Metropolitan Museum of Art, New York. Marquand Collection, Gift of Henry G. Marquand, 1889. www.metmuseum.org.
Fig. 10: Royal Collection Trust / © Her Majesty Queen Elizabeth II 2022
Fig. 11: © bpk / Staatliche Kunstsammlungen Dresden / Wolfgang Kreische
Fig. 12: © The Fitzwilliam Museum, Cambridge
Fig. 13: © bpk / Nationalgalerie, SMB / Jörg P. Anders
Fig. 14: Alex Ramsay / Alamy Stock Photo
Fig. 15: Deepak Dogra / Alamy Stock Photo
Fig. 16: © Succession H. Matisse / DACS 2021. Photo: Helly Nahmad Gallery